GOVERNMENT BEYOND THE CENTRE

SERIES EDITOR: GERRY STOKER

The world of sub-central government and administration – including local authorities, quasi-governmental bodies and the agencies of public-private partnerships – has seen massive changes in recent years and is at the heart of the current restructuring of government in the United Kingdom and other Western democracies.

The intention of the *Government Beyond the Centre* series is to bring the study of this often-neglected world into the mainstream of social science research, applying the spotlight of critical analysis to what has traditionally been the preserve of institutional public administration approaches.

Its focus is on the agenda of change currently being faced by sub-central government, the economic, political and ideological forces that underlie it, and the structures of power and influence that are emerging. Its objective is to provide up-to-date and informative accounts of the new forms of government, management and administration that are emerging.

The series will be of interest to students and practitioners of politics, public and social administration, and all those interested in the reshaping of the governmental institutions which have a daily and major impact on our lives.

GOVERNMENT BEYOND THE CENTRE

SERIES EDITOR: GERRY STOKER

Local Government in the 1990s

Edited by

John Stewart

and

Gerry Stoker

MACMILLAN

This book replaces *The Future of Local Government* (1989, reprinted 1991, 1992)

First published 1995 by
THE MACMILLAN PRESS LTD
Houndmills, Basingstoke, Hampshire RG21 2XS
and London
Companies and representatives
throughout the world

ISBN 0–333–61683–9 hardcover
ISBN 0–333–61684–7 paperback

A catalogue record for this book is available
from the British Library.

Copy-edited and typeset by Povey–Edmondson
Okehampton and Rochdale, England

Printed in China

Contents

III WHAT PAST? WHAT FUTURE?

List of Tables

Notes on the Contributors

Peter Garside is a research associate at the European Institute of Urban Affairs, Liverpool John Moores University. He was a member of the research team that recently completed an assessment of the impact of natural urban policies for the Department of the Environment and he has particular expertise on the role of advanced service industries in urban regeneration. He is currently involved in evaluation of the City Challenge at the national level and at Hulme, Manchester.

Alan Harding is a Senior Research Fellow at the European Institute of Urban Affairs, Liverpool John Moores University. He has published widely on urban development and urban policy issues within the UK and in Europe and is currently conducting a cross-national research project on the politics of urban change as part of the Economic and Social Research Council's *Local Government Initiative*. He is co-author of *Urbanisation and the Functions of Cities in the European Community* (1993) and co-editor *of European Cities in the 1990s: Profiles, Policies and Prospects* (1994).

Desmond King is a Fellow of St John's College, Oxford. His publications include *The New Right: Politics, Markets and Citizenship* (1987) and (co-editor) *Challenges to Local Government* (1990).

Steve Leach is a Senior Lecturer at INLOGOV, University of Birmingham. He has written widely on local politics, policy planning and most recently, local government reorganisation. One of his most recent publications, written with John Stewart, is *The Politics of Hung Authorities*.

Karen Mossberger is a PhD candidate at the Department of Political Science, Wayne State University, Detroit, USA. During 1992–3 she was a research assistant to Gerry Stoker, funded by Strathclyde University.

David Prior is Head of Policy Development in the Strategic Management Department of Birmingham City Council. He also manages the Public Policy Partnership, a joint venture between Birmingham City Council and the School of Public Policy at the University of Birmingham. He has written on various aspects of local government management and is currently co-authoring a book on citizenship and its significance for local authorities.

Stewart Ranson is Professor of Education in the School of Education at the University of Birmingham. He has written widely on the changing government and politics of education and is leading the major education management study with the ESRC Local Governance Programme.

Kenneth M. Spencer is Professor of Local Policy, Head of the Department of Local Government Studies and Director of INLOGOV at the University of Birmingham. He has written books and articles on housing policy and management, the voluntary sector and on regional economic development. He is a member of the European Union's Committee of Experts advising the Regional Policy Directorate.

John Stewart is Professor of Local Government and Administration at the Institute of Local Government Studies (INLOGOV), University of Birmingham. His previous books include *The Future of Local Government* (with Gerry Stoker).

Gerry Stoker is Professor of Politics, University of Strathclyde, and Co-ordinator of the five-year ESRC Local Governance Research Programme. His previous books include *The Politics of Local Government* and *Remaking Planning* (with Tim Brindley and Yvonne Rydin).

Tony Travers is Director of Research, Greater London Group, London School of Economics and Political Science. He has published widely both in book and journal form.

Kieron Walsh is Professor of Local Government Management, Institute of Local Government Studies, University of Birmingham. He has worked extensively on issues of contracting and competition and the public service. He has recently published *Competition and Service: The Implications of the Local Government Act 1988*. He is presently completing a study of the use of market mechanisms in public service management. He is author of a number of books and articles on management in the public service.

Martin Willis is the Director of the Social Services Management Unit (SSMU), in the Department of Social Work and Social Policy at the University of Birmingham. SSMU is a self-financed provider of training, consultancy and research to local government, voluntary and private organisations. His past experience encompasses social work, management and economics. A recent publication is *Older People and Equal Citizenship* (1992).

Preface

When we edited *The Future of Local Government*, which was published in 1989, we felt then that the pace of change facing local government was considerable. Nothing has happened over the last five years to change our minds! Indeed because local government has experienced so much change we thought it appropriate to produce a second edited text to provide an up-to-date picture of the emerging system. The chapters in this new book are provided by many of the authors from *The Future of Local Government* along with several new faces. All of the writers have operated to very tight deadlines and in the context of shifting targets in relation to changing policy and practice. The book is as up-to-date as it can be but we hope that readers will bear in mind that most of the authors completed their writing in January 1994. Overall, our aim has been to place the extraordinary set of changes within local government in context and provide some insight into likely future directions.

We would like to thank all of those who helped to produce the book. Steven Kennedy at the publishers was as helpful as ever. Kathy Bonehill at Birmingham and Fiona Thorpe at Strathclyde helped greatly to smooth the production of the book. Thanks also to Teresa, Deborah, Bethany, Robert and Benjamin.

John Stewart
Gerry Stoker

1   Introduction

John Stewart and Gerry Stoker

'Local authorities are in the throes of a revolution. The immediate cause is a wave of legislation changing their methods of raising revenue, their ways of working and the range of their functions. But this, like all revolutions, has deeper roots. The political, financial and social environment in which local government operates began to change some time ago.'

Audit Commission, *The Competitive Council*, 1988, p. 1

When auditors write of a revolution in local government clearly something unusual and significant is happening! In the 1987–92 Parliament the Conservative Government introduced a programme of legislation and other measures that are changing the nature of local government. Towards the end of that Parliament, the then Secretary of State announced an internal departmental review of local government, which led to the publication of consultation papers on the structure of local government, local government finance and internal management. That led on to further changes which are continuing with the re-election of the Conservative Government in 1992. This book aims to provide an up-to-date account of the major changes occurring in local government and examine the implications of the programme of restructuring for the future of local government.

The programme of restructuring follows a period in which the consensus about the role of local government has increasingly come under challenge. From the 1970s onwards elements of the Left, Right and Centre of the political spectrum have increasingly challenged the belief that the established form of local government is capable of solving social and economic problems. Scepticism, doubt and a willingness to experiment with other methods have emerged as major themes. Indeed many local authorities have come to the fore, developing new forms of service delivery and initiatives in economic development, crime prevention, environment protection and in many other areas.

During its first two terms Mrs Thatcher's Government was far from inactive in relation to local government. In total some forty Acts dealing with local government were passed between 1979 and 1987. The emphasis of many of these measures and the central thrust of the Government's concern was with increasing the control of central government over local authorities and in particular on restraining local authority expenditure. A fuller examination of the measures and counteractions by local authorities of this period can be found elsewhere! This book, however, is premised on the view that from the mid-1980s the Government's concern about local government became wider in its focus and more far-reaching in its implications. The Government's programme moved beyond the search for public expenditure restraint to a more broad-ranging attempt to restructure local government. The commitment to financial restraint remained but a wider range of goals aimed at transforming the nature and organisation of service delivery came to the fore.

The measures of the 1979–87 period in many instances weakened or destabilised local government. This made the likelihood of further change greater, and given the nature of the Thatcher style it was likely that a substantial restructuring would be promoted. But it should not be assumed that the Government had a predetermined strategy; rather it learnt its strategy through experience – even as with the community charge going into reverse as part of that learning. The commitment to the community charge reflected a dissatisfaction with earlier financial measures. The extension of compulsory competitive tendering built on its initial applications to house building and maintenance work and then spread to a wider range of manual work. The education and housing reforms built on earlier legislation and are now leading on to further change. The post 1987 programme drew on earlier initiatives but it transcends the earlier changes because of the breadth and common themes of the restructuring it proposes. Out of a process of trial and error a comprehensive programme of reform began to emerge.

The arrival of Major in Downing Street signalled retreat on some fronts such as poll tax but continuation of much of the broad thrust of the post-1987 package. Structural reorganisation introduced in a piecemeal way by the 1986 abolition of the Greater London and metropolitan county councils became a strong theme with the extension of the reform process to non-metropolitan areas.

Key themes of the programme as seen by the Government are:

- *financial constraint*: the growth of the post-war era has given way to spending constraint. In some instances real cutbacks in service provision have occurred and in others increased spending has failed to fully compensate for rising need. Accompanying financial constraint has been the search for efficiency and value for money defined in terms of achieving more output in service provision for fewer resources.

- *the fragmentation of local government*: elected local authorities will increasingly share their service delivery, regulatory and strategic responsibilities with a range of other institutions and agencies. Educational and other responsibilities are to be removed from local government and given to a complex of institutions and agencies.

- *a commitment to competition*: a range of services are to be subjected to competitive tendering from the private sector. In addition, schools are expected to compete for pupils. Housing departments are to compete with other social landlords for tenants. Social services departments are to work towards a mixed economy of scale.

- *the separation of responsibility for a service from the act of providing the service*: a local authority will retain responsibility for some services but it will increasingly pass on the doing.

- *the development of an enabling role*: there is a preference for the development of an enabling authority. While its meaning is contested, enabling clearly implies a local authority will work increasingly with and through others.

- *a closer relationship between paying for and receiving a service*: the rationale of the community charge was that it extended the net of contributors to local government. Its repeal meant the end of that aspiration but higher council house rent and charges for other services remain themes of the programme.

- *a greater emphasis on customer choice*: citizens are to be seen as customers in the terms of the Citizen's Charter. They are to choose from within a market plan of public and private sector providers.

- *a greater scope for individual and private sector provision*: individuals are to become more self-reliant and provide for themselves (supported by public sector subsidies). Voluntary

associations are seen as having an expanded role. Private sector
provision is set to increase. Local authorities are encouraged to
concentrate on those services really 'needed' by the public,
abandoning 'unnecessary' functions and allowing scope for
individuals and private sector provision.

- *producer interests within local government are to be challenged*:
  public sector trade unions and professional groups are to have
  their influence checked, as too are the welfare lobbies and client
  groups with which they have forged alliances to expand public
  services and expenditure. Competition and choice provide
  counter-measures to the perceived dominance of producer
  interests. More flexible employment contracts, pay and working
  practices are to be demanded of service producers.

- *a commitment to developing more 'business-like' management*:
  councillors are encouraged to perceive themselves less as engaged
  in detailed casework and administration and more as directors,
  giving a strategic vision and clear policy objectives to their local
  authority. Chief Officers are encouraged to delegate and work
  through target-setting and performance appraisal. Service
  deliverers are encouraged to adopt an ethos of commercialism:
  developing business plans, marketing skills and managing their
  cost centres.

- *an increased emphasis on new forms of accountability to the centre
  and within the locality*: central government will contract with
  local authorities and other agencies to achieve its policy
  objectives. It will be able to choose to which organisation to
  allocate resources and lay down performance targets and
  criteria. Decisions over local spending above centrally approved
  levels will be limited by capping. Business representatives are
  given control over some local institutions – for example Training
  and Enterprise Councils – and a greater influence in other areas.
  Self governing institutions are created. Parents are given an
  enhanced role in the government of schools.

- *a challenge to the mechanisms of local representative democracy*:
  the planning of some officer decisions beyond the direct control
  of councillors, new rules covering practices and procedures, the
  removal of functions from local government, and the exclusion
  of many officers from the right to stand for political office in
  neighbouring councils are likely to make the operation of the
  institutions of local representative democracy more problematic.

Market democracy and the choice it gives to individual consumers is seen as an alternative to decentralisation to local authorities.

The programme is so broad in its agenda and so wide in its scope that it is far from certain how the reforms will work out in practice. In particular the actual nature of the restructuring of local government and the extent of change to remain uncertain. What the cumulative impact will be is a matter for debate. There is no doubt that the role of local government is changing but in what way and how the process will be played out remain open questions. The Government's agenda pushes change in a number of directions. The aim of this book is to provide a basis for an assessment of the likely future role of local government in the light of the overall impact of the Government's proposals.

Part I of the book details changes in structure, finance and management. Chapter 2 deals with local government finance. Chapter 3 considers the introduction of competitive tendering. Chapter 4 examines the process of structural reorganisation. Chapter 5 looks at the debate about internal political management. Chapter 6 reviews progress on the Citizen's Charter.

Part II of the book examines developments in key services and functions. Chapter 7 analyses changes in education. Chapter 8 deals with social services and community care. Chapter 9 considers housing. Chapter 10 reviews policies concerned with urban and economic development.

Part III examines the context and implications of the Government's programme. Chapter 11 provides an evaluation of fifteen years of local government restructuring. Chapter 12 links changes in local government to a broader pattern of economic and social development. It also outlines the uneven processes of local change. Chapter 13 examines the New Right normative arguments underlying government policy. These are contrasted with the Left's perspective on local government. Chapter 14 provides one scenario for the future development of local government.

Notes and references

1. G. Stoker, *The Politics of Local Government*, 2nd edn (Macmillan, 1991).

I STRUCTURE, FINANCE AND MANAGEMENT

2 Finance

Tony Travers

The funding of local government has long been believed to have important implications for local autonomy and democracy. A system of local authority finance where councils have freedom to raise taxation and to determine how resources are used is clearly different from one where authorities rely largely or wholly on resources allocated by an upper tier of government. In the words of the Layfield Committee:

> If local authorities are to exercise discretion over the way they carry out their functions and to determine the level and pattern of expenditure on them, they should be responsible for finding the money through local taxes for which they are accountable.[1]

The system of local government finance in Britain was massively reformed in the years from 1989 to 1993. A new local tax was introduced and then abolished. Capping of local authority revenue expenditure was extended to the point where all councils are, in effect, capped. The proportion of income raised from local taxation was cut from about 60 per cent to under 20 per cent. Capital expenditure controls were tightened. The future of local government will be much influenced by the funding changes of the early 1990s.

The background to financial reform

During the late 1970s and throughout the 1980s, attempts to find new methods of raising revenue were accompanied by efforts to constrain revenue and capital expenditure. These efforts led the Government to pass a number of laws to change the financing of local government. However, the changes made to grant systems, rate-raising powers and capital controls generally fell short of a root-and-branch reform.[2]

The relentless legislative effort to curtail local authority expenditure has been well-documented.[3] The 1974–79 Labour Government first attempted to constrain revenue spending during the economic crisis which beset the mid-1970s.[4] These early pressures to cut were made within existing legislation: grants were reduced so as to discourage spending. Indeed, expenditure *did* level off and fall in 1976–77 and 1977–78. From 1979 onwards, the Conservative administration started to introduce new laws in order to give itself greater powers to discourage and then force down local expenditure.

First a new 'block grant' was introduced in 1981–82, giving the Government powers to taper off grants from authorities which chose to spend above centrally determined benchmark spending levels. This new grant system was backed up (during 1981–82) by 'targets' and 'penalties', which allowed severe grant penalties to be imposed on high-spending councils. Supplementary rates (i.e. the power to increase the local tax level more than once a year) were abolished in 1982. Rate limitation (widely known as 'capping') was foreshadowed in the Conservatives' 1983 manifesto, and introduced from 1985–6.[5] Many other smaller changes were also made.

The tightening of central government's financial control over local authorities had a negative impact on the relationship between local and central government. The fact that local elections in most years during the 1980s brought about a significant increase in the number of non-Conservative councils made matters worse. By the middle of the 1980s, a radical Tory Government faced many radical Labour administrations in local government. The stage was set for a continuing struggle about how local government was funded, and about how much it spent.

A further ingredient in the pressure for major reform of local authority finance was provided by the Conservative Party's interest in abolishing domestic rates. In the Party's October 1974 manifesto, the abolition of the domestic rating system was put forward as a lure for householders. By 1979, this commitment had been weakened somewhat, with the promise that domestic rates would go only after other direct taxation had been reduced.[6] Nevertheless, the association of the Conservatives with the idea of getting rid of the rates helped to build up pressure for their abolition.

The process of moving to the abolition of domestic rates had been tortuous. Official reports and consultative papers published during the 1960s and 1970s (and for that matter before) had failed to produce a new system of local authority finance and taxation that was acceptable to the government of the day. Issues of structure, functions and finance were invariably considered separately. The Conservatives' abolitionist sentiments of 1974 and 1979 had to wait until 1989 (in Scotland) and 1990 (in England and Wales) to reach fruition.

The reasons why it took so long to produce a full package of reform derived in part from the resilience of rates. Property taxes similar to rates had been in use since the sixteenth century,[7] were easy to collect, and the public were used to paying them. Other taxes looked relatively expensive to collect, while the introduction of any new system would produce millions of gainers and, more importantly, losers. Successive governments felt it was easier to keep the rates for a few more years, rather than risk unpopularity and expense by undertaking reform.

The failure to examine structure and finance together is more difficult to explain. Political issues, such as public resentment against the regressiveness of rates in the 1960s[8] or against massive rate rises in the 1970s and 1980s,[9] were perhaps seen as immediate problems, requiring short-term solutions and not as the starting point for all-embracing studies of local government. The Royal Commission on Local Government, 1966–69, could, if it had chosen, have decided to make recommendations about finance as well as structure as its terms of reference did not explicitly rule out the consideration of finance. In fact, although the Commission did discuss finance, it made no proposals for change. It appears that the commissioners assumed that their brief did not include financial proposals.

Moreover, during the 1960s and the early 1970s, growth in the economy was generally sufficient to pay for increases in Rate Support Grant from year to year. So long as rising local government expenditure could be financed out of national taxation, ratepayers could be shielded from the impact of the rising cost of local government services. It took the very large rate increases that accompanied the 1974 structural reorganisation in England and Wales to galvanise the Government into a full review of finance (though without reference to structure or funding). In the review, the Layfield Committee[10] examined all aspects of local authority finance, and concluded by offering the Government a choice between a more centrally controlled system of local government and one where there was greater local discretion. A majority of the Committee favoured the latter proposal, which would involve the introduction of a local income tax. The Government chose not to accept Layfield's analysis or proposal, and opted to leave local authority finance unreformed. Thus, at the end of the 1970s, there were many unresolved problems with local government funding.

The Conservatives, once in office, took a long time to get round to fulfilling their promise to abolish domestic rates. It is clear that when the Heath Government originally made its commitment in 1974, a local income tax was seen as the most plausible replacement for the property tax. By 1979, the Conservatives were committed to reducing direct taxation. The idea of giving local authorities the power to set income taxes was inconceivable by this time. After the publication of a Green Paper on *Alternatives to Domestic Rates* in 1981, the Prime Minister was reported to be in favour of replacing domestic levels with a local sales tax. But it was argued that having different rates of sales tax within metropolitan parts of the country would lead to border-hopping, as mobile consumers bought goods in areas with low tax rates. In addition, it was suggested that a local sales tax would contravene European Community obligations. Rates-capping was introduced from 1985–86 as a surrogate for full reform.

In the spring of 1985, a rating revaluation in Scotland made the Government deeply unpopular. The Conservatives were by now well into their second term, and had a majority of over 100 in the House of Commons. Siren voices from right-wing think-tanks, notably the Adam Smith Institute, pressed for a flat-rate poll tax, on the grounds that it was 'fair' that everyone within an authority should pay the same price for a similar basket of services. Moreover, by spreading the burden of paying for local authority services over all adults within an area, the consequences of increasing local government spending would be felt by the whole electorate. A review (by ministers and civil servants) of local grant finance in Britain, which had been set up in the autumn of 1984, had already started to reconsider the possibility of replacing domestic rates with a poll tax. The Prime Minister was convinced by the Scottish experience and by the enthusiasm of ministers involved with the 1984–85 review that poll tax should replace the rates.

The need for 'fairness' and 'accountability' underpinned the wholesale reform of local government finance proposed as a result of the 1984–85 review. It is clear from official documents published in the 1960s and early 1970s that fairness at this earlier time was taken to mean that local government should be redistributive. Local taxation was criticised in the 1960s for being regressive, while reforms such as the introduction of rate rebates were intended to reduce such regressiveness. Provision by local authorities, particularly of education and social services, was expected to assist poorer individuals and areas.

By 1986, the Government interpreted fairness in a different way. Surely, it was argued, it would be fair if everyone living in an authority's area made a contribution towards the provision of local services: everyone enjoys the benefit of using refuse collection, street cleaning, street lighting, and roads, and has the insurance offered by fire and police services. Thus, it is fair that all adults should contribute towards the cost of these services.[11] Of course, the vast majority of adults are also electors, and can therefore vote at local elections.

Strengthening this link between paying for local government and voting in local elections was at the heart of the Government's drive to strengthen local accountability. The Conservatives had become convinced that weak accountability allowed councils to spend in ways and on things which the majority of their electorate would find unappealing. Such irresponsibility was possible, it was argued, because many local authorities were able to raise the rates without most local people feeling the impact of the increase. Non-domestic ratepayers paid over half of any rate increase in most urban authorities, while in urban areas a large proportion of domestic ratepayers were protected by rebates.

Community charge and the National Non-Domestic Rate (NNDR) were designed to solve the problem of weak accountability. NNDR would be set by the Government, and thus be outside local authority control. Grants would also be fixed, in advance, by Whitehall. Community charge would be paid by virtually all adults, and would reflect any marginal change in spending by an authority. Thus, in the eyes of the Government, the new system of revenue finance was intended to improve fairness and strengthen accountability.

Much less effort was made between 1979 and 1989 to reform the control of capital expenditure. For a start, capital spending accounted for only about one-tenth of local authority spending. In addition, although control was less than perfect, sometimes there was massive *under-* rather than over-spending. However, as authorities accumulated capital receipts from the sale of assets such as council houses, and, at the same time, the Government found it increasingly difficult to target resources or to achieve precise control over borrowing, it was decided to accompany the reform of revenue financing in 1990 with a reform of capital financing.

The Government also reformed the funding of local authority housing at the end of the 1980s. Changes in the Housing Revenue Account (HRA), like the introduction of the community charge, were intended by the Government to improve accountability and to move towards a more market-oriented kind of local government. The consultative document which first described the HRA changes talked of moving towards a more business-like system of housing finance. The possibility of increased charging for local authority services, under provisions in the Local Government and Housing Act 1989, was also part of the ideological drive towards a greater market influence in local government.

The HRA and charging initiatives, taken with the requirements for services to be put out to compulsory competitive tender from August 1989, were clear evidence of the Government's desire to improve efficiency and effectiveness in local government. This drive for greater economy, efficiency and effectiveness was indicative of the strong desire within the Government to change the culture within local government from one of mass public providers towards a kind of publicly run holding company or 'enabler' for local services.

The community charge experiment

The poll tax was given the user-friendly official name of 'community charge', although opposition politicians, the media and most of the public have continued to refer to it as the poll tax. Even Government ministers and the then Prime Minister herself occasionally forgot to use its official name. The money raised from domestic rates in 1989–90 – about £10 billion – was to be collected from community charge payers in 1990–91. Incidence shifted from 20 million householders to virtually all (40 million) adults in England and Wales. A similar system started in Scotland on 1 April 1989.

The £10 + billion raised by councils from non-domestic, i.e. business, ratepayers was to be determined by the Government and called the *National Non-Domestic Rate*. All business ratepayers would pay the same rate in the pound on newly determined rateable values. Local authorities were to continue to collect non-domestic rates, but now had to hand the money over to the Government. The national total of rates was to be recycled to councils as a flat-rate amount. In effect, therefore, the non-domestic rate became an assigned revenue.

Finally, the £12 + billion of government grants – *Revenue Support Grant* – to local authorities continued, though distribution was altered, with the bulk of the allocations to authorities being designed to equalise for variations in spending need. 'Need' would be measured by a formula known as 'Standing Spending Assessments'. Any grant not needed for need equalisation purposes would be allocated to authorities as a flat-rate amount per adult.

The new ways of allocating non-domestic rates and government grants left some local authorities with more income from these sources than they used to receive, and others with significantly less. Where an authority gained from the new distribution of resources, it was possible to reduce the burden on domestic taxpayers, i.e. community chargepayers. Where an authority lost from the new allocations of grant and non-domestic rates, the burden on local domestic taxpayers was increased. These inter-authority shifts were to be introduced gradually over two to four years between 1990 and 1994.

In general, authorities in the South East of England, outer London, the South West, East Anglia and the West Midlands were expected to gain in the long term, while inner London, the North, the North West and Yorkshire and Humberside would lose. This meant that during the first few years of the new system, local tax bills would generally fall in the more economically affluent parts of the country and rise in the less buoyant areas.

Table 2.1 below shows the scale of the inter-authority shifts of resources, at its most extreme, brought about by the move from the

Table 2.1 Largest redistributions of resources between authorities

'Gainers'	£ per adult	'Losers'	£ per adult
Westminster	⁺345	Greenwich	−254
South Buckinghamshire	+225	Tower Hamlets	−216
Chiltern	+219	Southwark	−195
City of London	+172	Lewisham	−193
Wycombe	+163	Calderdale	−175
Kensington and Chelsea	+163	Barnsley	−153
Elmbridge	+138	Hammersmith and Fulham	−150
Epping Forest	+134	Barking and Dagenham	−143
Chelmsford	+131	Wandsworth	−138
Uttlesford	+129	Kirklees	−138

Source: Chartered Institute of Public Finance and Accountancy, unpublished
figures.

1989–90 system of local government finance to the new one. The
authorities shown as 'gainers' received a significant increase in
overall income from grant and business rates, while those shown as
'losers' received less.

Of course, the figures in Table 2.1 show only the biggest gains and
losses, and thus the largest implications for the community charge.
The majority of authorities saw smaller resource shifts. A system of
'safety nets' was introduced by the Government to slow down the
movements of resources from authority to authority.

Safety nets worked in such a way as to reduce the gains to gaining
authorities in 1990–91 and to introduce the losses to losing areas
over a number of years. Thus, the authorities in the 'gainers' column
received only a part of their extra resources in 1990–91, while those
in the 'losers' column lost little or nothing in 1990–91. This apparent
subsidy from gaining authorities to losing authorities proved very
unpopular with government back-benchers.

There were also considerable shifts of resources *within* each
authority. Households which paid relatively large rate bills in 1989,
and where there were only one or two adults, tended to pay less
under poll tax. On the other hand, households which had previously
paid relatively small rate bills, and where there were three or more
adults, generally paid more in local tax. The table below shows, in a
simplified form, what took place. The table shows what happened to
households of different types with the move from rates to
community charge in 1990–91. Households with the national

Table 2.2   Impact of the move from rates to community charge (all figures in £s per year)

1989–90 rate bill:	275	550	1100
Adults in household			
1	−75	+150	+750
2	−425	−150	+400
3	−775	−500	+50
4	−1125	−850	−300

Note: + indicates a gain, − indicates a loss.
Source: Constructed by author from national average rates and community charge figures.

average rate bill (about £550) are exemplified, as are those which had half and those which had double the average bill. The impacts on households with one, two, three, and four adults are shown. A charge of £350 is used to exemplify the impact. The actual average charge in England for 1990–91 was £363 per adult. The figures in the table are shown *before* the impact of any social security payments.

Two adults paying £700 in rates in 1989–90 would have paid, on average, £700 (£350 × 2) in 1990–91 and would thus have been unaffected, but a single adult paying £700 in rates would have gained £350 under community charge. Similarly, a three-adult household with a £700 rate bill would have lost £350. Households with additional adults lost more.

Households which previously paid rate bills of £350 and below will have paid more in 1990–91 in almost all cases. In the table above, two adults living in the average property would have paid about £150 more in 1990–91 than in 1989–90. Households with only one adult paid less in many cases, which meant that many single elderly people gained because of the abolition of rates. On the other hand, households with three or more adults have paid more, except where the previous rate bill was very high.

Gains and losses were in many cases very much greater than those exemplified in the table above. As the overall level of local taxation increased by about 30 per cent between 1989–90 and 1990–91, a majority of households lost out. Losing households outnumbered gainers by three or four to one. Short-term 'transitional arrangements' were implemented to slow down the losses for some households, while up to nine million people received rebates.

A massive political impact of the community charge started to take effect during the spring of 1990. Most local tax bills were set by local authorities in March and delivered in April or May. Enormous political and media activity attended the introduction of the 'poll tax'. Indeed, it is hard to exaggerate the political furore which built up during the early months of 1990. Hundreds of newspaper articles and television programmes were devoted to the subject, a by-election in the Midlands was fought as a virtual referendum on the new tax, the setting of the charge in many areas was accompanied by disturbances and, finally, at the end of March, a major march in central London ended in a riot.

Opinion poll evidence[12] suggested that many lower-income households were aware that, notwithstanding transitional arrangements and the benefit system, they had lost heavily in the move to the new tax. These lower-than-average-income households contained many marginal voters. The impact of the community charge on politically marginal households, more than any other effect, galvanised political and media attention. Turn-outs at local elections in May 1990 were generally well up on those in earlier years.

The political fall-out from the poll tax was predictable. In the May 1990 local elections, the Conservatives lost council seats from an already poor position. Only in London, notably in the boroughs of Wandsworth and Westminster, did the Conservatives do reasonably well. The two flagship authorities had undoubtedly been assisted by the fact that they had been able to set very low poll taxes. Tory politicians made much of the Wandsworth and Westminster results, while playing down the national electoral disaster inspired by the community charge.

The introduction of the community charge involved moving from a tax paid by 20 million householders in England and Wales to one where all 40 million adults paid. The increase in administration required was even greater than these figures suggest, as about 4.5 million of the 20 million ratepaying households were council tenants who received a single rent bill which combined rent and rates payments. The real increase in the number of tax points was thus from about 15 million to about 38 million.

This increase in the number of taxpayers was compounded by the fact that whereas under the rating system only a minority of householders paid rates by instalments, in the new system the legislation stated that all adults would pay by instalments unless they opted not to do so. Thus, there were perhaps 350 million tax instalments to collect under the poll tax as compared with under 100 million rates instalments.

A register had to be compiled by each authority in England and Wales. As no comprehensive register of adults already existed, each district council had to canvass every property to find out who lived where. This process was not without political controversy, given concerns about civil liberties and data protection. Despite dire political predictions of failure, the process of registration was broadly successful. About 99 per cent of the estimated adult population registered for the charge, though there was some dispute about the accuracy of the official population estimates. Registration tended to be most comprehensive in rural and suburban areas, and most incomplete in inner-city districts.

Registration, billing, the need to send out reminders and the day-to-day correction of the register proved to be labour- and computer-intensive. The cost of setting up the new system was estimated at some £300 million. Running costs were at least double those of domestic rates (an extra £250 million per year).[13]

Payments of tax to local government proved to be very slow at the start of the 1990–91 financial year. A survey showed that by the end of June 1990, 22 per cent of adults had paid no community charge at all. In some inner London boroughs, more than 60 per cent of the population had made no payment, though in some rural areas the proportion of non-payment was small. Overall, local authorities had collected about 18 per cent of their expected annual local tax by 30 June 1990, as compared with 31 per cent of rates at the same date in 1989.[14]

The local government taxation reform in England and Wales (and Scotland) was of considerable political and economic importance for the government of Britain. Years of uncertainty about the rating system was, at least for the time being, resolved. A major shift of incidence and accountability took place. National and local politics were affected. Hundreds of millions of pounds were spent on inplementing and operating community the charge.

However, the unpopularity of the new tax proved so great that it contributed to the downfall of the then Prime Minister (Mrs Thatcher) and was abandoned by the Government within a year of its introduction in England and Wales. It was replaced by the council tax.

Capital controls

The first day of April 1990 was an important day for local government. Not only did the community charge come into operation in England and Wales, but a new capital control system came into effect. Like the poll tax, the new capital arrangements were designed to achieve greater control over local authority expenditure. However, while the community charge was originally supposed to put control into the hands of local electors, the capital control system was very much a top-down mechanism.

Previous arrangements to control local authority capital spending in Britain had always given the Government enormous capacity to limit councils' overall activity. But the post-1990 system was a highly sophisticated attempt to ensure that the Department of the Environment could limit both net and gross expenditure, and also regulate the use of capital receipts. In addition, the definition of the activities to be brought within the scope of the new system was very wide indeed, and included leasing, barter deals and other kinds of capital-related expenditure.

The system to operate in England and Wales involved the Government in setting each authority an 'Annual Capital Guideline' (ACG) which was generally made up of assessed capital spending needs (agreed by the relevant Whitehall department) for each of a number of services. From this ACG, the Department of the Environment would take away a total of 'Receipts Taken Into Account' (RTIA). The amount thus deducted would depend upon the propensity of a particular authority to sell off capital assets. The difference between the ACG and the RTIA, known as the Basic Credit Approval (BCA), would be the amount that an authority would be allowed to fund out of borrowing and other credit.

The BCA would therefore vary with the size of an authority's ACG and of its RTIA. A council which had very high needs and a low propensity to produce capital receipts would receive a large BCA. Similarly, an authority with lower spending needs and high yields from receipts might get little or no BCA. In addition to their BCA, authorities may receive a 'Supplementary Credit Approval'. These supplementary amounts may only be used for the precise purposes determined by the Government.

The 1990 capital control system proved effective and robust. Although authorities complained about the relatively low levels of capital expenditure allowed, the system itself worked reasonably well. However, the degree of central control over local authority capital activity now available to central government is very considerable.

Council tax

Council tax was born in the aftermath of the Conservative Party leadership election which saw the removal of Mrs Thatcher and the arrival of John Major as Prime Minister. During the leadership campaign in November 1990, all three candidates (Major, Douglas Hurd and Michael Heseltine) promised to review the community charge if they won. When John Major arrived in Downing Street, he appointed Michael Heseltine as Secretary of State for the Environment and gave him the task of conducting the review.

Heseltine announced that civil servants would examine the finance, structure and internal management of local government. During the months between December 1990 and March 1991, a review team was created within the Department of the Environment which started to produce possible solutions to the poll tax problem. Successive leaks to the newspapers suggested the Government was looking at a number of options, from ameliorating the community charge to its replacement by a new property tax.

The 1991 Budget resulted in the Chancellor cutting all community charge bills by £140, at a total cost of £4.5 billion. Value Added Tax was raised from 15 to 17.5 per cent to pay for this major shift of resources. Additional transitional relief of £1.2 billion was paid out on top of this £4.5 billion, which meant that the proportion of local government income which was funded from the centre increased sharply.

In March 1991, Heseltine announced that the community charge would be abolished in favour of a new property-based tax, to be called 'council tax'.[15] The new tax would replace the community charge and, like it, would raise about 20 per cent of local authority revenue income (10 per cent in Wales). A short consultation paper was published.

The proposed replacement for community charge would

comprise a personal and a property element . . . where there are two or more adults living in the property, the basic bill will normally have to be paid in full. Single adult households will receive a personal discount, expressed as a percentage reduction off the basic bill. The Government propose a 25 per cent discount . . . liability for the new tax will fall on the occupier, normally the head of household. It will be up to that person to decide how the bill will be shared if there are other adults in the household.[16]

Each property would be allocated into one of seven bands (this number was later increased to eight). Houses and flats would be placed in an appropriate band according to how their capital value related to the national average for all properties in England, Scotland and Wales. The amount of the basic bill for each household would be determined by the band into which the property fell. This system of banding was designed to 'ensure that there is no need for regular or frequent revaluations'.

The tax would be set up so that the ratio of tax paid in the highest band would be 2.5 times the payment in the lowest. There would be fixed ratios for each intermediate band, Local authorities would not have the freedom to vary these relative payments by properties in particular bands, though they could (within capping rules) set any level of local tax they chose.

Capping would be used to restrain local expenditure and taxation. In the consultation paper, the Government stated:

> no tax will be acceptable if it is levied at very high rates as a result of excessive spending by local authorities. Central government has a duty to protect local taxpayers from unacceptably high bills as well as to control the level of public expenditure. The new system will therefore need to incorporate effective arrangements to ensure proper restraint in local spending and taxation.[17]

The Revenue Support Grant (RSG) system would ensure that differences from authority to authority in the need to spend and in the number of properties within bands would be compensated. The RSG would thus work in such a way that all households in properties in the same band would attract the same bill for a standard level of spending, wherever they were located within the country.

Council tax would require a single bill for each household and, crucially, would not need the maintenance of a register of all adults. Households with very low incomes would not be required to make any payments (unlike the community charge, where even the poorest individuals had to pay 20 per cent of their local tax bill).

The new tax closely resembled the old domestic rating system which had been swept away in 1990 by the community charge. The consultative document that unveiled the council tax included the Government's rationale for abandoning the tax which Mrs Thatcher had once described as the 'flagship' of her fleet. Paragraph 1.6 of the 1991 consultative paper accepted that 'the public have not been persuaded that the scheme [community charge] is fair'. That was that, and local government embarked on its third tax within 1100 days.

Aftermath

The ease with which council tax was introduced in Britain proved surprising to most commentators. Following the disastrous community charge experiment, it was expected that there might be public resistance to the council tax and, most particularly, to any redistribution of burden that might occur at the point of its introduction in 1993. In fact, there was very little public reaction. Council tax operates effectively in virtually all authorities.[18]

The reasons for the success of the council tax include its perceived fairness; the relatively low levels of the tax (compared with the first year of community charge); the economic and political profile of those who paid more as a result of the move to council tax; professionalism in central and local government; ease of administration; and, perhaps, a certain public weariness with the subject of local government finance.

Perceived fairness (or the lack of it) is widely believed to have damaged the community charge. The return to a property-based tax where people in bigger homes pay more than those in smaller ones was evidently seen by the public as being more equitable than a flat-rate tax on all adults.

In addition, the average level of council tax bills in 1993 was well below the figures for the first year of poll tax in 1989 (Scotland) and 1990 (England and Wales) because of the 1991 Budget cut in local taxation. These lower bills were less likely to cause an uproar than the relatively high ones sent out in 1989 and 1990. Capping ensured that no authority could push up spending at the point when the new tax was introduced.

Moreover, the Government set up a new system of transitional relief to assist those who found themselves facing higher local tax bills in 1993–94. Household losses were limited to amounts ranging from about £75 to £200 per year. Compared with losses of over £1000 suffered by some households in 1990, the 1993 figures were modest indeed.

The economic and political profile of losers in 1993 was very different from that in the first year of poll tax. In 1990, most of the households which lost large sums consisted of people who were 'not quite poor' – just above the point where they would receive social security help. Many of them were marginal voters, whom the Conservatives could ill afford to alienate. The 1993 losers tended to be better off, and were far less likely to change their vote as a result of the (relatively small) losses they suffered because of the move to council tax.

Professionalism in both town halls and Whitehall meant that the introduction of a third local government tax within three years was achieved without misery. Central government departments made great efforts in the run-up to 1993 to ensure that they assisted local authorities in every way possible. Regulations were published as early as possible. Local authorities responded with speed and effectiveness.

The fact that the council tax is far easier to administer than the community charge also ensured the new tax a relatively smooth passage. The Government's decision to remove the '20 per cent rule', whereby even the poorest had to pay local tax, made administration very much easier than for the community charge: it was no longer necessary to collect millions of very small amounts of money from people with little or no income. One bill per household, as opposed to one bill per adult, also made administration easier.

Finally, after several years of public attrition between central and local government over local taxation, it is possible that the media and the public had become a little weary of local government finance. 'Poll tax riots' made headlines, while 'council tax introduced with few problems' was less newsworthy.

The future of local government finance

Whether or not the council tax can provide a robust local tax in the long term is still uncertain. Because it raises only some 20 per cent of authorities' revenue income, local government remains heavily dependent on central support. Small changes in the level of Revenue Support Grant (RSG) can have a far greater effect on local taxation and expenditure than decisions made by councillors. The formulae underlying the RSG – most notably 'Standard Spending Assessments' which are designed to achieve equalisation for authorities' relative needs to spend – are much criticised and come under relentless pressure for change.[19] So long as local government relies on Whitehall for such a large part of its income, the future of local taxation must be in some doubt.

First, there is the 'why bother?' argument. Local government raises very little of its income from local taxation, so why not simply transfer the remaining proportion to VAT or some other national tax? Second, because authorities are being forced by capping to move their spending closer and closer to Government-set Standard Spending Assessment levels, they will soon all be setting very nearly the same tax rate. Once all authorities have the same tax rate, what purpose is there in having a local tax?

Third, if there were a sudden bout of inflation, there would be a risk that (unless grant increased steeply) council tax would have to increase by a large percentage. Such an increase would be caused by the high 'gearing' between percentage rises in spending and changes in central support: an additional 1 per cent on spending will lead to a 5 per cent rise in taxation if central grants were unchanged.

Fourth, as the valuations used for the council tax (based on prices in 1991) become out of date, the tax base will come to look unconvincing. Capital values – as opposed to notional rentals used for domestic rates – are widely known and understood. If the valuation lists become grossly unrealistic, council tax could be undermined.

The Conservative Government evidently believed, even following the poll tax débâcle, that local taxation was an important feature of local democracy. Both Labour and the Liberal Democrats have maintained their support for local government taxation during the upheavals of 1986 to 1993. Labour flirted for several years during the 1980s with the idea of a local tax based on income *and* property. By the 1992 general election, they had come to support a property tax (called 'fair rates'), coupled with the return of non-domestic rates to local control. The Liberal Democrats have stuck firmly to their long-term commitment to introduce a local income tax.

It is likely that local government finance will be further reformed in the years ahead. Both the major opposition parties will probably want to make changes. Labour appears to have accepted that the council tax, with some amendments, could form the basis of 'fair rates'. The Liberal Democrats will continue to press for local income tax.

As long as the Conservatives remain in power, universal capping of expenditure will remain in place. Whether this policy will lead to long-term spending levels that are lower (or higher) than what would have been achieved without capping remains the subject of debate. Labour and the Liberal Democrats remain opposed to capping. Nevertheless, whichever government is in power at Westminster, it is likely that powerful downward pressures on local budgets will be maintained.

Local government finance has not reached a stable position. In the medium and longer term, changes will have to be made, either to strengthen the local tax base (and thus local democracy) or to accept that local government is merely an agent of the centre, perhaps with little or no local tax-raising power. The 1990s should point the way to the long-term future for the funding of local government.

Notes and references

1. *Local Government Finance: Report of the Committee of Inquiry* (Chairman Frank Layfield QC) (HMSO, 1976) p. 286.
2. See T. Travers, 'Conclusion', *The Politics of Local Government Finance* (Allen & Unwin, 1986).
3. See, for example, J. Gibson, *The Politics and Economics of the Poll Tax: Mrs Thatcher's Downfall* (EMAS, 1990) ch. 2.
4. *Public Expenditure to 1979–80*, Cmnd 6393 (London, HMSO, 1976), pp. 12–13.
5. See T. Travers, *The Politics of Local Government Finance*, ch. 8.
6. *The Conservative Manifesto 1979* (Conservative Central Office, 1979) p. 14.
7. C. D. Foster, R. Jackman and M. Perlman, *Local Government Finance in a Unitary State* (Allen & Unwin, 1980) pp. 152–71.
8. *Committee of Inquiry into the Impact of Rates on Households: Report,* Cmnd 2582 (HMSO, 1965).
9. See T. Travers, *The Politics of Local Government Finance*, p. 160.
10. *Local Government Finance: Report of the Committee of Inquiry,* Cmnd 6453 (HMSO, 1976).

11. *Paying for Local Government,* Cmnd 9714 (HMSO, 1986) ch. 10, para. 10.5.
12. Opinion polls were conducted for the *Local Government Chronicle* in each year from 1987 to 1990. Such polls consistently showed that lower-income households were aware that they would lose because of the move to poll tax.
13. *Implementation and Collection of the Community Charge, Volume 1: Forecast of Costs* (Price Waterhouse, 1988).
14. Survey by IPF Ltd for BBC '*Newsnight*', 14 August 1990.
15. Local Government Review, *A New Tax for Local Government: Consultation Paper* (Department of the Environment, 1991).
16. Ibid., Summary, paras 5–7.
17. Ibid, para 7.2.
18. Audit Commission, *The Sooner the Better: Progress Report on the Council Tax* (HMSO, 1993).
19. Rita Hale and Tony Travers, *£36 Billion and Rising* (Joseph Rowntree Foundation, 1993).

3 Competition and Public Service Delivery

Kieron Walsh

The Government's attempt to introduce market disciplines into the operation of local authorities through the introduction of competition for services has two main components: the requirement to subject some services to competitive tender and the imposition of internal trading and markets. The tendency is to focus upon the requirement to put work out to tender, but the requirement to operate an internal market has had at least as great an impact, because it has created an ethos of commercialism within the local authority. It is increasingly possible to see the local authority as a set of contracts and quasi-contracts, involving a network of internal and external trading organisations.

This chapter is concerned with the development of the policy of competitive tendering and contracting in local government. I start by examining the origins of the policy in the thinking of the New Right and in the activities of specific local authorities. I go on to examine the form that the policy has taken in the Local Government Planning and Land Act 1980 and the Local Government Act 1988 and in the development of voluntary tendering. We will see that the Government has slowly tightened the rules, as it has done in other areas of policy such as trade union legislation. Rather than attempt to change things completely all at once the Government has developed and, indeed, learnt its strategy as it has gone along. I shall argue that, from the Government's perspective, competitive tendering has the virtue that it can gradually be extended and can be changed to meet varying circumstances. The impact of competitive tendering will be considered under five headings: the financial implications, the effect on service quality, the effects on the management of local authorities, the impact on the role of the politician, and the impact on staff and industrial relations.[1]

28

The pressure for competition

The pressure for the introduction of competition in local government came from within the Conservative Party, from the various 'think-tanks' of the New Right, such as the Centre for Policy Studies, the Institute of Economic Affairs and the Adam Smith Institute, from the private sector and the academic world, and from within local government itself.[2] Contracting out fitted easily into the new market-oriented philosophy of conservatism that developed under Mrs Thatcher, and its value as a strategy was enhanced by the public sector strikes of 1979, which gave powerful ammunition to those who wished to reduce the influence of the producers of public services.

The support for competitive tendering grew through the early 1980s, particularly on the Conservative back benches, and a number of its major proponents, notably Michael Forsyth and Christopher Chope, entered Parliament and became ministers. The 'think-tanks' pressed for legislation on competitive tendering, and there was a strong overlap between the politicians and the think-tanks, with the Adam Smith Institute publishing two of Michael Forsyth's pamphlets.[3] Private sector lobbying for the extension of competitive tendering has grown stronger as the number of firms in the market has increased. There are some differences between contractors, notably in the extent to which they favour formalistic tendering, as against more flexible approaches.

There were two sources of pressure for competition and trading within local government itself – the Chartered Institute of Public Finance and Accountancy (CIPFA) and individual authorities. In 1969 CIPFA recommended that Direct Labour Organisations (DLOs) should compete for a representative proportion of their work, and in 1975 that local authorities should run their DLOs as trading organisations, that tendering should be adopted for the vast majority of contracts and that accounts should be based on value rather than cost. These principles were accepted by the Labour Party[4] and a government report on the running of DLOs in 1978 argued that they should 'act as trading bodies and charge on a formal contract basis',[5] that they should make a rate of return on capital and that there should be limited tendering. The same report carried the principle of competition further by stating that DLOs should also be allowed to compete for some kinds of work in the private sector. The approach to the operation of DLOs established by the Local Government Planning and Land Act 1980 followed this model closely, while denying local authorities the right to compete for private sector work. The introduction of a competitive regime for building and highways construction and maintenance can be seen as an expression of an existing stream of policy thinking, rather than a break with the past.

Competitive tendering and internal trading for services other than construction, for which there was a well-developed external market, had different roots. There had been no significant advocacy of competition from professionals or Government before 1979, but, following the public sector strikes of that year, in which a number of authorities used contractors to carry out services on an emergency basis, some, such as Southend, decided to put services out to tender, arguing that the contract resulted in a considerable saving. Other authorities, notably Wandsworth, followed the example and tenders were invited for services such as school meals, school cleaning, road sweeping, grounds maintenance and building cleaning. The extent of voluntary tendering in the 1980s was not great; the *Local Government Chronicle* survey in 1988 found that between 1981 and 1988 131 councils had contracted out services and claimed savings of £42 million.[6] But most contracts are small and the total value of work put out was less than £100 million. Most of the authorities contracting for services were Conservative-controlled and in the South-East of England. There is little evidence that, left to themselves, local authorities would have introduced contracting and competition on a significant scale. Change was only likely to follow from government pressure and legislation, though the action of individual authorities was valuable in providing exemplars.

Legislation on competition in local government

The first move in the Government's initiation of competition in the provision of local authority services was the introduction of the Local Government Planning and Land Act 1980, which required local authorities to engage in competitive tendering for the construction and maintenance of buildings and highways, and to maintain trading accounts which had to make a surplus sufficient to enable them to make a rate of return on capital of at least 5 per cent. If local authorities wished to carry out work by direct labour then they had first to invite bids for the work and were only allowed to carry it out if they won the right to do so in competition.

The impact of the Local Government Planning and Land Act was limited by the various exemptions that were made. Local authorities were not required to bid for any building maintenance work valued at less than £10000, or any highways work costing less than £100000. Small DLOs were exempted from the legislation; emergency work was excluded; and local authorities were allowed to allocate extension contracts to the DLO. Various specific types of work were excluded, such as the maintenance of street lighting. These exclusions gave the local authority a good deal of leeway. Local authorities were also able to let contracts in a form that was unattractive to some potential bidders, by asking for tenders for very large amounts of work, or combining different aspects of work in a way that makes it unattractive. Local authorities did not, in practice, have to win the majority of their work in competition except in the case of new construction, which was, in any case, declining as housing expenditure was cut back.

In the shire counties in particular the Act had a relatively limited impact on the amount of work that the authority had to compete for in the early years and most county DLOs were allocated more than 90 per cent of their work. The Federation of Civil Engineering Contractors was moved to produce a report claiming that the competition was 'neither fair nor frequent'.[7] Generally, though, the pressure from private contractors was relatively limited.

The fact that many local authorities were able to avoid competition in the early years did not mean that the Act had no effect. There was competition, especially for building work, and some trades, notably painting, for which the market is easy to enter, were very strongly affected. Some types of authority fared worse than others, with London boroughs and Welsh counties finding the greatest difficulty in maintaining their share of the work. But the major effect was through the requirement to keep separate trading accounts for the competitive services. Many DLO managers now saw themselves as having commercial priorities. They were encouraged, as one metropolitan district treasurer put it, to 'Think Profit'[8] and many contrasted that with a service orientation. DLO managers saw themselves as subject to market pressures and behaved accordingly. Many who felt that they could not make the transition to the new values left and new managers rose quickly to head DLOs. Pressure grew on trade unions and pay and conditions of their members. DLO managers became assertive about their needs within the authority.

The impact of the Local Government Planning and Land Act has increased as the Government has continually tightened the regulations. Authorities have been required to tender for increasing proportions of work that they do, and the areas for manoeuvre have gradually been closed down. By the 1990s the vast majority of local government building and highways construction work was subject to competition in an increasingly tight market. The private sector had more than 50 per cent of the building maintenance market, compared with 36 per cent in 1982–83. Failures to meet financial targets are common, and a number of DLOs have been closed down, or had the work they are allowed to do restricted.[9]

The requirement to compete was extended by the Transport Act 1985, which required bus undertakings to operate commercially. The Government also extended the requirement to operate on a commercial basis to some local authority airports. The legislation on public transport has had a major impact on bus services, with higher fares and lower subsidies, though frequencies have increased in many cases.

The major extension of competition came with the Local Government Act 1988, which required competition for a number of defined activities – refuse collection, street cleaning, building cleaning, catering, schools and welfare catering, vehicle maintenance, grounds maintenance and sports and leisure management. As in the Local Government Planning and Land Act 1980, the local authority, if it wins, must keep trading accounts, which may not be subsidised, and may not cross-subsidise each other. A rate of return on capital of 5 per cent, or break-even, for building cleaning and sports and leisure management must be achieved in trading accounts.

The Local Government Act 1988 was more tightly drawn than the Local Government Planning and Land Act 1980 and the regulations governing competition and trading have continually been tightened, restricting the freedom of local authorities. The Act required local authorities not to 'act in a manner having the effect or intended or likely to have the effect of restricting, distorting or preventing competition'.[10] This catch-all clause is the most powerful in the legislation since it means that local authorities must examine everything that they do to ensure that it is not anti-competitive. Detailed regulations have been produced by the Department of the Environment, covering such matters as how contracts are to be let and what may be taken into account in the process of evaluating tenders. Trade associations and individual companies have been active in policing the legislation and in taking cases to the Secretary of State, who has taken action, such as requiring retendering, in a number of cases.

The powers of the local authority are further restricted by the contract compliance sections of the legislation which define a number of matters as being non-commercial and which forbid the local authority to ask questions about them or to take them into account in the award of contracts. The matters defined as non-commercial include terms and conditions of employment, the use of labour-only subcontracts and restrictions on the country of origin of materials. The Secretary of State has laid down specific questions that may be asked by local authorities in carrying out their duty to prevent unlawful racial discrimination. The limitations on contract compliance have reduced the local authority's ability to vet companies that wish to tender for their work and prevented it applying contractual conditions such as fair wages clauses. This situation may change because of the implications of the Transfer of Undertakings (Protection of Employment) Regulations 1981, which make cutting staff numbers and pay and conditions more difficult.

There was a further extension of competition, to cover waste disposal, in the Environmental Protection Act 1990. Local authorities, if they wish to carry out this work, must form internal local authority waste disposal companies, which then compete for the work. It is likely, in the future, that local authorities will contract out waste disposal work or engage in joint ventures with the private sector, because of difficulties in access to capital for the major investments that will be needed.

Competition is now to be extended to central support services, such as law and finance, construction-related services, such as architecture and surveying, and housing management. It is also being considered for libraries and museums. The extension of competitive tendering is to be phased in over a number of years, and, initially, only a proportion of the work will be subject to competition. The process is likely to be delayed, and made more complex, by the reorganisation of local government.

Tendering for professional services such as law and finance poses new problems for the local authority, because such services are difficult to specify and the monitoring of quality is more difficult. It will also be necessary to distinguish the democratic 'core' of the authority and those elements of professional services that exist to support front-line services. The requirement to compete for professional services is leading to radical rethinking of the organisation of the local authority.

Competition in education and social services

The introduction of competitive tendering has been complicated in the case of education by the delegation of budgets to schools and by schools opting for grant-maintained status. The money allocated to the school includes an amount to enable it to pay for competitive services. School catering services are still to be provided centrally unless the school can show that it could provide the service more efficiently itself. In cleaning, grounds maintenance and vehicle maintenance the school is free to opt into or out of the service that the local authority is providing. Even if it wishes to stay with the authority the school can ask for a particular level of service to be specified. Small schools are exempted from the requirements of the legislation.

The schools have strong staffing powers over DLO staff. The governing body of the school has the right to 'require the removal from the school of a particular DLO worker'[11] and to select a replacement, a power that has been little used. Schools that opt out of local authority control and become grant-maintained may stop using the DLO even if the authority won the tender. The Education Reform Act places great powers in the hands of the headteacher and governors who may well differ from the authority in their approach to competitive tendering. Further education colleges, now with independent status, have commonly operated tenders both for manual services and financial services such as payroll, commonly letting contracts to the private sector.

Generally schools and colleges are still contracting through local authorities for the majority of their support services, though there are indications that they will, in future, want more individually tailored provision.[12]

In social services contracting has been introduced by the National Health Service and Community Care Act 1990. Social services departments have taken over funding and responsibility for the purchase of care from the Department of Social Security. They are required to spend the majority of the finance transferred in the private sector. More generally the Act requires a move to a more market-based approach to care involving contracts, competition, purchaser–provider splits, and internal markets.

Voluntary tendering

The voluntary use of competition by local authorities has increased rapidly in the 1990s. It has developed particularly in information technology, where facilities management agreements are widely used. Externalisation of professional services has become increasingly common, particularly in shire districts and shire counties. The most extreme example is Berkshire, which has a programme to externalise the majority of its services, including core support services such as finance. Other authorities have externalised services ranging from housing and property management to audit and budget preparation. A variety of mechanisms have been used for externalisation, including management buy-outs and buy-ins, joint ventures and trade sales. Even without the legislation the strategy of externalisation can be expected to become more common. Interest from the private sector in providing services as contractors is increasing rapidly. A mixed economy of provision is rapidly emerging.

The impact of competition

The most obvious immediate effect of competition is that a higher proportion of local authority work is done by private companies than in the past. The Local Government Management Board[13] figures show that the private sector has won about 40 per cent of the contracts let under the Local Government Act 1988, though, because they tend to have more success in winning smaller contracts, they have won only 17 per cent of the work by value. Private contractors have been most successful in winning building cleaning contracts, in which local authorities are unwilling to match the poor pay and harsh conditions operated by many contractors. The success of contractors is steadily increasing.

The total value of the services subject to competition is higher. Carnaghan and Bracewell-Milnes[14] estimate that the number of staff involved is between 250 000 and 300 000 and the annual cost of the work about £5000 million to £6000 million.[14] This figure excludes housing management, which will involve about 55 000 staff and a cost of about £1500 million. Markets of this size are bound to attract competition, particularly where there are few barriers to entry and exit, as in the case of building cleaning. Even if the local authorities wins the right to provide the service, competitive tendering and internal trading will have a great impact on the operation of local government.

The financial effects

Studies of competitive tendering in British local government have generally found that it results in a reduction in costs. The Audit Commission's study of housing maintenance found that 'costs tend to be higher when work is not subject to competition',[15] and for refuse collection[16] it found that privatised services had lower-than-average costs, but that some services provided by direct labour did equally well. Generally the Commission concludes that:

> The most competitive DLOs have costs that are lower than the prices quoted by the average private suppliers; but an average DLO's costs are more expensive to ratepayers than private suppliers. That is, most DLOs are not fully cost effective.[17]

In a study of highway maintenance the Audit Commission found savings of about 14 per cent following competition.[18]

The major early studies of the financial impacts of competitive tendering in local government in Britain were those by Domberger *et al.*[19] and Cubbin *et al.*[20] which were both concerned with refuse collection. Domberger *et al.* found that:

Costs are lower (by about 22 per cent) where private contracting is taking place. This result suggests that the introduction of private contracting has yielded substantial cost savings – a conclusion confirmed by analysis of the trend in costs in authorities where private contracting has been introduced. Real costs have fallen in these authorities.[21]

They also found cost savings where tenders had been awarded in-house and argued that:

> it is the introduction of competition, rather than awarding contracts to private firms, which is the critical factor in achieving lower costs.[22]

Cubbin *et al.* took this work further and attempt to find the source of the savings. They find that:

> for those authorities with private contractors, the bulk of the savings can be attributed to improvements in technical efficiency – that is, physical productivity of both men and vehicles. Only a small residual remains that can be attributed to other, pecuniary factors.[23]

Overall the early evidence suggested that there were large savings to be made through subjecting services to competitive tendering, some of which would come from reducing pay and conditions, some from new methods of working and some from increasing the pace of work and reducing the total labour input. These studies were all based upon the relatively limited experience of voluntary contracting for refuse collection, mostly by small local authorities, before the introduction of the Local Government Act 1988; it would be dangerous to generalise from them.

Evidence on the financial impact of competition following the introduction of the Local Government Act 1988 suggests lower savings than for earlier voluntary competition. Szymanski and Jones studied refuse collection following competition and found that direct unit costs had fallen by 27 per cent, but, after allowing for administrative costs, they estimate the final savings figure as being between 10 and 20 per cent.[24] Other studies suggest lower figures. A *Local Government Chronicle* survey in 1990, which covered 476 contracts, found average savings of 5.6 per cent.[25] A detailed study of 40 local authorities by Walsh and Davis found an average saving of 6.5 per cent, though with considerable variation from service to service and authority to authority.[26] There was some tendency for the level of saving to increase over time, reflecting market conditions and the economic problems of the recession. These findings cannot be extended to professional services, which will face quite different market conditions. Those authorities that have voluntarily contracted services generally claim to have made savings, but they have been able to determine the conditions of competition more than will be possible under the compulsory regime.

The main sources of savings have come from the reduction of the number of staff employed to do the work, commonly by 20 to 30 per cent. Pay and conditions have been cut, but this has been a secondary source of saving. Methods of work have also been changed, and new equipment has been introduced, for example larger refuse wagons. Any full social costing would have to take account of the unacknowledged costs of unemployment and increased benefits following pay reductions.

The nature of the market

The claim that there are savings from contracting out because of the competition for the work can be countered by the argument that the initial competitive market will give way to monopoly or oligopoly as time passes and as large firms acquire smaller firms that have won contracts. Certainly there is some evidence of amalgamation of contractors, both in manual and professional services. The initial saving to the authority may be eroded over time as contractors exploit local monopolies. Amalgamation may well increase as firms attempt to increase their capacity to offer combined contracts, for example for cleaning, catering and grounds maintenance, and try to buy firms in the relevant industries. So far, though, there is little evidence of growing monopoly, and the number of firms entering the market has been growing. Nor is there any evidence of winning contracts through 'loss-leader' bids, though there are plenty of examples of bids being entered that have turned out to be too low, both by contractors and internal providers.

The argument that the savings that result from competition will be eroded by the growth of monopoly has, in turn, been countered by three arguments. First, there are still competitive pressures even when there is a monopoly because of the nature of the stock market and the labour market for managers. There will be a threat of takeover for those firms that do not use their assets effectively whatever the structure of the industry. Managers will also want to ensure that the firms for which they work perform well so that their value in the market and their own rewards are enhanced. This is likely to be a particularly strong argument in service industries that are technologically simple and where the key skill is the effective management of staff. If a firm has a poor record of performance both it and its managers are likely to be vulnerable.

Second, many of the large firms that are active in the services that are subject to competition operate through subsidiaries, and they are harsh in the way that they will treat subsidiaries that are failing to make adequate returns. Though they are part of larger firms, individual subsidiaries will be expected to make an adequate rate of return on capital and managers will have detailed performance targets to meet. Third, according to the theory of contestable markets,[27] the fact of concentration need not destroy competition, which will depend on the conditions for entry to and exit from the market. When the barriers to entry and exit are low then firms will be forced to behave as if there was competition, because otherwise new firms will force their way into the market. It is not the pattern of ownership that is important but the nature of the industry, and in most local authority services entry and exit are not likely to be difficult. It is possible that firms in industries where concentration is high will collude with each other to control potential competition, and there is some evidence that this has happened. Much of the justification for competitive tendering assumes a degree of effectiveness in the working of markets which is only weakly supported by the evidence. The need for regulation of the market may increase.

A different perspective on the effectiveness of competition is offered by Williamson's work on transaction costs,[28] which compares the advantages of internal organisation of the production of goods and services with those of buying them on the market. Williamson argues that the appropriate form of organisation will depend upon the cost of transactions under the alternative forms of organisation which will depend, in turn, on three variables – bounded rationality, opportunism and asset specificity. Bounded rationality means that we cannot know everything, and that gaining information costs money. Opportunism refers to the presumption that people will pursue their interests whenever the chance arises, and they will do so with 'guile'. Asset specificity refers to the fact that some assets are highly specific to the uses to which they are put, while others can be moved quickly and easily from one use to another.

The presence of bounded rationality makes it difficult to write contracts because future circumstances cannot be fully anticipated. The less certain is the future the more contracts will need to be written to allow variation, but contractors will always look to variation as a means of making high profits. Opportunism will be greater the more difficult it is to state precisely what it is that is wanted and the standards of performance. Asset specificity is higher the less there is a market for the labour skills or the equipment used in the production of the service. When the local authority can simply go elsewhere to purchase the same skills or equipment then the power of the supplier is reduced and purchase on the market is a more effective way of obtaining goods or services.

The greater are bounded rationality, opportunism and asset specificity, the less effective is contracting on the market and the more effective is internal production. It is easier for an organisation to obtain information on those whom it employs, to change their patterns of work, and to take sanctions against those whose opportunistic behaviour will damage the organisation. Most of the services that are to be subject to competitive tendering, so far, do not come high in the scales of bounded rationality, opportunism and asset specificity. As competition is extended it is involving services where these factors are important. In professional services bounded rationality is high. Indeed professionalism is partly justified by the difficulty the lay person has in knowing what should be done in complex areas of work.

Opportunism arises in professional services because of the information advantages professionals have over lay people. Asset specificity may also be high because professionals are likely to acquire specialist knowledge of the organisation, making contract-switching more difficult.

Transaction costs are likely to vary with the nature of service, and the extent to which the contractor can be trusted. Walsh and Davis estimated the costs of preparing for competition under the Local

Government Act 1988 to be about 7.5 per cent of the annual value of contracts, and about 1.8 per cent of the total value. The Audit Commission[29] estimated the average costs of managing contracts as ranging from 1.4 per cent of the annual contract value for education and welfare catering to about 12.5 per cent for vehicle maintenance. It is not clear whether transaction costs for professional service contracts will be higher or lower than those for manual services. It may be that, for more complex services, difficulties of monitoring and contract specification are so great that lower costs may result since local authorities may be forced to trust contractors. The experience of the United States of America, though, is that the management costs of contracting can be high.[30]

Williamson's analysis is valuable in emphasising the structure of information rather than ownership. The ability of the authority to obtain an effective service on the market will depend upon the information that it is able to obtain. The more difficult it is to develop an information system that will allow the client to control the contractor the more likely it is that internal production will be more effective than purchase on the market. Poor information is one of the major difficulties that local authorities have faced in contracting.

Quality of service

The impact of competition on the quality of service is disputed, with the Department of the Environment arguing that standards have improved, and the trade unions claiming that it is a disaster for quality. In the early stages of competition there were certainly significant problems, but total failure is rare. The Local Government Management Board found that only 85 contracts had been terminated out of a total of 4421 let, that is, about 1.9 per cent. This may not be a good indicator of the level of success. It is likely that local authorities will persist with contracts even if there are some problems of service delivery because of the costs of reletting them and the disruption involved. The Local Government Management Board found that difficulties were particularly likely in refuse collection, street cleaning and building cleaning. Walsh and Davis found that the standards specified in contracts were being attained in about 90 per cent of cases, though failings were more common in some services, notably cleaning.

The main causes of failure are threefold. First there is simply poor standard of work, which is most likely in building cleaning and grounds maintenance. The second difficulty is incomplete work, and the third is not completing work on time. At the same time improvements in service standards have resulted from the requirement to specify work, and to be clear about the relationship between cost and quality. Local government officers involved in contracting tend to argue that the process has been valuable in forcing them to review existing practice. Local authorities are focusing more clearly on service quality and standards as they learn to manage competition. Formal quality assurance systems are increasingly being introduced.

It is difficult to draw clear conclusions about the impact of contracting and competition on the quality of service. There have obviously been failures, but, at the same time, there is no evidence of any significant breakdown in public service standards. A number of conclusions seem justified. First, service failure is most likely at the beginning of contracts. There are problems of transition to the contract mode of operation, particularly when there are significant changes in the pattern of service. New providers may not have a detailed knowledge of the work or of the local area, and must go through a period of learning. Second, though there are some differences between the public and private sector, they are both equally competent in most cases. Third, the standards of service have tended to become more uniform as a result of competition.

The impact on management

Local authorities are changing their patterns of management and organisation in response to competitive tendering and internal trading. The major change is the need to separate the role of client and contractor within the authority. This separation may be made within a department or by creating separate contractor departments. A few authorities have also created technical client units to advise on such matters as specification and contract conditions. It is becoming increasingly common for authorities to bring together the various services that are to be subject to competition in a single trading department, in order to reap economies of scale, gain flexibility, and concentrate managerial expertise. The effect of change as a result of competition is being felt most strongly in shire districts because a greater proportion of their work is subject to competition compared to other authorities, but all authorities are facing the need to change their management structures. The separation of client and contractor will result in increasingly complex organisational structures as competition is extended to professional services.

The requirements to keep internal trading accounts, meet financial targets, and put in successful bids has led direct service and direct labour organisations to put pressure on the rest of the authority to make changes. The costs of central support services such as law, personnel and accountancy are recharged to the various service accounts. These central recharges mattered little in the past, since they were not treated as part of the core budget, but are now seen as an imposition by the DSO managers, who often feel that they are excessive and that they have too little control over the charge or the way it is calculated. Pressure is being put on central services to justify the charges they levy and on the authority to allow greater freedom for the managers of trading departments to decide the level of service that they want and, perhaps, to purchase services outside the authority. Internal quasi-contracts, service-level agreements, are increasingly being set up for central support services. The tendency for trading services to go their own way is heightened by the fact that they need new skills which may not be available in the authority: for example, cost and management accountancy, marketing and estimating. Competitive tendering is leading to more decentralised control of resources and the development of cost centres with freedom to decide how their budgets are spent. Authorities are being forced to consider the role of central services, distinguishing between corporate functions, such as committee administration, control, such as internal audit, and support, such as computer services. This pattern will obviously be enhanced by the extension of competition, and the local authority will become a network of contracts.

Competition and the politicians

There are pressures for the separation of client and contractor role among the elected members, just as there are in the officer structure. The major development in the pattern of committee operation is the emergence of boards for dealing with DLO and DSO affairs. Boards may be subcommittees of policy committees, full committees, or officer–member working groups. These DLO and DSO boards are likely to have strong delegated powers and can react more quickly than the somewhat ponderous full committee. They are normally small, in order to make speed of working easier and so that the board can work closely with the DLO manager. The development of boards is a move towards a more executive style of working and a style in which the officers and members work closely together. Boards are typically served directly by DLO and DSO managers rather than central committee administrators.

The introduction of competitive tendering affects the way that members' complaints are dealt with. It is less easy to take account of complaints because of the client–contractor split and the requirement to work to a prior specification. What members see as an unsatisfactory service, perhaps because of complaints that they are getting from their constituents, may be closely in accord with the specification for the work. Changing specifications, even if there is a variation clause written into the contract, may be expensive. It is difficult to influence DLOs and DSOs or contractors because they will be at one remove from the client, and subject to a set of pressures that may override the interests of the client.

The contracts that are to be let vary in length from three to seven years. There may be break clauses written in, but, in the main, the authority needs to ensure that the contracts and specifications that are developed will be satisfactory over a long period of time. This means that major policy decisions have to be made before contracts begin, because significant changes in the middle of the contract period lead to high variation costs. If the authority wants to introduce wheeled bins for refuse collection, mechanised street sweeping or new methods of food preparation, then it is best to do so before the contract starts. This level of forward planning is difficult for more complex services such as leisure, in which changes in taste are likely to have a major effect, or in housing management and social care, in which service needs may change. The need to write contracts that will stand for a number of years requires the authority to plan its service well into the future. The ability of elected members to influence services is limited because they are tied to contracts which they will have to honour whatever the platform on which they have been elected.

The need to plan is even more clear in the case of budgets. Unless there are clauses that allow the authority significantly to vary the level of service, and these have proved difficult to develop, then the cost of the service to be provided must be set for a number of years ahead. The need for budget variations then falls more strongly on the rest of the budget if the trading services cannot be varied. On the other hand the client service department may gain some certainty by being clear on the charge that it will face from the DLO or private contractor, which will only be able to vary its prices within the limitations of the contract. Moreover it may be possible for the service department to force the contractor to bear the impact of shortage of money by varying the amount of work that is ordered. But generally the legislation on competitive tendering forces local authorities to plan their services and budgets over a longer time-period and with greater accuracy. The role of the elected members in future in a contract culture involves more work on planning and the development of clear statements of the quality of services that they want to be delivered, whether by DLOs and DSOs or by the private sector, and the development of effective systems of monitoring to ensure that those standards are delivered.

The introduction of competition and markets raises issues about the nature of accountability. The separation of client and contractor certainly clarifies roles at one level, but at another it divides and, perhaps, confuses accountability. It is not always clear who should be held to account for failure, those who did the work, those who specified it, or those who monitored it. Members may find themselves facing difficulties of conflicting interests, as they consider services that are divided into client and contractor roles. The tendency has been for elected members to become less involved in overseeing services that are subject to competition.

The impact on industrial relations

The introduction of the competition legislation was intended to have a major effect on the power and influence of the trade unions and the operation of industrial relations in local government, and has clearly had such an effect. The obvious impact has been on pay and conditions of service and on the level of employment. Local authorities have, traditionally, been good employers and offer rates of pay for some of the services subject to competition that are much greater than those offered by the private sector, particularly in less skilled work such as cleaning. Even when the private sector offers comparable basic pay rates it is unlikely to offer bonus payments, and sick pay, holidays and superannuation are likely to be inferior. Part-time working has increased as contractors and DLOs and DSOs have reduced the hours worked by individuals so that they can avoid paying National Insurance. The impact of competition has been greater for women, people with disabilities and workers from ethnic minority groups, since they are more likely to work in those jobs affected by competition. Local authorities have found it difficult to maintain good employment conditions, though the Transfer of Undertaking (Protection of Employment) Regulations may reduce the damaging impact of competition on employment conditions.

Trade union membership declined following the introduction of competition because of the reduction in numbers employed, and because the private sector is less likely to recognise unions. Few local authorities, about 30 or so, have opted out of national bargaining completely, but national agreements are playing a smaller part in the determination of pay and conditions. Bonus systems are being simplified, and managers are taking a tougher stance on issues such as absenteeism and sickness. Competitive tendering has strengthened the hand of management. Industrial bargaining has also been decentralised within local authorities, with managers searching for mechanisms that bypass cumbersome central negotiating committees. Managers are more likely to deal directly with staff rather than go through trade union representatives, particularly in shire counties and shire districts. In some cases changes in pay and conditions have simply been imposed.

Conclusion

Competitive tendering is a major weapon in the Government's armoury as it attempts to change local government. It has the virtue of apparent simplicity, and, if local authorities argue that there is a great deal of work involved in specifying work for competition, they are open to the accusation that they should have had the necessary information long ago in order to manage effectively. If they point to the cost of managing and monitoring contracts, the Government will argue that these costs are small compared with savings, and that client-side costs can be reduced.

Competition has the virtue of forwarding a number of different Government policy objectives. It provides more work for the private sector, it reduces the power of the local authority and it weakens the public sector trade unions. The policy is flexible because the Secretary of State can add further services to the list for competition, and can easily change the rules for tendering and for trading accounts. Loopholes in the legislation can quickly be closed by the issue of regulations, and if the Government does not see the policy as having the effects that it wants as quickly as it wants them, then it can easily change the rules. Competition on its own has had a huge effect on the way that local authorities operate, especially when combined with change in services such as education and social care. It is now much easier to envisage the local authority as an agency for the purchase rather than the provision of service.

Notes and references

1. This chapter draws extensively upon research work conducted for the Department of the Environment and the Economic and Social Research Council. See K. Walsh and H. Davis, *Competition and Service: The Implications of the Local Government Act 1988* (HMSO, 1993).
2. For a study of the development of competitive tendering, see K. Ascher, *The Politics of Privatisation: Contracting Out Public Services* (Macmillan, 1987).
3. M. Forsyth, *Reservicing Britain* (Adam Smith Institute, 1980), and *Reservicing Health* (Adam Smith Institute, 1982).
4. See, for example, *Building Britain's Future: Labour's Policy on Construction* (Labour Party, 1977).
5. *Working Party on Direct Labour Organisations. Final Report* (Department of the Environment, August 1978) para. 5.3.
6. Local Government Chronicle, *Supplement*, 8 July 1988.
7. The Federation of Civil Engineering Contractors, *Neither Fair nor Frequent: A Review of the Impact of the Local Government Act 1980 on Highway Work by County Direct Labour Organisations* (no date).
8. Phrase used at a private local authority seminar on the Local Government Planning and Land Act 1980.
9. For a review of the experience of building maintenance DLOs see B. Walker, *Competing for Building Maintenance: Direct Labour Organisations and Compulsory Competitive Tendering* (HMSO, 1993).
10. Local Government Act 1988, s.7(7).
11. Department of the Environment, *Education Reform Act: Local Management of Schools,* Circular 7/88 (September 1988).

12. See the discussion in Audit Commission, *Adding Up the Sums: Schools' Management of their Finances* (HMSO, 1993).
13. The Local Government Management Board runs an information service on compulsory competitive tendering. The figures quoted are taken from the latest report available at the time of writing: Local Government Management Board, *CCT Information Services: Report No. 7*.
14. R. Carnaghan and B. Bracewell-Milnes, *Testing the Market: Competitive Tendering for Government Services in Britain and Abroad* (Institute of Economic Affairs, 1993).
15. Audit Commission, *Competitiveness and Contracting Out of Local Authorities' Services*, Occasional Paper 3 (HMSO, 1987) p. 2.
16. Audit Commission, *Securing Further Improvements in Refuse Collection* (HMSO, 1984).
17. Audit Commission, *Competitiveness and Contracting Out*, p. 2.
18. Audit Commission, *The Impact of Competitive Tendering on Highways Maintenance* (HMSO, 1991).
19. S. Domberger, S. Meadowcroft and D. Thompson, 'Competitive Tendering and Efficiency: The Case of Refuse Collection', *Fiscal Studies*, vol. 7, no. 4, pp.69–87.
20. J. Cubbin, S. Domberger and S. Meadowcroft, 'Competitive Tendering and Refuse Collection: Identifying the Sources of Efficiency Gains', *Fiscal Studies*, vol. 8, no. 3, pp. 49–58.
21. Domberger *et al.*, 'Competitive Tendering and Efficiency', p. 79.
22. Ibid.
23. Cubbin *et al.*, 'Competitive Tendering and Refuse Collection', p. 54.
24. S. Szymanski and T. Jones, *The Savings from Compulsory Competitive Tendering of Refuse Collection Services: A Statistical Analysis* (CDC Research, 1993).
25. *Local Government Chronicle, Supplement*, 6 July 1990.
26. See note 1 for full reference.
27. The major text on the theory of contestable markets is W. J. Baumol, J. Panzer and R. Willig, *Contestable Markets* (Harcourt Brace Jovanovich, 1982). For a more accessible discussion, see G. Davies and J. Davies, 'The Revolution in Monopoly Theory', *Lloyd's Bank Review*, July 1984.
28. O. E. Williamson, *Markets and Hierarchies* (Free Press, 1975), and *The Economic Institutions of Capitalism* (Free Press, 1985).
29. Audit Commission, *Realising the Benefits of Competition: The Client Role for Contracted Service* (HMSO, 1993).
30. J. Rehfuss, *Contracting Out in Government: A Guide to Working with Outside Contractors to Supply Public Services* (Jossey-Bass, 1989).

4 The Strange Case of the Local Government Review

Steve Leach

There are two concepts which characterise the way in which the Local Government Review has developed (and survived) in England and, in a different form, in Scotland and Wales. The first is 'policy drift' – the survival of a policy initiative beyond the time when there is any real political commitment to it, because it is perceived to be more difficult to halt it than continue with it. The second is the 'garbage can' model of policy-making in which:

> Policy making is a collection of choices looking for problems, issues and feelings looking for decision situations in which they might be aired, solutions looking for issues to which they might be the answer, and decision- makers looking for work. The result is that policy making becomes a 'garbage can' into which various kinds of problems and solutions are dumped by participants as they are generated.[1]

In the first section of this chapter the origins of the Review are considered. The way in which the Commission has been operating – its assumptions, metholodogy and processes – is next examined. By July 1983 six initial reports had been published by the Commission, and the contents of these reports are compared and evaluated in the third section. In October 1993, revised 'policy guidance' to the Commission was issued by the Government, and the implications for the future course of the Review of this new guidance, together with the Commission's 'final recommendations' so far published, are explored in the final section.

The origins of the Review

The idea of a reorganisation involving a move to unitary authorities does not seem to be related to any of the central elements of the current ideology of the Conservative Party. Nor does it have a basis in the transparent malfunction of the existing two-tier system. In the 1960s there was a good deal of tangible evidence of the need for a reorganisation, including the palpable inability of large numbers of small authorities to deal effectively with the growth-associated problems of development and movement, particularly in the more urbanised parts of the country. It is difficult to identify similar problems that underpin the present reorganisation, in which far too much has been made of the supposed 'problems' of conflict, overlap and duplication in the existing two-tier system,[2] Indeed, it can be argued that the last thing local government needs at the present time is a structural reorganisation. Local government is currently undergoing a considerable upheaval and huge strain resulting from a wide range of other legislation (e.g. council tax, community care, education reform, CCT). To superimpose a reorganisation in an already extremely demanding period of legislative and functional transition is hard to justify. There are thus a number of compelling reasons for *not* reorganising local government at present.

The most convincing explanation centres on the political ambition of one individual. It was part of the vision (and personal election manifesto) of a contender for the leadership of the Conservative Party, who (as it turned out) became instead Secretary of State for the Environment, where he was subsequently given the scope to implement his own personal manifesto. The reorganisation proposal was linked to a more fundamental element of that vision, that of strong mayors in local government (which arguably would be more congruent with a 'unitary' system). The introduction of elected mayors was, in the event, watered down on cabinet insistence. But the reorganisation proposals whose publication preceded those of elected mayors by some three months have survived.

Indeed, they have survived the intervention of a general election and a change of Secretary of State. Although the 1992 Conservative manifesto did contain a commitment to reorganisation, this would have been relatively easy after the election to rescind or delay or water down. With the move of Michael Heseltine from Environment to Trade and Industry, the policy lost its main internal champion. There is no evidence that the new Secretary of State, Michael Howard, was particularly committed to, or even interested in, local government reorganisation. Indeed, a very authentic sounding *Times* 'leak'[3] suggested that Michael Howard was understandably concerned about the costs involved in the Commission's five-year programme and the extremely tenuous nature of the possible financial benefits of reorganisation. The article implied a movement towards a more limited reorganisation, focused on the 'big nine' (plus one or two additions). However, a week later John Redwood, the Minister of Local Government, was emphatically stating that the Review would go ahead as originally planned. The impact of its dilution on his own ministerial portfolio, civil service pressure and the effects of the 330 outraged faxes received from shire districts at the DoE may all have helped to swing the balance. The appointment of a high-profile chairman of the Commission – Sir John Banham – shortly before the general election may also have been influential in preventing a retreat. Whatever the reasons, the opportunity to stop the Review in its tracks was lost, although a further opportunity presented itself in the summer of 1993 (see below).

Assumptions, methodology and processes of the Commission

On the face of it, local government reorganisation in England appears a more clearly articulated and rational policy process than its counterparts in Wales and Scotland. The mysterious emergence of options from the depths of the Welsh and Scottish Offices has not taken place. Instead, a Local Government Commission has been set up, at least some of whose members have direct experience of local government as councillors, officers, or representatives of a relevant national organisation. A good deal of policy guidance has been issued to the Commission, and research projects into certain aspects of reorganisation commissioned and published (though not necessarily taken much notice of). It is accepted that different solutions may be appropriate in different parts of the country. The Local Government Commission has thus been left with a good deal of scope for choice (or, rather, recommendation) in a way which appears to enhance some elements of rationality (as indeed one would expect in a major constitutional change of this nature).

It has already been argued that the origins of the Review have more to do with political opportunism than they do with a thorough examination of the problems and objectives. In so far as it has a philosophical basis, it is based on two central ideas – the concepts of the 'unitary authority' and 'the enabling authority' between which there is presumed to be a logical link which justifies the process of reorganisation. But neither of the two central ideas, nor the reality of a link between them, has been thought through in the rigorous way which would be necessary to justify a major reorganisation on the basis of the two ideas. They remain in the stratosphere of vague generalities. The way in which the enabling concept covers a wide range of possible interpretations is now widely recognised. Where the discussion of enabling in the Consultation Paper and various versions of the 'Policy Guidance' particularly falls down is in its failure to recognise that local authorities are not merely 'service-providing' agencies (the function to which the enabling concept is more directly applicable). They are also currently endowed with the important functions of regulation, strategic planning and promotion and advocacy. Enabling as an idea is much less applicable to each of these three functions. Yet the Policy Guidance hardly recognises their existence. Nor is the Guidance at all clear on the governmental role of local authorities which overarches all these more specific functions. 'Enabling' as set out in the relevant papers does not provide an adequate basis for a reorganisation.

The same can be said of the apparent commitment to the benefits of 'unitary authorities'. The dominance of the 'unitary' principle is an interesting feature of recent thinking about local government, on the part of academics as well as governments. No other Western democracy except Finland and Luxembourg has a unitary system of subnational government; indeed several are multi-tiered rather than merely two-tiered. What is so problematical about the two-tier system in England? INLOGOV research in the mid-1980s revealed considerable degrees of cooperation and a significant lack of substantive inter-tier problems in many parts of the country. Indeed, if the 'enabling' principle is all about the need to work cooperatively with other agencies to achieve local goals, why is this not felt to be possible for counties (with respect to districts) or vice versa? Thus the second pillar of the reorganisation – the benefits of a unitary system – remains in the realms of assertion rather than demonstration, and does not draw upon a growing body of evidence which questions the viability of the unitary principle. Arguments, for example, about the benefits of a so-called unitary system in the metropolitan areas can be shown to be almost totally spurious.[4]

It can be argued that the unsatisfactoriness of the Review's starting point – the Policy Guidance and other briefing material provided to the Commission – cannot reasonably be used as a basis for criticising the work of the Commission itself. It had no part in the establishment of its own term of reference. What can however legitimately be examined is the way it has interpreted its brief.

The Commission has always been in difficulties because the Government has never made a clear statement of its views on the role of local government. In this sense the Review is a 'reorganisation in a vacuum'. Even while the Commission has been deliberating, fundamental changes have been underway in the role of local authorities in relation to education[5] and the police[6].

As John Stewart has pointed out the fact that the Government has not made such a statement placed the onus on the Commission itself to clear its mind on the nature and role of local government, and to test its views in public debate before it began its work in particular areas.

> Instead of that, the Commission has sent out its members to the areas without agreement on what was to be aimed at. Without debate, discussion, public testing and agreement on the principles to be applied, there is a danger that the Commissioners in each area will do their own thing. The rolling programme places a special obligation on the Commission itself to have agreed the principles and approaches to be used. It has been said that what Commissioners are doing is to judge local circumstances. But unless the principles that should guide the judgement are agreed and understood, what we will get is not a reorganisation which varies with local circumstances, but one which varies with local Commissioners.[7]

When the Commission's 'first tranche' reports are discussed in the next section, it is clear that these predictions have been borne out. The case for the status quo has not been properly considered (except in one instance). The principles underlying the recommendations have not been made clear, nor have they been weighted. The reliability of information on costs and community identity has not been properly examined. And where recommendations between areas differ, it is not clear what evidence justifies the differences. All these problems can be traced back to the failure of the Commission to develop its own perspective on the role of local government and the principles to be adopted in the Review.

The situation in Scotland and Wales

The nature of the process followed in Wales and Scotland has been even more unsatisfactory. The Secretaries of State for Wales and Scotland respectively were convinced of the case for unitary authorities across the whole country, and did not see any need to establish a Commission to look into these matters (an interesting example of the inconsistencies which can develop between approaches to the same problem in the three countries). If a uniform unitary solution is right for Scotland and Wales, why not for England? If a Commission is needed in England, why not in Wales and Scotland?

In each country consultation papers have been published setting out alternative patterns of unitary authorities,[8] drawing on the same kind of arguments which formed the basis of the brief to the Commission in England (see pp. 51–2). In each case the favoured solution involves a size of unitary authority intermediate between county (or region) and district. In Wales, where there are currently eight counties and 39 districts, 23 unitary authorities have been proposed.[9] In Scotland, where there are currently twelve regions and 52 districts, 28 unitary authorities have been recommended.[10]

In Wales David Hunt ended his period of tenure as Secretary of State for Wales in July 1993 with the reorganisation facing an impasse due to the non-cooperation of the counties and the Welsh Labour Party. His successor John Redwood made the judgement that the process of reorganisation had gone too far to be reversed, and the requisite Bill was published in January 1994, by which time the policy of non-cooperation was already beginning to weaken, mainly because of pressure from the local authority trade unions. The proposed changes are now scheduled to take place in 1996. However a sense of unease about the arbitrariness of both process and proposals remains,[11] and the reorganisation has hindered rather than benefited the quality of central–local relations in Wales. The same conclusion applies to Scotland where the Scottish Office proposals have been subject to accusations of political gerrymandering[12] and the policy of non-cooperation of Scotland's authorities association (COSLA) is in January 1994 still in operation, despite the fact that the Scottish reorganisation Bill had also just been published. As Alexander and Orr argue:

There is a paradox in the fact that the representative body of Scottish local government has come out in opposition to a change that is argued to enhance the discretion and autonomy of local authorities. On the other hand, it can also be argued that these concessions to local autonomy scarcely begin to balance a reform process which will greatly increase the powers of the Secretary of State and which, in the details of the new local government map, reveal a single-minded pursuit of partisan advantage which has led to gross anomalies of population size between adjacent authorities. There is, perhaps, a certain symmetry between the political imperatives that caused the reform process to begin and the political outcome that ministers now seem determined to ensure.[13]

The 'first tranche' reports

In May 1993, the reports on the groups of authorities in the first tranche of areas covered by the Commission began to appear.[14] The publication of the report on Durham and Cleveland was quickly followed by the report on Derbyshire. A month later the Commission's report on Avon, Gloucestershire and Somerset was published, quickly followed by separate reports for North Yorkshire and North Humberside and Lincolnshire and South Humberside respectively. By the end of June 1993, proposals had been made for ten county council areas, affecting 75 authorities in all (ten county councils and 65 district councils). It was thus possible by this stage to try to discern patterns in the proposals made by the Commission, and to attempt to deduce the criteria which had been given priority, in a way which had not been possible beforehand.

The variety of proposals, hinted at before the publication of the reports, is striking. In one county area (Lincolnshire) the retention of the two-tier system is proposed; in all other areas considered by the Commission a unitary solution was the preferred option. In one county only – Cleveland – the preference is for unitary authorities based on existing districts. In four county areas – Isle of Wight, Somerset, Durham and Derbyshire – the preferred option is a unitary county solution (although within the last two counties unitary status for Darlington and Derby respectively was recommended). In the remaining county areas – North Yorkshire, Humberside, Avon and Gloucestershire – the recommendation is for a unitary system based on areas of intermediate size, i.e. smaller than the existing county but (with only one or two exceptions) larger than existing districts. In North Yorkshire and Humberside, the proposed new authorities are an attempt to reconstruct North, East and West 'ridings' of Yorkshire. In none of the cities and major towns so far considered is a boundary extension proposed, with the exception of the City of York.

It is important to stress that all the 'preferred structures' identified have the status of proposals. There has been a period of public consultation, which, at the time of writing, has just been completed in all the areas concerned (the unitary Isle of Wight proposal was confirmed earlier in the year). There is the possibility that the Commission may change its mind, as a result of the public consultations. Indeed, there has been so much recent emphasis on 'giving the public what they want' that it would be difficult for the Commission to reject a strong public view in favour of an alternative option. The present set of proposals, however, may be taken collectively as indicative of the Commission's assumptions, priorities and analytical approach as at August 1993.

It is interesting to compare the extent to which existing districts and counties respectively have been earmarked for unitary status. There has long been a strenuous ADC campaign for unitary status for all districts on existing boundaries. The ACC approach has been less unequivocal, arguing the benefit of larger as opposed to smaller unitary authorities, but unitary status for counties on existing boundaries is certainly compatible with these arguments. On this basis, the county success rate is 40 per cent (in addition, the ACC were not unhappy about the status quo proposal in Lincolnshire) whereas the district success rate is 17 per cent. Only eleven of the 65 districts so far considered have achieved the aim of a recommendation of unitary status on existing (or marginally extended) boundaries. Of these, seven are cities or large towns which had in the past enjoyed county borough status (Derby, Bristol, Hull, York, Middlesbrough, Darlington and Hartlepool); one is a district relatively small in population (76 000) with a strong community identity – the Forest of Dean; whilst the other three – Stockton, Woodspring and Langbaurgh – can realistically attribute their proposed unitary status to the fact that after the Commission had dealt with other parts of the county areas in which they are situated, there was little option but to make a recommendation of that nature! Of the remaining 54 districts, seven will retain their identity in a two-tier system, whilst the remaining 47 will on current proposals be amalgamated in groups of two, three or four, or submerged within a unitary county.

The patterns which seem to be emerging are thus as follows. Unitary solutions have been the norm, the retention of a two-tier system the exception. There has been a preference for large unitary authorities (the average size of the 24 such authorities so far proposed is around 200 000). Relatively small unitary authorities (i.e. around 100 000 or below) have been recommended only when there is a strong argument on community identity grounds *and* the overall solution in which the small unitary authority is included is estimated to save enough money (in operational cost terms) to overcome the transitional costs concurred over a relatively short (up to five years) time-span. In this respect, being a former county borough helps (Hartlepool, Darlington, York) but is no guarantee of success (cf. Gloucester, Grimsby, Lincoln). Counties are more likely to survive as unitary authorities where there are no large towns or cities (or where the county consists of one such settlement together with a large tract of more rural territory) for example Somerset, Durham, Derbyshire. But such a settlement pattern is no guarantee of success (cf. Gloucestershire and Lincolnshire). There is a readiness to give unitary status to large cities (Derby, Hull, Bristol) but not to extend their boundaries. Indeed the Commission has so far shown great reluctance to modify boundaries (i.e. to split existing districts, or to merge districts across existing county boundaries) at all.

On the basis of what principles and evidence has this portfolio of proposals been advocated? As implied in the previous paragraph, in *prima facie* terms there appear to be a number of inconsistencies. If the continuation of a two-tier system is appropriate in Lincolnshire, why not in Durham, Gloucestershire, Somerset and (outside York) North Yorkshire, where the settlement patterns appear similar? If it is considered appropriate to recommend the extension of York's boundaries, why not the equally constrained boundaries of Hull, Derby and Bristol? If large parts of Avon are redesignated as

Somerset or Gloucestershire (and then considered as part of the study area for these two counties) why is not most of Langbaurgh redesignated as North Yorkshire, and reconsidered as part of a North Yorkshire solution, given the strength of identity with Yorkshire in that district?

To some extent these seemingly arbitrary discrepancies are a reflection of the unsatisfactory nature of the terms of reference which the Commission was saddled with. If a unitary solution is proposed for the City of York, then a two-tier solution cannot be considered for the rest of North Yorkshire. The future of Langbaurgh cannot be considered in conjunction with that of North Yorkshire, because Cleveland and Durham were considered as a separate project (with a different pair of Commissioners) from North Yorkshire. But of much greater concern has been the way in which inconsistencies have developed through differences in approach and emphasis on the part of different pairs of Commissioners. It is beginning to look as if the predictions by John Stewart and George Jones are correct, and that what we are being presented with is a set of proposals which reflect not differences in local circumstances, but differences in the views of local Commissioners.

All the reports so far published by the Commission share a common format. Indeed, substantial sections of their contents reappear in identical form in each report, with only the occasional allusion that it is Durham (and not Derbyshire) that is being dealt with. (The advent of word processing has a lot to answer for!) In so far as they have a consistency it is that they use in each area the same model (developed by the consultants Ernst & Young) to estimate the transitional costs and future operational costs (or savings) of each option, and the same MORI questionnaire format (with one or two notable exceptions) to assess the strength of identity with a range of different areas within each county. Although other factors are also given weight – for example, the strength of local feeling for or against specific options (where tested), and the scope of joint arrangements which are perceived to be required in association with particular options (in the Commission's view, the more joint arrangements the worse, because of their adverse effects on accountability) – the main foundation for the recommendation in each area is a juggling around of the Ernst & Young financial data and the MORI 'community identity' data.

The Ernst & Young model incorporates a quite unmistakable 'economies of scale' effect.[15] The model indicates that up to a population of one million, the ratio of indirect costs to total population decreases. Thus if costs were to be major criteria, then a comprehensive introduction of the 'unitary county' solution would be implied. Indeed on this basis there would be a case for amalgamating Durham and Cleveland, North Yorkshire and North Humberside, and Avon and Somerset, to reap the full benefits of these potential savings. The application of the Ernst & Young model also shows that if a county is divided into four or five unitary authorities, the potential savings (once transitional costs have been taken into account) become negligible or negative. A unitary solution based on existing districts is eliminated by the Commission in all counties (except Cleveland) on the basis that such a solution would be likely to result in increased costs.

The main emphasis in the MORI survey is placed on the answers given to a rather strange question. Residents were asked how strongly they identified with the range of different areas (town or nearest town, village or neighbourhood and so on etc) including the 'area of the county council' and the 'area of the district council' in which they lived. A comparison between the levels of identity ('very strong' and 'fairly strong') felt with these two areas was made in each study. In cases where there was a significally stronger identity with county than district (e.g. Somerset, Durham) this was regarded as an important and sometimes clinching consideration.

In relation to both the Ernst & Young evidence and the MORI 'community identity' information, the problem is that the Commission drew conclusions which are much firmer than can be justified by the tentative and inconclusive nature of the evidence concerned. First there is the problem of the spurious precision attached to the Ernst & Young estimates. In each area, these estimates differ from all the other sets of estimates produced by counties, districts and external consultants. What special qualities of expertise do Ernst & Young have, one wonders, that so much weight should be given to their guesstimates rather than anyone else's? The important point is that *all* estimates of costs and savings are intrinsically speculative – i.e. based on assumptions about what different types of authority *might* do if they were established and unproven hypotheses about the economies and the diseconomies of scale. Data of this nature could have some limited value for the

Commission, so long as it is recognised for what it is – hypothetical, full of qualifications, and certainly not definitive. What is quite inexcusable is the way such tenuous material has been bandied around in press statements which assert that particular proposals will save council tax payers £54 per year. Such statements are grossly misleading. In any event, the Commission's main concern should be with the cost-*effectiveness* of different solutions, rather than costs and savings *per se*. That is what the DOE's Policy Guidance asks them to consider. Yet although the potential capacity of larger authorities to provide strategic services more effectively is discussed, the potential capacity of smaller authorities to provide personal and community-based services more effectively is never explicitly addressed.

In all the reports, the term 'community' is interpreted almost exclusively in terms of 'perceived identity' as revealed by limited questions in opinion surveys. These questions do not attempt to relate the question of identity to the actual process of government and yet the very meaning given to 'community' varies with the context in which it is used. The evidence on which most reliance is placed by the Commission (see p above) presents particular difficulties. It is difficult to know what meaning would have been attached by respondents to the question 'how strongly do you identify with the *area* of the county (or district council)?, a view which is substantiated by the fact that whilst 78 per cent of respondents identified strongly with the City of Bristol (a more comprehensible concept) only 40 per cent identified with the *City Council area* of Bristol. The most likely explanation for the difference is that the public probably did not understand the question. Yet in most cases it is this question that the Commission relies on in its analysis.

Equally worrying is the fact that other equally plausible interpretations of the term 'community' – for example, the pattern of activities of residents in relation to work, shopping and leisure – are largely ignored in a way which is quite unprecedented in previous reviews of local government structure.

The catalogue of shortcomings does not end here. The Commission displays no real understudy of the strengths, weaknesses and potentialities of existing and other possible forms of two-tier systems (including the internal devolution of powers to community councils favoured in several of the county submissions).

There is little appreciation of the different forms of joint action which are possible, their appropriateness to different types of services and their (varied) impact on accountability. The real nature of the strategic role in relation to land-use, transportation, planning and economic development is not recognised, with strategic capacity being confused with size, and the potential benefits of city regions as a basis for strategic planning almost totally ignored. Consultation leaflets which are palpably biased in favour of the Commission's preferred option have been circulated. And there is no attempt to respond to the strong levels of identity with the neighbourhood/local town level which the MORI surveys reveal, beyond a set of proposals to strengthen the role of *parish* councils (which do not necessarily relate to towns/neighbourhoods).

The change of direction

By August 1993 considerable pressure had developed for the brief and the way of working of the Commission to be reviewed and changed. The growing body of criticism of the Commission's operation and output came from three different directions. There was the body of academic criticism, epitomised by the increasingly critical stance of George Jones and John Stewart in the *Local Government Chronicle*[16] and supported by others[17] which argued that the Commission was not behaving in the tradition of such bodies. As we have seen, principles had not been clearly laid down, the evidence collected was too limited in scope, the quality of analysis was questionable and the Commissions recommendations inconsistent. Second, there were the criticisms from the authorities whose existence had been threatened by the Commission's recommendations, and their representative bodies (particularly the ADC), where the concerns were about both methodology and proposals. Third, there were expressions of concern (and no doubt lobbying of individual ministers) from Conservative MPs whose constituency interests were affected by the proposals. MPs whose constituencies are wholly or mainly coterminous with district council areas typically perceive benefits in the strengthening or at least survival of the district tier, and will certainly come under considerable pressure from local councillors and party members to defend districts. Criticism from MPs was particularly strongest in relation to the Derbyshire proposals[18] where the anticipated demise of the much maligned Labour-controlled county council had not been recommended, but rather (City of Derby excluded) it was to achieve unitary status. But rumblings of discontent were apparent also in response to the proposals for Gloucestershire, North Yorkshire and Humberside, and Somerset.[19]

The new guidelines

Once it became apparent that the Review was running into difficulties, there were a number of choices open to the Government. It could have wound up the Commission and the Review forthwith, which would have been the boldest and most imaginative choice, but is now an opportunity sadly missed. It could have allowed the Review to continue on its present timetable within the existing Guidance. It could have limited the further work of the Commission beyond the first or second tranche of authorities to specific circumstances (e.g. some measure of expression of public opinion that change was wanted or a reworking of the organic change principle). It could have accelerated the Review timetable to ensure that the task was completed before 1997. Finally it could have clarified (i.e. changed) the terms of reference of the Commission so that the criteria upon which it was expected to reach its conclusions were 'clearer' (and, inevitably, to some extent 'different from' existing criteria).

Prior to the summer recess, it became apparent that John Gummer's preference as successor to Michael Howard at the Department of the Environment was for the third option – limitation of the Review to 'special circumstances'. He was not able to convince the Prime Minister that this was the best course of action.[20] Instead the Government announced on 1 October 1993 new guidance for the Local Government Commission and a new timetable, involving a speeding up of the review process.[21] The intention now is to complete the Review by the end of 1994.

The choice which has now been made is a combination of the fourth and fifth options – the speed-up of the Review and changes to the terms of reference. All the choices facing the Government were fraught with difficulties, as any major change in the operation of a supposedly independent Commission in the middle of its programme of work must be. However the choice which has been made is probably the most unsatisfactory of all.

The Environment Secretary argues in the Press Release that 'the principles behind the Review remain exactly the same – to secure effective local government reflecting the interests of local people.[22] That kind of benign generality should not be allowed to obscure the reality, as argued earlier, that the Review has always suffered from a *lack* of clear principles. As John Stewart argues,[23] unsubstantiated assertions about the benefits of 'unitary' systems of government and vague references to the growth of enabling do not provide an appropriate basis for a major review of territorial structure. What the new guidance does in fact provide is not a 'clarification of principle' but a preemptive indication of preferred solutions.

Apart from the process of speeding up the Review itself, the major changes proposed in the revised guidance are as follows. First the expectation that unitary solutions will be recommended is strengthened, with the retention of the two-tier system seen very much as an exception.[24] Second, there is a new predisposition against 'very large' unitary authorities, which it is claimed would need 'special justification in terms of community identity'.[25] Third, the Commission is expected to attach particular weight to intermediate solutions – i.e. amalgamation of districts or disaggregations of counties and to apply special sorting proposals to make existing councils unitary authorities. Intermediate solutions are expressly identified by the Environment Secretary as 'the most promising starting point for the Commission' in its search for solutions.[26] Other significant changes (or clarifications) include the requirement that the Commission should more explicitly address the four major elements of the Community Index – identity, accessibility, responsiveness and democracy – and an indication that solutions which are 'marginally more expensive' than the status-quo should not be excluded if the 'extra cost would be outweighed by other considerations'.[27] Previously the Commission has ignored the Community Index and excluded the 'more expensive' solutions.[28]

With the exception of these last two changes, all these 'clarifications' are not of course clarifications of principle or criteria, but indications of preferred solutions. Thus we have the bizarre situation in which not only have the work programme and operating assumptions of a Commission been significantly modified in mid-stream, but also the guidance issued to it has changed from *input* criteria (however partial and unclear) to *output* criteria. If the Commission has not so far behaved in the way one expects a Commission to behave, the Government's own treatment of the Commission appears to challenge the long- established expectations about the proper relationship of governments to such bodies.

What are likely to be the effects of the revised guidance? The first problem for the Commission and the Government was a potential incompatibility between the proposals in the 'final' reports of the Commission for the first tranche of counties, which were almost finalised by the time that the new guidance was confirmed (November 1993), but which had been written on the basis of the earlier (September 1992) guidance, and those expected in the remaining tranches, which would be subject to the new guidance. The 'final' reports for Durham proposed the retention of a two- tier system outside Darlington (which involved a change in the original proposals for a unitary Durham County). The final report for Derbyshire proposed unitary authorities for Derby and Greater Chesterfield, with the status quo in the remaining area of the county. At the same time as these recommendations were being publicised, Sir John Banham and John Gummer were exchanging correspondence which paved the way for these recommendations to be reconsidered in the light of the new guidance, a cause of events which led to an application for a judicial review from Derbyshire. Similar references back are anticipated for Gloucestershire (where the Commons changed its original proposal for three unitary authorities to the retention of the two-tier system) and Lincolnshire. Judicial reviews have also been set in motion by Cleveland (where the final recommendation is for unitary districts which is also out of line with the revised policy guidance) and Somerset (where the Commission's original proposal for a unitary county was replaced by one for three unitary authorities, despite a strong public preference for the status quo). By January 1994 the internal contradictions of the process had become transparent.

Second, counties and districts will now be expected to try to reach agreement over 'intermediate' solutions – in many cases involving arbitrary divisions of existing counties or equally arbitrary amalgamations of districts (often themselves the product of the arbitrary amalgamation on the 1974 reorganisation) which neither the counties nor the districts concerned really favour. Nor, on the basis of some of the MORI survey evidence which is becoming available is it the case that the residents of these areas will have much enthusiasm for such solutions either. This will present something of a dilemma for the Commission given its requirement to place a good deal of emphasis on public opinion. What is the Commission expected to do if the intermediate solutions now favoured by the Government prove less popular than other proposals, for example the continuation of a two-tier system, for which there is increasing evidence of public support? John Gummer himself referred in the press statement to the need to create councils with a strong local identity which people actually want!

Why has the Government chosen to go in this particular direction? There is evidence in the changes of some successful lobbying by the ADC, particularly in relation to authority size, the Community Index and the treatment of costs. However the dominant influence is likely to have been pressure from disgruntled back-bench Conservative MPs and constituency parties, particularly in relation to the Commission's 'doughnut' proposals (a unitary Derby City Coucil as the whole in the centre of a unitary county wide authority) for Derbyshire, where unrest has been apparent for some time. With a Party Conference looming at the time, political pressures are a more likely explanatory factor of the change than a considered change of policy in relation to local government reorganisation (for which there is anyway no evidence). In responding in this way however, the Government has altered the character of the Review from one which *differed* in its 'independence', from the Welsh and Scottish minister-determined reorganisation to one which is increasingly similar in nature since a preference for an authority wide pattern of unitary authorities which are intermediate in size between existing counties and districts has been built into the guidelines. The only potential source of effective resistance (short of a joint ACC/ADC boycott) is the Commission itself.

The future role of the Commission

A High Court ruling in January 1994 indicated that the stronger commitment to unitary status in the revised guidance had no legal standing. The Commission will undoubtedly take note of the new guidelines but remains in the position of having to find its own way forward.

There are two possible approaches the Commission could adopt. The Commission is still being expected to take into account local preferences[29] and to minimise the need for formal joint arrangements.[30]

An emphasis on public preference seems likely to lead in most areas – on the basis of preliminary evidence – to status quo recommendations, and in a very few areas to an intermediate solution, involving amalgamation of districts. Thus one tenable and consistent line for the Commission to take would be to continue to recommend status quo solutions in circumstances (as in Lincolnshire) where they can see little case for change in terms of governmental effectiveness or public preference.

The second possibility, if the unitary solution is felt to be unavoidable, is to use the city region and the rural region as the basis for change rather than the political deals which emerge from county–district bargaining processes. For 'local consensus', if indeed it can be reached, is much more likely to be on the basis of the prospects of party control in the new units, and is likely also (because of local interest-based resistance to boundary extension) to arbitrarily continue to separate cities and large towns from their natural suburbs and hinterlands. A city (or rural) region solution would produce unitary authorities – but it would be a solution that would minimise the need for joint arrangements in relation to strategic planning, transportation, economic development, waste disposal and many specialist services, in a way other intermediate solutions would not.

For such a solution to be possible four changes would have to be made. The first tranche proposals would have to be reconsidered (but that will probably happen anyway). All areas would have to be considered at the same time (opening up possibilities of solutions which straddle county boundaries). The preoccupation in favour of not changing existing district boundaries would have to be withdrawn. And the power of veto currently being permitted to the residents just outside the existing boundaries of large cities and towns would have to be removed. A requirement on the new unitary authorities to decentralise power to the smaller towns or neighbourhoods with which, as MORI shows, there is the highest level of community identity would also help.

If the Commission were to adopt either of these two positions or a combination thereof, it could be seen to be taking the initiative, and would be likely to regain the early respect it has lost. It is facing what is probably its last opportunity to establish itself as a credible Commission. Sadly, it is unlikely that either of these alternative approaches will be taken. Michael Clarke has referred to the Review in terms of 'a tragedy being played out'[31] and that is not an over statement. It is difficult to over-emphasise the negative consequences of the Review for local government. If all goes according to the Government's plan, the map of local government in Britain will by 1995 have been transformed, by a Government that no longer has any reason or plausible rationale for doing so, working (in England) through a Commission which has shown little sign of behaving like one, and which is drifting towards a role of symbolic legitimation of a governmental 'quick fix'. The 'solution' produced will in most areas be supported neither by existing authorities (county or district) nor, more importantly, by public opinion. The change will not result in real unitary authorities (because of the need for joint arrangements), will not (on the Commission's own calculations) result in significant savings in operational costs, and will generate substantial transitional costs which local authorities and council tax payers will themselves have to bear. The only other democratically elected institution outside Parliament is being played around with in an astonishing way.

Notes and references

1. See M. Cohen, J. March and J. Olsen, 'A Garbage Can Model of Organisational Choice', *Administrative Science Quarterly*, vol. 17, no. 1, (1972) pp. 1–25.
2. See S. N. Leach, C. A. Vielba and N. Flynn, *Two Tier Relationships in British 'Local' Government* (INLOGOV, 1987) for a research-based appraisal of such problems.
3. See *The Times*, 28 April 1992.
4. See S. N. Leach, H. Davis, C. Game and C. Skelcher, *After Abolition* (INLOGOV, 1992).
5. Any growth in the number of grant-maintained schools will raise new issues since they will entail not merely the removal of local authority responsibilities, but new responsibilities for a Funding Council for Schools.
6. The proposals put forward by the Home Secretary for new police authorities, of which only half the members will be appointed by local authorities and the majority of the remainder being appointed by the

Home Secretary and the rest being magistrates, raise an important issue of accountability.

7. See John Stewart, *The Local Government Review Itself Reviewed* (European Policy Forum, July 1993) p. 11.

8. The Scottish Office, *The Structure of Local Government in Scotland; Shaping the New Councils*, a Consultation Paper, October 1992.

9. Announcement by David Hunt, Secretary of State for Wales, March 1993.

10. Scottish Office, *The Structure of Local Government in Scotland*, September 1993.

11. See G. Boyne, G. Jordan and M. McVicar, *The Reform of Local Government in Scotland and Wales: A Comparative Evaluation* (draft report) (Joseph Rowntree Foundation).

12. Ibid. p. 28.

13 A. Alexander and K. Orr, 'The Reform of Scottish Local Government', *Public Money and Management*, vol. 14, no. 1, p. 37.

14. The Local Government Commission for England, *Report on the Future of Local Government in the Isle of Wight* (February 1993), *Derbyshire* (May 1993), *Cleveland and Durham* (May 1993), *Avon, Gloucestershire and Somerset* (June 1993), *Area North of the Humber* (June 1993), *Area South of the Humber* (June 1993).

15 Ernst & Young, *Local Government Review: Financial Appraisal of Options* (DoE, June 1993).

16. For example, G. Jones and J. D. Stewart: 'Where the Arguments Fall Down', *Local Government Chronicle*, 11 June 1993, p. 12; 'Off the Rails', *Local Government Chronicle*, 9 July 1993, p. 14.

17. For example, Michael Clarke, 'The Local Government Perspective', *Local Government Policy Making*, vol. 20, no. 2 1993; Steve Leach, 'Local Government Reorganisation in England', *Local Government Policy Making*, vol. 19, no. 4 (March 1993) pp. 34–5; and *The Local Government Review: A Crisis of Credibility* (European Policy Foundation, December 1993).

18. See *Local Government Chronicle*, 23 April 1993, p. 1.

19. See *Local Government Chronicle*, 9 July 1993, p. 8.

20. See *Local Government Chronicle*, 30 July 1993, p. 1.

21. See DoE Press Release, 1 October 1993 p. 30.

22. Ibid.

23. J. D. Stewart, *The Local Government Review Itself Reviewed*, pp. 3, 8.

24. DoE, *Draft Revised Policy Guidance*, 30 September 1993, para. 3.

25. Ibid., para. 11.

26. DoE, *News Release 630*, 1 October 1993

27. DoE, *Draft Revised Policy Guidance*, para. 9.

28. See, for example, Local Government Commission, *The Future of Local Government: Avon, Gloucestershire and Somerset Report* (1993) p. 24.

29. DoE, *Draft Revised Policy Guidance*, para. 6.

30. Ibid., para. 15.

31. M. Clarke, 'The Local Government Perspective', p. 6 (see note 17).

5 The Internal Management of Local Authorities

John Stewart

The Government's approach to the issues of the internal management and organisation of local authorities differs from most of the other changes discussed in this book. The legislation in this area was based on a considered response to a Committee of Inquiry (the Widdicombe Committee). Since that legislation there have been other developments which have added to the difference.

Within two years of the enactment of that legislation in the Local Government and Housing Act in 1989 the new Secretary of State Michael Heseltine produced a consultation paper which contained proposals that, as we shall see, undermined some of the principles underlying that legislation. It proposed changes in internal organisation but, and this is the unusual feature, on an experimental basis inviting local authorities to volunteer for such experiments. The paper recognised 'that change may not be appropriate for all local authorities and that it would be prudent to pilot changes in a few authorities'.[1] It was an argument which some felt could have been applied to some of the other changes set out in this volume.

The story does not end there. After considering the responses from local authorities, a further Secretary of State – Michael Howard – set up a departmental working party to review the responses and the need for legislative change. Not merely did this again represent a resort to a form of inquiry little used in preparing the other changes discussed, but the working party was largely composed of representatives of the local authority associations or those knowledgeable about local government.

The process has gone through four stages:

- the Widdicombe Inquiry
- the government response in a White Paper, later carried into legislation
- the Consultation Paper on Internal Management
- the Working Party on Internal Management

Most of that process has been marked by an unusual depth of investigation and especially later by a concern to consult with and involve local government in an exploration of the issues.

The Consultation Paper on Internal Management changed the nature of the debate. It focused attention on issues which the Widdicombe Committee had chosen not to pursue. Whereas the Widdicombe Committee had accepted the existing decision-taking model, recommending changes to the way councils conducted their business considering the composition of committees and their procedures, but not challenging the committee system, the consultation paper put forward radical alternatives.

The Widdicombe Committee defined the existing model as follows:

(a)   the council is a corporate body;
(b)   decisions are taken openly by, or on behalf of, the whole council – without any separate source of committee authority;
(c)   officers serve the council as a whole.[2]

The Widdicombe Committee recognised that councils can and do delegate their functions to committees who in turn can delegate functions to subcommittees and that councils, committees and subcommittees delegate functions to officers. They saw however the three principles set out above as defining the basic model.

They briefly considered alternative models, which were mainly based on a separate executive that could be constituted by the council or separately from it. While the assumption that all decisions made in the local authority rest upon the authority of the council has been taken for granted in our system, other systems of local government do not necessarily make that assumption. Executives carry authority in their own right, as indeed does the Cabinet in central government, based as it is on the ministerial model.

The Widdicombe Committee felt that the existing model ignored the reality of party politics which meant that in most authorities decisions were not made in the council or committees but through group machinery. The leadership of the group might in reality be the effective executive controlling the work of the council although it was likely to operate through informal meetings rather than through the formal machinery of the council. Despite this the Widdicombe Committee rejected alternatives to the present model.

They rejected these because they did not see major problems in the present structure and because most of those giving evidence had defended the existing model. They saw that model as being one that was adaptable to local conditions. In these circumstances they stated that

> we believe that the onus of proof should always be on those who propose institutional change, especially where this is of a major structural character. Great Britain has a strong tradition of evolutionary change and improvisation in its institutional arrangements and a healthy suspicion of solutions that are theoretically logical or transplanted from elsewhere. Unless there is a clear case to the contrary it is preferable to build on what is already there.[3]

They therefore focused their recommendations on ensuring that the three fundamental points of the existing model were 'reinforced and clarified: At the same time we seek – within this framework – to bring the formal machinery of local government more into line with political reality and thereby to give it greater substance'.[4]

Certain of those proposals or rather the response of the Government were to be the focus of attention in the discussions of the Consultation Paper on Internal Management which was to open up the issue of a separate executive and to challenge the existing model.

Thus the Widdicombe Committee recommended that all committees and subcommittees with delegated powers to take decisions on behalf of the council should have a composition reflecting the political balance of the council. This was a careful formulation because it permitted deliberative committees to have a different composition. As we have seen, while reaffirming the existing model they were concerned to ensure it was brought in line with political reality. They considered it proper for deliberative committees to be composed of one party – normally of the majority party. Noting the widespread practise of an 'inner circle' of the majority leadership meeting regularly, they argued:

> It is wrong that authorities should have to resort to informal devices of indeterminate status. If the political reality is that the general policy of the council is formulated by the majority party, we see no reason why this should not be recognised by the creation of a single party policy and resources committee within the formal structure and with full access to officers' advice.[5]

Indeed they went further, arguing that such deliberative committees need not be subject to the requirement of the Local Government (Access to Information) Act 1985 with regard to the rights of members of the public and the press to attend meetings and inspect documents:

> It is a simple reality, which no legislation can alter, that politicians will develop policy options in confidence before presenting their final choice for public decision. We do not think this is unreasonable. If the law prevents them from conducting such discussions in private informal committees, then they will conduct them less formally elsewhere. We have heard that some local authorities have been creating informal mechanisms expressly to avoid the effects of the 1985 Act. It is unsatisfactory to force policy deliberations out of the formal committee system into groupings of indeterminate status. It is also unnecessary. No decision can be taken by a local authority without it eventually being referred to a decision taking committee or the council, where there will be full public access to the meeting and the documentation. Given this basic safeguard, we can see no benefit in applying the Act also to deliberative committees.[6]

These recommendations follow from the position taken by the Committee. Because of their support for the existing model they are concerned to maintain and enhance the formal structure of decision-making, but also to recognise the reality of political control and give that recognition through deliberative committees.

This recommendation was however rejected by the Government. They accepted the recommendations about the composition of committees, but argued that they should apply to deliberative committees as well as decision-making committees. They did not see any justification for a distinction between them. They did not therefore see any reason why deliberative committees should be exempted from the requirements of access to information. They accepted that

> while the main business of local authorities should be carried on through the normal committee structure based on reports prepared by politically impartial officers, the Government consider it reasonable for leading members of a party group to meet from time to time to discuss policy co-ordination or sensitive issues. Indeed, there is no way of preventing this from happening away from council premises if inhibitions were placed on it happening as a formal council activity, and there may be advantages in ensuring that such groups have access to proper officer advice. However that does not mean that such groups need, as the Widdicombe Committee proposed, to be given the special status of deliberative committees and to be exempted from the requirements of the Local Government (Access to Information Act) 1985 or the new pro rata representation requirements.[7]

They considered that such groups should remain informal. As a result the Local Government and Housing Act 1989 recommendations introduced the requirement that all committees should have a membership related to the party balance on the council.

These changes meant that any move to give formal recognition to the reality of political leadership was inhibited. At least prior to the Local Government (Access to Information) Act there had been a growth in one party policy committees or subcommittees, normally on an advisory basis. Changes introduced by the Government in arrangements for the payment of councillors meant that attendance allowance could not be paid for meetings which were composed of members of one party. Whereas the Widdicombe Committee sought to give recognition to the reality of political control, while preserving the formal position of the council as a corporate body, the Government's response was, in effect, to keep political control in the shadowy world of the informal structure, almost as if it were something improper rather than the process through which most councils operated.

The Widdicombe Committee made many other recommendations, many of which were acted upon by the Government although
often in a modified form. Thus the Local Government and Housing
Act contained provisions restricting officers holding senior or
politically sensitive posts from standing for other councils or
engaging in other political activities; eliminating cooption except
in certain committees for specified purposes; restricting the
appointment of political advisers to one per party group; and
requiring the appointment of a Head of Service and of a monitoring
officer to maintain an overview of the legality and probity of an
authority's activities. This chapter has focused however on the
attitude of the Widdicombe Committee to the issue of political
leadership because that is the issue which has gained a new
importance because of the Consultation Paper on Internal Management and the subsequent work of the departmental working party.

The Consultation Paper on Internal Management

The Consultation Paper on Internal Management adopted a very
different stance to these issues from that adopted by the report of
the Widdicombe Committee and the Government's response, to
which it only made passing reference. Far from accepting the
existing model, it argued the need to challenge it and put forward a
range of options most of which were based on the separation of the
executive from the representational role of the council – a separation
strongly rejected by the Widdicombe Committee whose views on
this point had been accepted by the Government.

One reason for this difference was that the new Secretary of State
Michael Heseltine had been an advocate of elected mayors and it
was no surprise to see that proposal put forward in this consultation
paper. The consultation paper had a very different emphasis from
either the report of the Widdicombe Committee or of the
Government's response to it. The Widdicombe Committee was set
up in response to pressure at the Conservative Conference about
alleged abuses in Labour-controlled local authorities. It was
therefore an inquiry into 'The Conduct of Business' more than an
investigation of the political organisation of local authorities. In fact
it found no widespread evidence of abuses and in so far as it found

any, did not regard them as restricted to Labour-controlled authorities.

The origin and the emphasis of the consultation paper was very different. It was part of a wider review of local government whose implications for local government finance and structure are considered elsewhere. The emphasis of the consultation paper was on ways to improve the decision-making process. Its focus was less on the proper conduct of business and more on internal management. It paid less attention to the traditional model of the council than to its consequences in the committee system, which it described in its one reference to the Widdicombe Committee report as time-consuming and cumbersome.

Although the council has been a corporate body responsible for all that happens in the council, it has normally operated through committees and subcommittees, either acting through delegated powers or reporting upwards. The committee system has occupied the time of councillors. It has focused their attention on particular services. Committees have met on a regular cycle of meetings, sometimes as frequently as one a month. They can have lengthy agendas often concerned with the on-going work of the council and can be criticised as often involving the councillors in unnecessary detail. Against that the involvement of councillors in the workings of the council would be defended as both giving understanding of the services and necessary to detailed control.

To many in the United Kingdom the committee system seems an integral part of local government. It defines the role of councillors and determines their work patterns. The committee cycle sets the time table not merely for councillors but for much of the work of senior management. It is difficult to think about local government outside the workings of the committee system.

The consultation paper put forward a series of options, which were a challenge to rethinking. The first was a modification of the committee system through change in the legislative framework, including the removal of the requirement for minority representation on committees so recently introduced. The others involved more radical changes removing the need for the committee system as we know it.

These options departed from the model previously endorsed by the Widdicombe Committee. They drew a distinction between the executive and representative roles, although the nature of what was covered by each role was never fully spelt out. In putting forward these models, the consultation paper drew upon foreign experience.

A broad distinction can be drawn between political executives and officer executives. A political executive can be a single individual or a collective executive and can be appointed from the council or can be separately elected. Putting together those two sets of possibilities one can derive four options:

- the appointed collective executive described in the Consultation Paper as the cabinet system
- the elected collective executive similar to the cabinet system except that it is separately elected
- the elected individual executive described in the Consultation Paper as the elected mayor
- the appointed individual executive

Strangely the fourth option of the appointed mayor was not put forward, although it is the system found in France. The phrases 'elected mayor' and 'appointed mayor', although commonly used, can confuse because the reference is not to the ceremonial role known in the UK so much as to that of political leader.

The consultation paper recognised that some of the models 'would involve a small number of members of the local authorities concerned taking on a significantly enhanced role'.[8] It argued therefore that there was a case for reviewing whether they should be on a salaried basis.

In addition the consultation paper put forward the option of an officer executive described as the council manager system, following the model of the city manager in many US. towns and cities. In this option the council would appoint an officer to take over the day-to-day running of the authority. The council would retain overall policy responsibility, but would have little involvement in day-to-day decision-making.

The arguments for these models are not developed in the consultation paper, although by implication they are assumed to promote more effective, speedy and business-like decision-making which is stated to be one of the main objectives of any change.

Advocates of similar proposals have emphasised the greater visibility of political leadership and the enhanced accountability of a political executive and this relates to the consultation papers objective of increasing 'the interest taken by the public in local government'.[9] The existence of a separate political executive – and above all when it is a single individual and when separately elected – focuses attention.

The proposals change the role of the council making it more of a 'legislature' and a representative body. That can be argued to be a useful clarification of its role, enabling it to concentrate on those roles. The existing model supported by the Widdicombe Committee is seen as confusing, implying a responsibility resting on the whole council that it cannot properly exercise and concealing the actual existence of a political leadership which acts as a political executive. Indeed the existing model may prevent the council exercising proper scrutiny of the executive because, in form if not in reality, the council is the executive.

The consultation paper gave limited consideration to what the role of the council would be under its proposals. It recognised that there might have to be new arrangements for scrutiny of the activities of the executive and suggested the creation of scrutiny committees possibly modelled on parliamentary select committees.

It did not explore however the division of responsibilities between the council and the executive, what the councils representative role would mean in practice and how that would affect its conduct of business. One can only assume that the council would approve the budget and major policy proposals submitted by the executive. This might however require scrutiny of such proposals by committees of the council – giving such committees greater responsibilities than parliamentary select committees.

The consultation paper was an imperfectly developed document. It had relatively little to say about the role of councillors generally – a weakness almost calculated to ensure a sceptical response. It failed to elaborate how the executives would actually operate. The term 'executive' could cover a variety of different approaches. It suggests a body concerned with executive action but some of its advocates see its focus as strategic direction. The paper did not consider the role of the party groups, which may have reflected an unwillingness to enter into hidden territory, but whose workings would determine what any change would mean in practice.

Perhaps the greatest weakness of the paper was its limited scope. It focused on the need for an effective executive and ignored other needs to be met by internal management. It did not for example cover the need for responsive services as one would have expected at a time when the White Paper on the Citizen's Charter was being prepared, nor did it explore developments in decentralisation. It ignored thereby some of the most interesting innovations in internal management in local authorities.

The consultation paper had a largely negative response. While its stress on pilot projects rather than the imposition of changes was generally welcomed, barely a handful of authorities put themselves forward for those projects and most of these favoured cabinet systems as the nearest to present reality. Generally the committee system was defended and although a number of leaders and chief executives were interested in the proposals, they could not get support for them from councillors generally.

This was hardly surprising in view of how little attention was paid to the councillors' role, except for that of those on the executive. In any event, new ideas do not readily gain acceptance when they challenge assumptions previously taken for granted. Time is required. The Government's reaction to the responses, which was to set up a departmental working party with representatives of the local authority associations and others, provided the possibility for further consideration.

The departmental working party

The Working Party's terms of reference were to

- consider the suggestions for improving internal management arrangements which were received in response to the consultation paper;
- consult individual authorities supporting new management models;
- work up detailed options suitable for trial by volunteering authorities, including adequate safeguards to protect minority parties and to secure value for money and propriety; and
- draw up a list of changes to primary and secondary legislation that would be necessary to enable such experiments to take place.[10]

The committee met over an eight-month period. It appointed a task force to visit authorities which had developed new approaches within existing legislation or who had proposed experiments following the consultation paper. Its report was issued in July 1993.

The report represented a considerable advance in its analysis on the consultation paper. It recognised that consideration of internal management arrangements had to have a wider focus than the need for effective executive direction. The report began by stating that

In our view internal management of a local authority should secure effectiveness in:

- leadership in the community;
- effective representation of the citizen;
- clear accountability;
- effectiveness in decision making and implementation;
- effective scrutiny of policy and performance; and
- responsiveness to local people.[11]

This led the working party to identify two major objectives

(i) **To strengthen the role of all elected members** in formulating council strategies, leading and representing their communities and acting as consumer champions to help citizens in the area get the quality of services which is their right and hold to account those responsible for providing those services; and

(ii) **To develop the framework for effective leadership within local authorities** – including the provision of political direction, identifying the needs and priorities of their communities and overseeing the efficient provision of high quality services.[12]

The stress on strengthening the role of the elected member represented a significant difference from the consultation paper.

The working party was impressed by the degree of innovation taking place within the existing legislation. Its task force visited authorities in which change had taken place in formal and informal arrangements. It found that in practice many authorities had established an 'informal single group policy committee which in practice acts as an executive' outside the formal committee structure, which could be attended for all or part of its meeting by the chief executive and other chief officers. The legislation had in effect driven underground the development of a political executive.

In both majority and in hung authorities they found a variety of informal arrangements, many of which gave recognition to the reality of political control in local government.

The working party also recognised the extent of innovation taking place within the formal structure of the council. Three main directions were identified

- restructuring of committee systems to focus councillors' attention
- the development of policy and performance review panels
- devolution of responsibility including the creation of area committees

The working party welcomed these innovations and called upon all authorities to review their internal management arrangements. They did not however recommend any general change in legislation to enable that review, even though their evidence had shown that the present legislation was making it difficult to give formal recognition to the political executive and therefore for it to develop fully as part of the machinery of the council.

The only general change recommended was in the rules governing the allowance system, which was preventing local authorities giving recognition to attendance at these informal executives or giving recognition to the reality of the working within the authority. They recommended therefore changes to:

(i) give local authorities greater discretion over what allowances to pay and to whom: there should be a substantial increase in the headroom within which each authority has the discretion to incur expenditure on allowances and the government should specify only a minimum basic allowance to be paid to all members;

(ii) remove the upper limit on the payment of special responsibility allowances;

(iii) make specified party meetings and single member duties eligible for payment of allowances.[13]

They also recommended that the Secretary of State should review with his colleagues whether or not the limited statutory requirements to have certain specified committees should be lifted.

Wider changes, it was argued, should wait upon experiments, perhaps because the working party felt itself tied to its terms of reference linking its work to the consultation paper. In putting forward its proposals for experiment it differed in three important ways from the approach in the consultation paper.

First it based its approach on developments within the existing framework of local government. They considered overseas models but pointed out that 'all the overseas systems... evolved from the existing framework of local government in those countries. We believe that any new systems for internal management in local authorities in England should similarly develop from what is already there, by a process of evolution'.[14] This approach led them to reject, implicitly if not explicitly, models involving an individual executive or models involving separate elected executives (whether an elected mayor or, as recommended by the consultation paper an elected cabinet). Their analysis had shown that the process of evolution was towards a collective political executive, based in majority-controlled councils on the majority party.

The second contribution was to recognise that the political executive could take many forms and that for many of these forms the word 'cabinet' was inappropriate. Not all these forms required the separation of the executive from the council as representative body. The working party therefore set out a number of models of political executive, not to predetermine the experiment, but to encourage innovation by suggesting the range of possibilities.

These models were:

MODEL 1: The Single Party Executive Committee

In this model the council delegates to the single party policy committee a limited range of executive powers and formulation of a broad strategy. Decisions taken by the executive would become decisions of the council. The precise extent of the executive's control over policy would be at the discretion of the council and would be laid out in Standing Orders. Authorities could retain certain functions either with full council or with other specialist committees – for example approving the budget, and planning decisions. The executive would retain only an advisory role in such matters. The policy executive would set the broad strategic framework within which day to day matters were dealt with by the service committees or officers and have a right to call in committee and officer decisions. Its decisions could be challenged and/or vetoed by the full council. Standing Orders would prescribe the circumstances in which recall and veto could take place, and the mechanisms for doing so.[15]

MODEL 2: The Lead Member System

In this model the council delegates executive powers to named lead members rather than to a collective political executive. For example the council would delegate control over social service decisions to the chair of the Social Services Committee. Lead members could form themselves into a non-executive committee and its members would now have individual executive powers to carry out the policies agreed in their meetings.

The committee system could still operate but they would be used for scrutiny rather than executive purposes. However the extent of committees' powers would vary.[16]

MODEL 3: The Cabinet System

This model extends the principle of delegation to lead members to include a single party policy committee the membership of which has individual and combined executive powers. It is imprecisely referred to as the cabinet model, and we use that term here only as a form of useful shorthand. Much of what was outlined under models one and two would also apply in this model.

Decisions taken by the executive would be decisions of the council. Individual members of the executive would have delegated areas of responsibility, and the attendant decision taking powers; but the broader strategy would be decided by the executive.[17]

MODEL 4: The Strong Political Executive – Separate Legal Entity

In this model there would be a separate executive with its own legal powers and status. It would take control of the decision taking process on behalf of the council. Its membership would be drawn entirely from the council membership. It would not need to be politically balanced and minority party input into the formulation of policy would be discretionary. The executive would decide how to apportion powers, i.e. whether to adopt individual and/or collective responsibility.

Under the most extreme version of this model the executive would take over all the decision taking powers currently with the full council. It would then be for the executive to decide to what extent it would delegate powers back to the full council, to committees, or to officers.[18]

The third feature of the working party report was that its models were analysed in their impact on other aspects of the authorities' working and in particular the role of the council, including committees, and the role of officers. It is possible that the working party did not go far enough in considering how the council would operate if it became in effect a quasi- legislature, as implied by some models. Such a council would need new procedures for scrutinising policy statements as if they were legislation. But the aim of the working party was to suggest possibilities rather than to predetermine outcomes.

The working party proposed that there would be legislation:

that the Secretary of State for the Environment should take powers to allow, in consultation with local government, experimental changes to their internal management arrangements proposed by individual local authorities; legislation would allow approval of experiments including the following ingredients, amongst others, subject to suitable safeguards:

(a) the replacing of the existing committee structure and the introduction of executive models and other structures of political management,
(b) the creation of deliberative committees whose membership consisted only of members of the majority group (or dominant coalition group),
(c) the decentralisation of decision-taking,
(d) new rights for councillors to review and scrutinise council decisions, and
(e) enhanced roles for councillors not in executive positions.[19]

Proposals for experiments would be approved by the Secretary of State advised by a panel on which local government would be represented and which would also keep the experiments under review with a view to recommending possible wider application and, one would hope, general changes in legislation.

The working party's report focused on this issue of the political executive. It devoted too little attention to such issues as developing the role of the councillor or decentralisation although it recognised their importance.

It remains to be seen what the response of the Government will be to the report of the working party although it seems likely to accept it.

Conclusion

As was argued at the beginning of this chapter, the approach adopted by the Government on this issue differed from that set out in other chapters. The Government has used committees or working parties to assess the issues of internal management. Recently there has been an emphasis on experiment rather on legislation. An evolutionary approach is favoured.

Nevertheless internal management is changing. This is partly under the impact of the ideas discussed in this chapter. It is perhaps more due to the wider changes affecting local government as a result both of the legislative and policy initiatives of the Government and of initiatives taken by local authorities themselves in response to a changing society. Thus the client–contractor split and an emphasis on closeness to the public have implications for internal management. At times, and in particular, in the consultation paper these changes seem almost disregarded in the official debate on internal management. A full consideration of internal management should cover not merely the ideas discussed in society but the overall impact of the changes in local government discussed in this book. This theme is taken up in Chapter 11.

Notes and references

1. See Department of the Environment *The Internal Management of Local Authorities in England* (Department of the Environment, 1991).
2. See Widdicombe Committee, *The Report of the Enquiry into the Conduct of Local Authority Business* (HMSO, 1986) para. 3.5.
3. Ibid., para. 5.33.

4. Ibid., para. 5.35.
5. Ibid., para. 5.58.
6. Ibid., para. 5.63.
7. See Department of the Environment, *The Conduct of Local Authority Business: The Government Response to the Report of the Widdicombe Committee*, Cm 433 (HMSO, 1988) para. 2.16.
8. DoE, *The Internal Management of Local Authorities in England*, para. 29.
9. Ibid., para. 24.
10. See Working Party on the Internal Management of Local Authorities, *Community Leadership and Representation: Unlocking the Potential* (HMSO, 1993) para. 1.2.
11. Ibid., para. 2.4.
12. Ibid., para. 2.6.
13. Ibid., para. 4.19.
14. Ibid., para. 5.4.
15. Ibid., para. 5.43.
16. Ibid., paras 5.50–5.51.
17. Ibid., paras 5.62–5.65.
18. Ibid., paras 5.72–5.73.
19. Ibid., 'Summary', para. 4.

6 Citizen's Charters

David Prior

The publication of the White Paper on the Citizen's Charter in July 1991 was significant as the first substantial policy initiative to be recognised as the distinctive product of John Major's premiership. The values and aims of the White Paper were closely associated with the personal philosophy of the new Prime Minister, articulated through a political rhetoric which appealed to the interests and concerns of the 'ordinary citizen'.[1] It was an approach with inevitable resonances for local government, given its acknowledged roots in Major's early political experience as a local authority councillor.[2]

According to John Major's foreword to the Citizen's Charter, the role of the ordinary citizen was a central concern:

> The Citizen's Charter is about giving more power to the citizen. But citizenship is about our responsibilities – as parents, for example, or as neighbours – as well as our entitlements. The Citizen's Charter is not a recipe for more state action; it is a testament of our belief in people's right to be informed and choose for themselves.[3]

However, enhancing the power of citizens, clarifying citizens' responsibilities and enabling individual choice were not to be achieved through a direct engagement with the status, rights and obligations of citizenship *per se* – through a redefinition of the constitutional relationship between state and citizen, for instance – but through a programme of reforms directed at the quality of the public services. If the relationship between government and citizen was to be transformed, it would be as a result of changes in the way individual public services were organised, managed and delivered so as to meet more satisfactorily the wishes of their various users.[4]

In this regard, the Citizen's Charter initiative was an explicit continuation of the overall political programme of restructuring Britain's public services which had been a central preoccupation of the Thatcher years. It appeared to mark a new phase of the programme, characterised by a more positive view of the potential role of the public services and an interest in raising the standards of service delivery across the public domain. It contrasted with the innate Thatcherite suspicion and dislike of public services, which generated reforms intended primarily to focus public service management on the goals of economy and efficiency: to reduce the 'burden' of the public sector on the citizen, rather than address the benefits the citizen might gain from an effective public service.[5] The continuity was evident in the emphasis on the *management* of public services as the critical arena in which the achievement of better outcomes for the citizen was to be secured.[6]

The significance of the Citizen's Charter initiative is that it signalled the Government's intention to make the improvement of *quality* in the public services a desirable goal alongside the continuing imperative to contain expenditure. It thereby represented an adjustment in the Government's attitude to the public services, not just as a result of changing political and personality factors, but from the continued recourse to managerialism for its source of ideas. Managerialism is itself a changing ideology, and it was during the 1980s that the buzzwords of 'quality' and 'customer responsiveness' came to the forefront of private sector management discourse and to dominate prescriptions for effective and successful organisations.[7] The Citizen's Charter was inspired as much by managerial philosophies as by political philosophies.

The Citizen's Charter White Paper

The Citizen's Charter is not, in fact, a charter in itself, rather it is an agenda for the future development of charters in a wide range of services:

> The White Paper sets the framework and gives some examples of what the new policy will mean in some key areas. It will be followed up by a programme of action across all public services.[8]

The framework comprises a statement of objectives, a set of themes, a statement of principles of public service, and a list of mechanisms for achieving change. Most of the White Paper is then given over to proposals for applying this framework across the public sector. Many of these proposals have subsequently been implemented, so that individual charters which use the concepts and language of the White Paper now exist in most areas of public service, and more are in the process of development. The Government, then, has succeeded in getting citizen's charters firmly established within contemporary public service culture, and it is important to try to understand the way in which the White Paper has shaped the development of service charters.

The White Paper is a curious document. The framework it offers is complex and confusing, with a number of internal ambiguities and inconsistencies.[9] It is not clear how the different elements are meant to relate to each other, nor what the basis is for the inclusion of certain items within different elements. For example, *accountability* appears as one of the four objectives in the introduction, but is then not explicitly referred to again; *quality* and *value* are listed in both the objectives and the themes, but do not appear in the principles and do not clearly relate to any of the mechanisms; *choice* is an objective, a theme and a principle, but varies widely in its meaning; and *non-discrimination* is stated as a principle but no mechanism is identified to realise it.

In order to understand the thinking behind the Citizen's Charter framework, it is helpful to limit the focus to the objectives and the mechanisms – the former because they figure strongly in Government claims about the purpose of Charters, the latter because they are the measures actually being introduced into public services to realise the objectives. The objectives are to:

- raise quality
- increase choice
- secure better value
- extend accountability.

The mechanisms are:

- privatisation
- competition
- contracting out
- performance related pay
- independent inspectorates
- published performance targets

- information on standards
- complaints procedures
- redress.[10]

Two basic points can be made here. The first is that there is no clear explanation of why these four particular objectives are given priority. If they are intended to relate to fundamental concerns of citizens, it might be expected that they would be grounded in an explicit understanding of citizenship.[11] Instead, the starting point seems to be an assumption that quality, choice, accountability and value are obviously desirable and compatible aims which do not require justification. Questions of the extent to which the pursuit of quality improvement and better value for money might generate conflicting pressures, or of the varied circumstances in which choice and accountability may or may not be a high priority for citizens, are not acknowledged. Similarly, the implications of such objectives for public policy are not addressed: is choice an appropriate goal in all circumstances?[12]

Second, there is an imbalance in the range of mechanisms proposed in the Citizen's Charter, in that they actually provide little scope for the direct involvement of the citizen. The first four mechanisms listed above are concerned with the creation of a market in public services and with introducing incentives for managers. The creation of independent inspectorates allows for the inclusion of lay members, but these are likely to be appointed rather than chosen by their fellow citizens and the criteria for selection are not given. The remaining mechanisms – published performance targets, information on standards, complaints procedures and redress – are clearly intended to enable citizens to assess service performance and to take action when services fail, but the citizen's role is essentially a reactive one, responding to the activities of service agencies rather than engaging proactively with them.

These limitations stem from the implicit understanding of the nature of citizenship contained in the White Paper. This understanding views the citizen as *an individual consumer of services*. From the perspective of the White Paper, the dynamic for change in the public services is to be found in the creation of a market relationship between consumers and providers, with the Government intervening to empower citizens as consumers by means of rights to receive information on services and performance, to assert choices and preferences, to complain and to receive redress. The framework of objectives and mechanisms can thus be understood in terms of the twin aims of creating market relationships in public services and empowering public service consumers.

The approach to citizenship which is based on the development of consumer rights and entitlements and the specification of service standards has been the dominant model in the proliferation of public service charters that have followed the White Paper.[13] The complexity of these charters varies considerably, largely depending on the nature of the service product and the relationship between provider and user. Where the service product is clear, users' needs are well understood, there is little user involvement in the service delivery process and users pay directly for the service, then charters tend to be simple, consisting of little more than a statement of standards and what to do if these are not met. In more complicated services, where the nature of the service is not easily defined, users' needs and expectations vary, the success of the service may depend on the involvement of users and the service is paid for indirectly, charters are correspondingly complex. They tend to incorporate a statement of basic values, rights which express those values, entitlements consequent on those rights, the services available, standards to be met and the process of complaint and redress. Such charters can raise difficult operational issues, particularly the relationship between rights, entitlements and standards.[14]

But the key point is that whether the service is simple or complex in its characteristics, the approach to charters is firmly rooted in the notion of the citizen as consumer; the task of the charter is to define the rights, entitlements and standards which the citizen can expect as a consumer in the market for public services. It is an approach which neglects other considerations of citizenship: that the citizen is also a participant in the process of government and a contributor to public life, and that the citizen is a member of a community and therefore shares in collective rights and responsibilities as well as bearing individual ones.[15]

Charters in local government

During the 1980s, the influence of private sector management approaches was felt not only by central government. Local government also responded to managerial ideas to do with quality, effectiveness and responsiveness, and adapted them to its particular circumstances.[16] Whilst this process reflected both differences in local politics and differences in the nature of local government in different areas, the common thread was a determination to move away from traditional provider-controlled forms of public service delivery towards an approach which centred much more on the needs and experiences of service users.

Thus, enthusiasm for market-oriented, contract-based management approaches was more likely to be found among Conservative councils than Labour authorities. The latter, especially where the influence of the "urban left" was strong,[17] were more likely to pursue quality and responsiveness through experiments with decentralisation and devolution.[18] County authorities tended to focus on the efficiency and effectiveness of existing services, while district authorities, particularly in urban areas, gave greater priority to the needs and characteristics of local areas. But, throughout local government generally, a new emphasis on making the process and the outcomes of local government activities more relevant and more accountable to consumers and citizens was apparent.

A striking example of this trend was the production of York City Council's Citizen's Charter, which predated the government's White Paper by some two years.[19] Like most local authority charters, the York Charter is complex in its structure: it includes statements of basic values about the nature of local government and the kind of city to be aspired to, statements of general rights that residents should enjoy as citizens, statements of the values and beliefs that should underpin the provision of council services, and promises regarding specific action to be taken in different service areas and the standards to which specific services will perform.

The York Charter is interesting not merely as an example of local government innovation anticipating a major central government initiative, but because of the way it attempts to weave together the concerns of citizens, customers and community. The commitment to citizenship – to people's civic rights as citizens of York – is explicitly stated in terms of rights to know; rights to be heard and to influence; rights to be treated honestly, fairly and courteously; rights to participate and be represented.[20] These general civic rights are subsequently translated into practical entitlements, through, for example, the establishment of:

- Area Committees where you can have your say about decisions affecting your neighourhood;
- special arrangements to involve some of the people who are not often listened to: people with disabilities and other special needs.[21]

Intertwined with the concern with citizenship is the importance attached to the notion of the local community. The charter includes rights, such as:

- a right to a council which is genuinely local and promotes the interests of York both regionally, nationally and internationally
- a right to a council which is so local, so rooted in the community, that it is forced to listen and respond.[22]

Here, the language of rights and entitlements is used to identify with the general interests of local people as members of a particular community and with the general role of the local authority as the expression of community government.

At the same time, the York charter is clearly concerned with the status of citizens as consumers and with the council's role as a provider of services. Indeed, York was one of the first councils to introduce customer contracts in services where clear standards could be specified, such as refuse collection and street cleaning, and these were seen as part of the new relationship between local authority and citizen which the Citizen's Charter embodied.

The theme of improved performance and responsiveness to service consumers has continued alongside the commitment to citizens and community in promises to:

- train our staff to provide the most accessible and helpful service we can
- make the best use of new technology to improve services to customers
- develop customer contracts for housing repairs, housing benefit services, swimming pools and allotments.[23]

At the level of service delivery, the distinction between customers and citizens is not always obvious, and nor can it be. Services such as refuse collection and street cleaning are 'used' by everyone – as the Customer Contract for Street and Environmental Cleaning says, 'everyone in York will get a contract'.[24] For such services, to be a citizen is to be a customer, although what 'customer' actually means is problematic. There is, for instance, no choice for the customer of either provider or product; and there is a 'contract', commendably precise in spelling out the nature and standard of the service to be provided, to which the customer is not a signatory.

However, the York Charter is also concerned with services where customers make a clear choice whether to use the service or not (and thus there are many citizens who are not customers) and services where the nature of the service is largely determined by the involvement of the individual customer with the provider. In some services the customer/contract model of service relationship may be highly appropriate, in others it will not.[25] The York Charter attempts to capture these variations in the service/user relationship within a broader understanding of the individual as citizen.

A contrasting approach is represented by the Hertfordshire County Council Citizen's Charter.[26] The development of this charter followed the publication of the Government's Citizen's Charter and it adopts a similar style and focus.[27] Like the Government's approach, and, as has been noted, like county council charters generally, it focuses on services and on the citizen as consumer. The basic charter is very brief, with a framework of four goals designed 'for us to provide better services to you':

- aiming for the highest quality, with targets set for individual services
- giving clear information
- making sure you know what to do and who to talk to if things go wrong
- giving you a bigger say, through questionnaires and customer surveys.[28]

Each of the Hertfordshire service charters lists the specific charter aims under the same set of headings: Communicating With You, Answering To You, Meeting Your Needs, Giving Customers A Bigger Say. These aims comprise a mixture of straightforward consumer rights and entitlements, for example:

We will respond to or acknowledge all letters within five working days, and aim to provide a substantive answer to all enquiries within 10 working days [Planning and Environment];

New consultation arrangements with customers, offering them more choice in care services, will be introduced [Social Services];

When you contact us, we will tell you exactly what we can and cannot do to help you. Early honesty will avoid later disappointment [Trading Standards];

together with aims that are more to do with the development of citizenship rights, for example:

We will involve local residents before, during and after implementing road improvement schemes in urban areas [Transportation];

We will be asking local communities what they think are the important issues which should be taken into account in planning Hertfordshire's future [Planning and Environment];

The library service endeavours to provide services for *everyone* in the community. In 1993 we will introduce a new 'Minicom' system at Hertfordshire Information Points to assist deaf people and those with hearing or speech impairment to make contact with the County Council [Libraries, Arts and Information].[29]

In contrast to the York approach, the Hertfordshire Charter starts from a concern with the rights of consumers of individual services, and where appropriate, develops rights of citizenship from within the service context. Whilst this avoids some of the complexities of the York Charter's 'dual status'' approach, which employs a clear notion of citizenship arising from residence in the city but also wishes to assign rights to consumers of different services, the Hertfordshire approach neglects the civic rights of the citizen *per se* and the role of the local authority in providing locally relevant governance to its citizenry.

This analysis of the York and Hertfordshire charters illustrates some of the dilemmas and uncertainties encountered in the early experiments with citizen's charters by local authorities. These difficulties arise from an ambiguity about what the purpose of a 'citizen's charter' should be. York's attempt to use the charter mechanism to construct an interactive relationship between council and citizens around an issue of fundamental mutual interest – what sort of city do we want and how can we achieve it together? – is complicated by the introduction of service contracts to the charter framework. This is not to argue that service contracts are irrelevant or unimportant to the activities of a local authority; rather it is to suggest that they address a set of purposes, and raise a series of questions, which are different from issues of citizenship.

In the Hertfordshire case a kind of reverse process seems to be occurring. The charter is about consumerism, and does not deal with citizenship in any holistic sense. Yet concerns with the broader relationship between citizens and local government evidently exist in the county. Parallel to the charter, although not mentioned in it, the county council launched its 'Community Government' project:

> Community Government will redefine the relationships between the tiers of local government, and other statutory, commercial and voluntary agencies, and the communities they are part of . . . The objective of Community Government is to give individual communities (towns, parishes, groups) more influence and control over services and how they are delivered. The role of elected council members is to determine priorities and represent individuals and the County as a whole. This role will be reinforced by the greater visibility, clarity and purpose which will be voiced by local communities.[30]

The core focus is still on local government as a provider of services, but these are now viewed in aggregate, as the overall outputs of the various agencies of government in the county, and the objectives are defined not in terms of efficiency, effectiveness and quality but of control, influence and responsibility. A stronger sense of place or locality than is evident in the citizen's charter is injected into the Community Government project by the creation of a series of local project teams to take the initiative forward in partnership with local citizens and communities.

The discussion of these two examples highlights an obvious point about the development of citizen's charters in local government. Local authorities are multi-function agencies; they offer an extraordinarily wide range of services with very different characteristics, as well as providing functions of democratic government to their localities. They are involved in complex relationships with the people who live and work in their area, some of whose lives are substantially controlled by the actions of the local council, and all of whom are affected in some way by its decisions. They necessarily deal with people as both citizens and consumers, and are thus concerned (if only implicitly) with people's *rights* as citizens and as consumers. Local authority citizen's charters, if they are to be understandable, relevant and useful, will have to be based on a very clear assessment of the diverse functions and activities of local government and an equally clear appraisal of the multiple roles and relationships in which local authorities and their citizens are involved.

The impact of charterism

The language and values of the citizen's charter movement have quickly become a familiar feature in the contemporary management of local government. What is less certain is the nature of charterism's impact: whether it has generated significant change in the way local authorities are managed and the way services are delivered, and whether it has changed the way citizens view the activities of their local authority.

As regards citizens' perceptions, early research evidence, though meagre, suggests that the public impact of charters has been limited. A government-sponsored survey found that 71 per cent of respondents had heard of the Citizen's Charter, but did not examine people's knowledge of what different charters contain.[31] More localised research suggests that such knowledge is extremely limited, with respondents unaware of the specific charters relevant to the services they were using or with little knowledge of the standards the charters proclaim.[32] No doubt the picture varies greatly between services: anecdotal evidence suggests that many users of British Rail have some understanding of the entitlements available to them via the Passenger's Charter, and this may be true for other national services with a clear public identity. For charters in local government, which still struggles with widespread public ignorance about which services councils actually provide, penetrating the public consciousness is likely to be more difficult, although, again, considerable variation can be expected. This variation may be geographical, with greater impact where charters emphasise local identity, or service-related, with greater impact where services are well-understood and the user group is easily defined; but further comparative research is needed here.

Some indication of how citizens have responded to the publication of an individual local authority charter and what use they make of it is available from research in Leicester.[33] Leicester City Council published its first charter in 1991. It commissioned a MORI survey on public attitudes to the charter in the following year, and used information from the survey in the production of a second council charter, published in 1993. Responses to this were also tested by a MORI survey. The surveys reveal a significant increase in citizen awareness and interest between the two studies. In 1991, 20 per cent of the sample remembered having seen the charter, this proportion rising to 50 per cent in 1993. Of these, the proportion who had kept the charter for future reference, rather than having thrown it away or lost it, rose from 36 per cent to 51 per cent. Moreover, when all respondents were shown the 1993 charter, an impressive 70 per cent thought it 'very' or 'fairly' useful, compared with 55 per cent for the 1991 charter. These seem to be very positive results, although the key difference between the two charters is that in 1993 the charter incorporated the already successful, and previously separate, 'A–Z of City Council Services'. The survey results show that overwhelmingly people found the 1993 charter useful as a source of information about council services, with far fewer citing its usefulness in indicating the standard of services to be expected or how to make complaints. This suggests that Leicester's charter, whilst clearly well-received, may not yet be making the kind of impact on citizens which would distinguish it from more conventional local authority publications.

It is also difficult to assess the extent to which management and service change in local authorities can be credited to the influence of charterism. As already noted, local government has been substantially influenced by trends in managerial thinking which emphasise concepts of service quality, customer responsiveness, competition and performance. The citizen's charter movement has to be located in the context of these trends rather than their being seen as a consequence of charterism.

Thus, the impact of citizen's charter initiatives in any area of local authority service will, to a greater or lesser extent, be shaped by the impact that other managerial and service developments are having. For example, services subject to CCT will, in most authorities, have undergone considerable redesigning of their managerial and service delivery processes to make them more competitive, introduce formal quality management systems, and define new performance standards and targets based on customer requirements.[34] In these services, the impact of citizen's charters is likely to be limited, perhaps having most significance as a way of reinforcing the key objectives, standards and targets already established for the service and informing users how to complain if these are not met.

In non-CCT services, there are many developments which, whilst consistent with charterist goals, have anticipated the charter movement and set a framework within which any subsequent charter initiative must operate. Across a range of services, changes in legislation and in political and professional thinking have moved practitioners towards forms of service delivery which prioritise charter-type goals of empowering citizens as consumers, via notions of openness, partnership, choice, and so on. The particular configurations of legislative requirements and political/professional norms thereby create service-specific contexts for the introduction of citizen's charters.[35] Charters themselves may have minimal effect as agents of change within such contexts. The conclusion is that for many services charters will function more as a confirmation of, and a means of making explicit, existing processes of change rather than initiating new citizen-focused developments.[36]

An area in which charterism appears to be having some significant impact is the development and application of performance indicators. An important aspect of the Government's initiative is the Audit Commission's project to develop a common set of published performance indicators for local authority services, linked to Citizen's Charter standards, which are expected to answer questions about performance that the 'ordinary citizen' might be interested in.[37] Unlike the Citizen's Charter itself, the Audit Commission's identification of citizens' interests and the selection of indicators is in part based on research amongst citizens. However, whilst the emphasis is on relevance to the citizen, the intention is also that the indicators should be of practical use to local authorities themselves. The production of performance information which enables comparisons to be made between authorities is a further key objective.

The Audit Commission's work has generated a substantial response within local authorities, with considerable effort devoted to meeting the deadlines for collection of data during 1993–94 and publication of the indicators by December 1994. Whilst many councils were already engaged in the business of developing performance indicators for their own purposes, the effect of the introduction of the Commission's 'statutory indicators' is to force local authorities to focus on issues to which they may not otherwise have given priority, for example telephone response times. Possibly a more general effect is that local authority responses to the overall Citizen's Charter initiative become weighted towards dealing with the specific performance indicator requirements, focusing on those aspects of service delivery susceptible to quantification and measurement, and neglecting other issues involved in the relationship between council and citizens, such as openness, participation, entitlements and redress.[38] At the present time, it does appear that the publication of Citizen's Charter Performance Indicators may provide the most obvious and concrete impact of the whole charter initiative.

Finally, there is the financial cost impact of the development of charters. In an era when public service expenditure is subject to ever greater scrutiny and constraint, any new initiative must be examined for its cost implications. The development of charters and their associated technology – performance indicators, market testing, complaints procedures and so on – is clearly not a cost-free endeavour. This must be an issue for the health service where charterism, driven by central government exhortation, is endemic. Even firm advocates of charter principles might acknowledge the risk of distorted priorities here: on the same agenda of one district health authority in 1993, there appeared a report on the authority's annual performance *vis-a-vis* its Patient's Charter targets - an impressively detailed, but, one assumes, considerably costly exercise, quantifying achievements across a wide range of services – and a report predicting a very substantial budget shortfall in its acute services in the current year.

This is not an argument against charters as such. It simply makes the point that part of the impact of charterism relates to its direct costs of staffing and administration, and that this needs to be weighed against the benefits it yields in improved service to citizens: a judgement for local government as well as any other public service.

Conclusion

The potential importance of local authority citizen's charters is that they make clear the nature of the relationship between the authority and its citizens. They do this by defining the relationship in terms of rights, entitlements and responsibilities which can be checked and monitored. A charter is a statement of commitments, a set of promises to take particular action, together with the means for enabling citizens to judge how far and how well these commitments have been met. The charter thereby denotes an openness and accountability in the relationship between local authority and citizenry that was rarely achieved in the past. But as well as reaching outwards to local citizens, the charter should also reach inwards to transform the internal political and professional management processes of the local authority. Delivering promises to citizens which are meaningful, relevant and responsive will require substantial change in the way the authority operates across all of its activities.

This is clearly an idealistic view. Citizen's charters arrived on the managerialist tide which flooded local government in the 1980s. They can, indeed, be read as public symbols portraying the particular management approach adopted by the local authority in discharging its service responsibilities to its various users. But they can also denote the role the authority seeks to foster as provider of local *government* to its citizens. This raises perhaps the key questions regarding the role of citizen's charters in the future of local government. Are they to be aimed at customers or citizens? Should they prioritise quality of service or quality of government? Will charters remain true to the Government's managerialist vision, providing a means for the more effective delivery of services to consumers? Or can they become banners proclaiming the values of local democracy and fulfilling the promise of their name as charters *for citizens*?

Notes and references

1. G. Bruce Doern, 'The UK Citizen's Charter: Origins and Implementa tion in Three Agencies', *Policy and Politics*, vol. 21, no. 1 (January 1993) p. 21.
2. Prime Minister, *The Citizen's Charter: Raising the Standard*, Cm 1599 (HMSO, July 1991), p. 2.
3. Ibid., p. 2.
4. Ibid., p. 4.
5. '. . . for all the fine talk about effectiveness and quality of service, the basic dynamic of reform was actually input-minimization which was in turn a response to a perceived overriding need to restrain public expenditure': C. Pollitt, *Managerialism and the Public Services*, 2nd edn (Blackwell,1993) p. 51. See also P. Hoggett, 'A New Management in the Public Sector?', *Policy and Politics*, vol. 19, no. 2 (October 1991) p. 250.
6. For descriptions and discussions of this approach to public service management see, for example, Pollitt, *Managerialism and the Public Services* ; N. Flynn, *Public Sector Management*, 2nd edn (Harvester Wheatsheaf, 1993); J. Stewart and K. Walsh, 'Change in the Management of Public Services', *Public Administration*, vol. 70, no. 4 (Winter 1992) pp. 499–518.
7. Pollitt, *Managerialism and the Public Services*.
8. *The Citizen's Charter*, p. 7.
9. D. Prior, J. Stewart and K. Walsh, *Is the Citizen's Charter a Charter for Citizens?*, Belgrave Papers No. 7 (Local Government Management Board, 1993).
10. *The Citizen's Charter*, pp. 4–5.
11. This is the core argument in Prior, Stewart and Walsh, *Is The Citizen's Charter a Charter for Citizens?*
12. Ibid., p. 14.
13. Examples include the Royal Mail Charter, British Rail's Passenger's Charter, the Benefits Agency Charter, the Courts Charter, the Patient's Charter and the Parent's Charter.
14. Prior, Stewart and Walsh, *Is the Citizen's Charter a Charter for Citizens?*, p. 22: 'The question that arises is whether rights are procedural or outcome based. The more complex the service, the more difficult it is to make the link from rights to specified standards, partly because needs will vary with individuals . . . In many cases it will only be possible to state rights in procedural terms, not to relate them to outcomes stated as standards.' Anna Coote argues that in seeking to secure citizenship rights to welfare as enforceable rights alongside legal and political rights, the focus should be on the more attainable goal of procedurally based rights: A. Coote (ed.), *The Welfare of Citizens*, (IPPR/Rivers Oram Press, 1992) pp. 8–9.
15. The question of the meaning of 'citizenship' and the nature of the rights of citizenship is highly contested. Useful – and brief – recent

discussions which emphasise the civic and community dimensions and defend the status of social rights are provided by: D. Held, 'Between State and Civil Society: Citizenship', in G. Andrews (ed.) *Citizenship* (Lawrence & Wishart, 1991) pp. 19–25; R. Plant, 'Citizenship, Rights and Welfare', in A. Coote, *The Welfare of Citizens*, pp. 15–29; D. Marquand, 'A Language of Community', in B. Pimlott, A. Wright and T. Flower (eds), *The Alternative: Politics for a Change* (W. H. Allen, 1990) pp. 3–13.

16. The substantial output from the Local Government Training Board during this period provides evidence of the interest in new approaches to public sector management.

17. See G. Stoker, *The Politics of Local Government* (Macmillan, 1988) ch. 9.

18. However, the most adventurous experiment in local authority decentralisation occurred in the late 1980s in the London Borough of Tower Hamlets, under one of the very few majority Liberal Democrat councils. See V. Lowndes and G. Stoker, 'An Evaluation of Neighbourhood Decentralisation, Part 1: Customer and Citizen Perspectives', *Policy and Politics*, vol. 20, no. 1 (January 1992).

19. York City Council, *Citizen's Charter, Year 4* (April 1992–March 1993).

20. Ibid.

21. Ibid.

22. Ibid.

23. Ibid.

24. York City Council, *Customer Contract for Environmental and Street Cleaning* (n.d.).

25. See K. Walsh, 'Quality and Public Services', *Public Administration*, vol. 69, no. 4 (Winter 1991).

26. Hertfordshire County Council, *Citizen's Charter*, (1993).

27. J. Sellgren, 'The Hertfordshire Citizen's Charter: A Charter for a Million People', *Local Government Policy Making*, vol. 19, no. 2 (October 1992) pp. 22–28.

28. Hertfordshire County Council, *Citizen's Charter*.

29. Ibid.

30. Hertfordshire County Council, *Community Government* (n.d.).

31. ICM Research, *Citizen's Charter Customer Survey* (ICM, 1993).

32. V. Beale and C. Pollitt, 'Charters at the Grass Roots: A First Report', *Local Government Studies* (forthcoming).

33. Leicester City Council, *Attitudes to Leicester City Council's Charters* (Leicester City Council, n.d.).

34. Beale and Pollitt, 'Charters at the Grass Roots: A First Report'.

35. P. Dolan, 'Citizenship and the Personal Social Services', paper presented to the Public Administration Committee Annual Conference, University of York (1993).

36. P. McKeown, 'Using the Tenant's Charter: A Case Study from Housing Departments', paper presented to the Public Administration Committee Annual Conference, University of York (1993); C. Pollitt,

'The Citizen's Charter: A Preliminary Analysis', *Public Money and Management* (forthcoming).
37. Audit Commission, *Citizen's Charter Indicators. Charting a Course* (HMSO, n.d.).
38. S. Rogers, 'Charters and Performance Measurement', unpublished paper (INLOGOV, University of Birmingham, 1993).

II SERVICES AND FUNCTIONS

7 From Reform to Restructuring of Education

Stewart Ranson*

The present phase of the Conservative Government's movement to reform education has taken a decisive turn. Under the mask of continuing the changes begun in 1988 the legislative proposals of 1992–93 in fact mark a final break with the postwar values of universalism in favour of an earlier tradition, never eliminated, of private and selective education. At the centre of the new programme lies an attack upon the public and democratic foundations of education and upon the equal opportunities they strive to constitute.

The 1988 Education Reform Act (ERA) sought to recast the government of education in the most radical reform of the service since 1944 while, arguably, retaining some of the defining characteristics of the postwar period which strove for equal educational opportunity for all young people. The 1988 agenda for reforming the quality of education revolved around a number of key principles. First, establishing *an entitlement curriculum*[1]: the creation of a National Curriculum (NC) would provide an entitlement to broad and balanced learning for all five- to sixteen-year-olds and would improve achievement by providing a better definition of what is to be taught and learned. Clearer assessment of what has been achieved would enable planned progression from stage to stage of the learning process. Such close monitoring of progress in learning would enable parents to know more clearly what was being studied, what objectives were being set and what was achieved individually and collectively. Second, *public accountability*: this would substantially increase the amount of public information available to parents

*This chapter draws on Ranson, 'Public Education and Local Democracy', in H. Tomlinson (ed.), *Education and Training 14–19: Continuity and Diversity in the Cirriculum* (Longman, 1993) and 'Markets or Democracy for Education', *British Journal of Educational Studies*, vol. 41, no. 4 (1993). I would like to thank the editors for their comments on an earlier draft.

about the curriculum and achievement, and the use of resources would enable schools and the service to be more accountable to parents. Third, *public choice*: the availability of such evidence about the performance of institutions would enable parents to make more informed choices. Open enrolment together with 'pupils as vouchers' formula funding of schools[2] would encourage competition between schools and lead to improved standards of education. Fourth, *local management*: better management and a better curriculum go hand in hand, and the 1988 reforms sought to delegate decision-making as close as possible to the point where the decisions bite. Schools and further education colleges would be granted the flexibility to use resources more effectively to respond to their own needs as articulated by the governors and parents as well as the teachers.

The juxtaposing of a planned curriculum (entitlement) and parental choice (markets) within this reformed system suggested a compromise between the universal values of postwar social democracy and the emergent perspectives of consumer democracy. Yet the dimensions of planning and market choice could also be interpreted as providing mutually reinforcing strategies for change that were designed to weaken the hold of the educational professionals: thus, the state would assume control of the internal processes of education to create (albeit equal access to) a conservative curriculum beyond the control of the teachers, while the frameworks for learning (the schools) would be placed in the market-place, beyond the control of local administrators, to ensure the virtues of competition and choice. Related political agendas for the reform of education required different yet potentially consistent instruments of change.

The ERA was also, arguably, an uneasy compromise between political factions within the Conservative Party.[3] While the Institute of Economic Affairs[4] was promoting the market as the sole mechanism for reform, the Hillgate Group[5] sought national controls to impose the academic traditions and cultural values of a grammar school curriculum. The 1988 reforms forged the two together. Yet, in the practice of implementation, the ERA became a further compromise between the political agendas of the New Right and the agendas of the Secretary of State and the officials, appointed to elaborate and implement the new law, who could without exception be described as moderate educators drawn from the establishment of the previous social democratic tradition.[6] The burden of this paradox was nowhere more apparent than in the reform of the LEA.

Although the ERA redefined responsibilities, both centralising and devolving powers, so as potentially to undermine the LEA, the law could equally be interpreted to accord the LEA a significant but different role in the reform programme.[7] The challenge for the new - style LEA was to set aside its traditional commitment to controlling the routine administration of local education and to concentrate instead on clarifying strategy, supporting and assuring quality in schools and colleges. A 'providing' authority was to give way to an 'enabling' authority.[8] A plural system of education governance was, therefore, maintained but authority redistributed within an integrated but devolved framework of institutional management for post- as well as pre-sixteen local education.

By 1991 the balance of power and influence within the Conservative Government began to shift as the 'moderates' were gradually replaced not only in the ministerial team but in the commanding heights of the system.[9] The policy agenda appeared to be subject to radical revision in a series of legislative proposals and altered priorities that began to unfold during 1992: in March the Education (Schools) Act 1992 (which privatised school inspections) and the Further and Higher Education Act 1992 (which nationalised further education) received the Royal Assent and in July the White Paper *Choice and Diversity: A New Framework for Schools* was published (promoting the movement of all schools to grant-maintained self-governance and thus threatening the future of the LEA). This became the Education Act 1993, the year in which the Queen's Speech proposed the restructuring of initial teacher training. The elements of the new paradigm – revealed in the restructuring of curricula, institutions and government – will be discussed in turn, emphasising the way in which the dual strategy of accelerating national state regulation *and* market forces combine not only to stratify educational opportunities but also undermine democracy within the public domain.

Back to a basic secondary education

Although there is the semblance of continuity between 1988 and 1992 there is actually a fundamental shift of policy. In place of 'progression', 'entitlement' and 'local management' is substituted a new emphasis upon 'standards', 'specialisation', 'selection' and 'autonomy'. In the foreword to *Choice and Diversity*, the Prime Minister said that 'the drive for higher standards in schools has been the hallmark of the Government over the last decade' and was now to be carried forward. The White Paper emphasised that the Government was 'absolutely committed to testing . . . as the key to monitoring and raising standards in our schools' (p. 9).

The White Paper reinforced other government announcements about standards. The proportion of coursework in GCSE had been reduced while that of exams had been increased. The concern about standards in GCSE was reiterated following the publication of the exam results in August 1992 when the Secretary of State announced a review of marking following a confidential report from inspectors which claimed a decline in standards. In earlier years simpler tests are being introduced to assess a more basic curriculum. Standard attainment targets (SATs) have been simplified with an increase in pencil and paper tests and some of the key curriculum Orders are being reviewed. Only three years after publishing its Orders on the teaching of English, the Government announced a review of the subject. The traditional 'basics' were to be reinforced with greater emphasis given to spelling, grammar and the speaking of standard English. In October 1992 the Prime Minister on the radio emphasised the importance of teaching facts in history.

What is emerging fitfully but surely from speeches, announcements and reviews is a different conception of learning: a move away from an emphasis upon progression in understanding, skills and capacity taking into account the needs of the child as a whole person as well as the requirements of learning through the NC. The move towards a basic standards model of the curriculum entrenches even more securely than the subject-based NC a conception of learning as acquiring separate bodies of knowledge and of assessment as selection. It reinforces a notion of fixed levels of ability, the 'normal curve' of achievement, and of different 'types' of aptitude and ability.

Piecemeal change, however, acquired coherence with the Dearing review of the National Curriculum and Assessment. The specificity of the NC and the overload caused by the testing and assessment system came to a head in 1993. What began as a protest by English teachers over ill-prepared tests in the subject for 14-year-olds rapidly became a boycott by most of the teaching profession of all the tests for 14-year-olds in which teachers refused to set, administer or mark tests produced by the Schools Examination and Assessment Council. This boycott was upheld by the Appeal Court and appeared to have wide public support. What was a particular dispute became a general dispute about the NC, testing and in particular the preoccupation with using information from the tests to create national league tables of school performance.

In April 1993 the Secretary of State invited Sir Ron Dearing, Chairman-designate of the new School Curriculum and Assessment Authority (SCAA) to review the manageability of the NC and testing system. The review would include the scope of the curriculum, the 10-level scale for graduating children's attainments and the complexity of the testing arrangements. Dearing, publishing an interim report in July 1993 and a final report in January 1994,[10] acknowledged that while the principle of the NC had wide support, teachers were experiencing many problems in trying to implement the ERA reforms:

- curriculum overload: the sum of the individual subjects accounts for virtually the whole of the teaching time available, leaving little time to pursue curriculum objectives outside the NC or to explore links between subjects across the curriculum.
- lack of training: many primary teachers did not possess the academic specialist training required by a very academic NC.
- the required teaching resources were often not prepared in time
- the pace of change: short lead times for implementation and the late arrival of key documents exacerbated teacher anxiety
- over prescription (higher than most West European Countries) limiting the proper exercise of professional judgement
- bureaucratic complexity: for example, the classroom teacher at Key Stage 1 with 35 pupils . . . who assesses all the class against all the statements of attainment would make and record some 8,000 judgements
- deep concern about the confused purposes of assessment: to benefit the pupil in diagnosing personal needs, the teacher and school in planning the curriculum, or parents in making competitive choices of school.

In proposing to address the issues of curriculum overload, prescription and administrative burden Dearing appeared to bargain a compromise between the teachers and a New Right Government: trust should be accorded to the profession in exchange for an acceptance that schools are accountable to parents and society for their stewardship. The report proposed that a broad, balanced foundation should be maintained at key stages 1–3, but the statutory requirements should be reduced (and be less prescriptive) at each key stage with the content of each subject divided into a statutory core and optional studies supplemented by material for use at the discretion of the teacher.

The most significant aspect of the Dearing Report, however, is its 'subtext' which presages a more significant restructuring of secondary education. Whereas the NC in 1988 sought to establish a broad, balanced traditional curriculum for all pupils from 5 to 16 the Dearing Interim Report argues for serious consideration to be given to a different approach to the post-14 age group. This is to see '14 as a distinctive staging post in the structuring of education [followed by] . . . a new approach to the education of students in the 14–18 age range [which would] specify a number of pathways which lead through in an easily intelligible and coherent way from Key Stage 4 to post-16 education and training' (p. 25). It is a continental model where 'in the rest of Europe 16 is not a particularly significant stage in schooling and post-14 many of our neighbours place particular value on technical and vocational education. In France, Germany and the Netherlands . . . about 25% of students go to schools which specialise in some form of technical or vocational education' (p. 25). The Final Report argues for new pathways to be developed for 14- to 16-year-olds: *'the academic pathway'*, and to be worked out over the next few years, *'the vocational pathway'*, which maintains a broad educational component, and the possibility of *'the occupational pathway'*, which might consider developing competence to do a job or a narrow range of jobs.

The Dearing proposals and suggestions are consistent with other policy developments and indicate a framework for restructuring which would gradually leave 5 to 14 as a general foundation of secondary education. A circular from the new Further Education Funding Council in September 1993, announcing that colleges would be free to recruit even 13- or 14-year-old students, prompted *The Times Educational Supplement*[11] to refer to the new 'watershed at 14 plus'. Students will be given the option not just of what they study – vocational courses as well as GCSEs – but where they study – college as well as school.

The Government's intention to strengthen vocational pro-grammes has been apparent for some time. The 1991 White Paper *Education and Training for the 21st Century*[12] sought to promote a vocational skill-based curriculum which would achieve or be given parity of esteem with the academic:

> Young people and adults need a clear framework of qualifications to measure their success in education and training. We need to build up a modern system of academic and vocational qualifications which are equally valued. They must both set a high standard and offer ladders of opportunity after sixteen and throughout working life . . .
>
> Vocational qualifications in this country have been under-valued and underused. A major reform is underway to produce clear, nationally recognised qualifications. The reform is led by the National Council for Vocational Qualifications . . . the NCVQ should work with others to develop criteria for accrediting more vocational qualifications.

At the same time, a framework of principles will be designed to ensure the quality of all A-level and AS syllabuses. New diplomas will encompass these academic (e.g. A-level) and vocational (NVQ) qualifications. (A range of general NVQs will be developed for young people to cover broad occupational areas and enable a variety of career choices.) The Government intends that these principles should control the development of syllabuses, limiting assessment by coursework and establishing examinations at the end of courses as the norm.

The narrow focus of NVQs has been the subject of much criticism. Smithers[13] believes that 'the qualifications have lost touch with reality. They are tailored to specific jobs. Rather than setting a core standard for maths for example, you just have to know the maths related to one job. This may be alright in the short term but what about a job in five years time'. Hilary Steedman,[14] of the National Institute for Economic and Social Research, argues that: 'NVQs need significant amendment to be suitable for young people because they are too focused on one or two areas and have no perspective of what will be needed in ten years time. They will be alright for adults because they encourage people to get recognition for skills they have already acquired and this can improve morale. But it does not improve skill levels. It simply certifies levels which already exist.' The piloting of the more general GNVQ, which emphasises cross-curricular themes and core skills, has been designed to counter criticisms of the narrowness of NVQs.

The principal thrust of government policy seems to be the creation of a foundation of secondary education leaving young people to enter a system of tripartite streams from 14 to 19 with an 'academic' stream (A Levels), a 'technical' stream (GNVQ: an advanced-level general vocational qualification) and a modern stream (NVQs) of practical skill development (see Green[15] and Ranson[16]).

Stratifying self-governing institutions

The 1992 White Paper celebrated 'diversity and parental choice [to] allow schools to develop in different ways' (p. 9). Diversity offers parents and children greater choice: private and state schools, county and voluntary; comprehensive schools of variety, grammar and bilateral; CTCs and grant-maintained schools. Some schools will choose to specialise in music or technology or in languages. Diversity, it is proposed, extinguishes the anathema of uniformity which 'in educational provision presupposes that all children have basically the same educational needs. The reality is that children have different needs. The provision of education should be geared more to local circumstances and individual needs: hence our commitment to diversity in education' (pp. 3–4).

This discussion in the White Paper implied, however, that specialisation might proceed beyond different emphases of subject into different *types* of learning and school – academic, technological and creative. These distinctions recall the terms of tripartite education – grammar, technical and modern – outlined in the 1938 Spens Report and the 1943 Norwood Report and introduced into the secondary system after the Second World War. Indeed the 1992 White Paper refers affectionately to this tripartite system of secondary schools which, it implied, would have proved an ideal education system if it had only been supported by a NC! Like the 1940s reports, the 1992 White Paper expressed its commitment to 'parity of esteem' between different types of school. It is argued that schools could develop such specialisation 'within existing powers': 'it generally does not constitute a significant change of character requiring the approval of the Secretary of State. If schools wish to develop in this way responding to the aspirations of parents and local economic needs, then it is entirely appropriate that they should use the discretion vested in them to do so.'

While the White Paper celebrated diversity and alluded to the virtues of a tripartite education system it denied that any such specialisation or differentiation of institutions entailed selection. 'Specialisation is often confused with selection . . . a school that specialises is not necessarily one that applies rigid academic criteria for entry to a non-selection school can choose to specialise.' Yet the word 'selection' appeared in a title of prescribed values together with 'specialisation' and 'standards' and, moreover, the White Paper acknowledged that selection *could* take place through parental choice: 'the selection that takes place is parent driven'. The emerging research evidence indicates that social selection, resisted but never eliminated by postwar social democracy, is once more being released and reinforced by the market mechanisms set in place by legislation.[17]

While the 1988 Education Reform Act introduced the possibility of schools 'opting out' into grant maintained status it is a contested issue whether the originating conception for GM schools was as the future of all schools, or as a privileged sector like the old 'direct grant' schools, or as an exception (for schools seeking to escape purported 'undesirable LEAs'!). The norm was, arguably, intended to be 'locally managed schools' within an LEA but accorded considerable discretion over the use of resources within local strategic policy planning. Yet since 1991 ministers have been promoting a very different policy that 'GM status should become a norm not an exception'. Institutional autonomy rather than discretion has now become the key value of Government. 'More diversity allows schools to respond more effectively to the needs of the local and national community. The greater their autonomy, the greater the responsiveness of schools' (p. 2), especially to parents who 'know best the needs of their children' certainly better than the professionals.

Following the 1993 Education Act the autonomy provided by GM status supposedly becomes the key to future quality of schools.

Yet the trend towards opting out has slowed considerably and the Government looks as if it will fall short of its target of 1500 schools by April 1994 (in October 1993 the number of GM schools stood at 693). The Government is planning to revive its flagship policy by funding three regional grant-maintained school centres to encourage schools in the Midlands and the North (East and West) where only 50 schools have opted out. Furthermore, despite pressures upon public expenditure, the Government is seeking to maintain the 'incentives' for schools to opt out of their LEA by 'giving almost twice as much capital funding to the GM sector'[18] and by giving schools up to £1500 to cover 'relevant expenses' where there has been a parental ballot.

Now the 1993 Education Act extends opting out to special schools and provides an opportunity for Christian or Muslim schools to opt into GM status even if there are surplus places in the area. The Act will require the governing bodies of all LEA schools to consider a GM ballot once a year and the Secretary of State has taken powers both to declare a ballot void if he or she believes there has been impropriety and to limit what an LEA can spend on its publicity efforts.

Privatisation, hierarchy and regulation

Accompanying the shift to institutional self-governance are parallel moves to privatise significant components of the service while at the same time strengthening the national regulation of education. Together these developments further erode the postwar tradition of public education nurtured within local democracy.

Section 66 of the 1993 Act allows GM schools to be sponsored by naming a member of the governing body as a sponsor of the school and permits up to four such sponsor governorships. Morris *et al.*[19] summarise the rationale for this' as enabling a number of developments to take place without the occurrence of legal obstacles to the involvement of private capital and revenue contributions to state schools' (p. 44). The authors quote the Parliamentary Under-Secretary of State:

> If there is an opportunity to gain additional resources, it is right to secure them if that is what the governors wish. That can benefit

the school and its pupils. it is a positive way of forging closer links between business and schools. (HC, cols 882–6, 19 January 1993, in Morris *et al.*, p. 44)

The 1992 Education Act had privatised school inspections. HM Inspectorate of Schools would be replaced by a system of registered inspectors who were to tender for the inspection of a school announced in a schedule published by the HM Chief Inspector of the new Office for Standards in Education (OFSTED). Successful tenders would win the contract for an inspection. The Act thus repealed the LEA's powers to inspect (s.77(3) of the 1944 Education Act) although LEAs could compete for inspection contracts if they so chose. OFSTED is given powers by the 1993 Education Act to identify schools which are supposedly failing and the Secretary of State can impose an 'educational association' of 'experts' to run the school.

The LEA has, therefore, since 1991 been placed in the eye of the storm as the purported cause of the service's problems. The very conception of education government embodied in the ERA – of a strategic LEA leading an integrated, albeit devolved, system of institutional governance was giving way to a very different vision of self-governing institutions with the local administration retained to provide for 'residual' services and special needs. The Prime Minister in May 1991 spoke of the need to break up the monolith of the local education system while a senior civil servant spoke of the need to 'plough the ground', a metaphor for dismantling the local system of education.

During the passage of the 1993 Education Act a new clause 1 was introduced which removed reference in s.1 of the 1944 Education Act to national policy being secured by LEAs under the 'control and direction' of the Secretary of State for Education. In so doing the 1993 Act not only withdraws the LEA from its preeminent position in the provision of state education, it terminates what was, in its introduction a constitutional settlement between central and local government.[20] Now the Secretary of State is given personal responsibility for overseeing education (although powers to direct education will not cover universities).

A new quango, the Funding Agency for Schools (FAS), is to be introduced, in the first instance, to administer GM schools and, as opting out accelerates, the FAS is conceived as replacing the role of the LEA in relation to primary and secondary schools. When 10 per cent of schools in an LEA have acquired GM status the FAS and the LEA are to share responsibility for planning provision until a 75 per cent point is reached when the FAS will assume overall control. The FAS will be an appointed Board. The Parliamentary Under-Secretary for State in Committee[21] announced that a majority of its initial employees will be former DFE officals providing a further indication of the trend in government to substitute appointed boards ('the new magistracies[22] for elected authorities. Any obstacles which may resist increasing the 'organisational flexibility' of the LEA in the evolution of its residual functions will be removed 'in particular the requirement to establish an Education Committee. Some local authorities may soon be in sight of no longer needing them'.[23]

The role of the LEA is considerably reduced: it is to maintain and plan its own schools, keep information in relation to its provision, and exercise responsibilities for school attendance and religious education. The LEA maintains a duty in relation to non-vocational further education and youth and community provision as part of further education. The principal role for the LEA will in future be in special education. The LEA will have a duty

- to pupils with statements of special need but will share responsibility with GM sector for those with special needs but no statement
- to collaborate with the FAS on arrangements for special education
- to encourage the GM sector to consult local authorites about special needs
- to fund 'pupil referral units' for truants and disruptive pupils

The LEA in matters of special needs is to be guided by a code of practice, produced by the Secretary of State, in special needs cases including national guidelines for issuing statements. An appeals tribunal will to be set up to hear disputes about special needs.

The lobby to give the LEA overall planning powers was defeated, as was the lobby to give the lead responsibility to the LEA in special needs. The Minister of State said, 'those amendments would have given a continuing strategic role to the [LEA]. That role was inconsistent with the new regime embodied in the Bill as a whole and inconsistent in particular with the autonomy of schools, especially those which have opted to leave their LEAs'.[24]

Thus the emphases of the 1992 and 1993 legislative changes mark a significant change for the government of education. The strategies of increasing both the powers of state regulation and the forces of market choice have served to erode institutions designed to support educational opportunity and local democracy. School segregation and social polarisation have been the fruits of market forces in education.[25] Whereas in Scotland the comprehensive system had 'increased social mix, reduced the attainment gap betwen pupils from different backgrounds and contributed to a rising standard of attainment among pupils from all social backgrounds'[26] the current legislation 'has quite clearly led to a widening of educational inequalities'.[27] The Conservative Party's agenda has congealed into a Platonic vision of education to secure social selection and social control during a period of social and economic crisis – a vision in which educational and political inequality go hand in hand.

Perhaps the defining characteristic of the present restructuring by the government of pre- and post-16 education is the attack upon the democratic foundation of local education. Its attempt to remove education (schools and colleges) from local politics presents the most significant indication of the termination of the postwar social democratic era in which local government played the pivotal role in the development of public services for all. The de-democratising of local education is not a peripheral element: it is, arguably, its central purpose. At this stage, the analysis of an American study which has been influential with the Government (a civil servant indicated that ministers had made it prescribed reading) needs to be critically examined.

The attack on local democracy

Chubb and Moe in their *Politics and Markets in America's Schools*[28] (popularised in the glossy *Sunday Times Magazine*)[29] argued that a generation of reforms to American schools failed because the underlying cause – the institutions of direct democratic control – were not identified. Schools fail because the 'game of local democracy' constitutes a perpetual struggle for power that creates winners and losers with the victors imposing their higher-order values (for example, the authors list 'sex education', 'socialisation of immigrants', 'the mainstreaming of the handicapped', 'bilingual education', 'what history to teach') on schools by bureaucratising control. Democracy is coercive, stifling the autonomy of schools, and demotivates the teachers. Institutions work when people choose them. The key to better schools lies, thus, in institutional reform creating markets in which consumers influence schools by their choices. Markets promote autonomy, enabling all participants to make decisions for themselves; markets are myopic, offering what people want. Because markets also select and sort, if schools are to be successful they will need to find a niche – a specialised segment of the market to which they can appeal and attract support: targeting particular values and learning – discipline, religion, socioeconomic and ethnic make-up of students. Although markets have imperfections these are preferable to those of local democracy. Thus the instititional conditions for effective schools are to de-democratise institutional settings and to create market settings which constitutes: decentralisation, competition, choice, autonomy, clarity of mission, strong leadership, teacher professionalism and team cooperation. This belief that strong markets together with increased internal professional control will secure improved schooling finds its expression in the UK in the writing of Tooley.[30]

Markets, however, as the emerging evidence emphasises,[31] deny opportunity for most: supporters as well as opponents acknowledge they create inequality. In education they work like this. Competition forces schools to see each other as rivals striving to gain the advantage that will secure survival. From this rivalry emerges a hierarchy of esteem with schools increasingly inclined to 'select' and 'exclude' pupils so as to produce a school population likely to shine in the national league tables, as well as in local 'coffee circles'! In this market hot-house only some parents are likely to acquire their 'choices': those with time, resources, knowledge and confidence to 'promote' their children; or those with 'able' children. Children with 'special' needs may struggle to secure a place with schools at the apex of the hierarchy that begin to celebrate 'academic' distinction above other learning achievements. Some schools may seek to specialise in providing for this market 'niche'. For policy-makers this illustrates 'choice and diversity'. Others believe this policy is covertly restoring a selective system in which access to 'an education' is confined to some schools where the social characteristics of parents will determine the chances of admission.

Although the market (a parent rejecting one school for another) may jolt this or that school into improving its relative position in the league table, it also inescapably entrenches the table. In this context, some schools, by definition, *will always* suffer invidious comparison. That is what competition creates. It is a zero-sum 'game' in which if there are to be winners there are sadly always going to be losers. Individually, schools and parents are forced to play a game which can only disadvantage most of them and leaves them powerless to change the rules. The power of resources is valued above the authority of reasons. A system of governance is thus created in which public policy is removed from public deliberation, choice and action, the only processes through which a community can devise a system of education that can meet the learning needs of all.

Markets cannot resolve the predicaments we face: indeed they ensure that we stand no chance of solving them. Those problems – the restructuring of work; environmental erosion; the fragmentation of society; opportunity for all – present issues of well-being, rights and justice which cannot be resolved by individuals acting in isolation, nor by retreating because we cannot stand outside them. Markets will merely exacerbate these problems which are public in nature and thus all should have a right to contribute to their analysis and resolution.

Democracy and public education

Only the democratic processes of the public domain can help our society face the difficult problems we confront. As Dunn[32] argues: 'In the face of the obscure and extravagantly complicated challenges of the human future, our most urgent common need at present is to learn how to act together more effectively.' Far from being a burden upon a community a system of local democracy is a key institution which can provide it with the freedom and justice to create the conditions for all to flourish. The educational arguments for democratic local government develop in three stages:

(i) learning is inescapably a *system*: learning is a process which cannot be contained within the boundaries of any one institution. Discovery and understanding occur at home, in the community, on a scheme of work experience as well as in college or school. Progress, furthermore, will unfold more securely between stages of learning when they are mutually comprehending and supporting. Improving achievement depends for its realisation upon enabling a wider system of learning: one element cannot be treated in isolation from another if each is to contribute to the effective working of the whole. Ensuring, for every school, the appropriate numbers of pupils, the provision of resources and teachers to support a balanced and comprehensive curriculum with choices at key stages to enable progression in response to diversity of need are characteristics which have to be managed at the level of the system as a whole, as well as the school, if all young people are to be provided with opportunities to realise their powers and capacities.

(ii) education needs to be managed as a *local* system: the system of learning is more effective if managed locally, as well as nationally and at the level of the institution. The different tasks need their appropriate tier of management and by creating a local system which delegated *and* enabled strategic leadership, the 1988 Education Reform Act enacted the conditions for excellence in the local management of education within a national framework. A local system of management is needed to ensure understanding of local needs, responsiveness to changing circumstances, and efficiency in the management of resources within geographic boundaries consistent with identifiable historical traditions. Such local systems need to be properly accountable and this requires location within a local democratic system.

(iii) education needs to be a local *democratic* system: if education is, as it should be, a public service of and for the whole community rather than merely the particular parents, young people and employers who have an immediate and proper interest in the quality of the education provided then education must be responsive and accountable to the community as a whole. The significance of learning for the public as a whole suggests the indispensable location of the service within a framework of democratic local government which enables all local people to articulate and reconcile their views and to participate actively in developing the processes of their education service. A learning society – enabling all to contribute to and respond to the significant changes of the period – will depend for its vitality upon the support of local democratic institutions which articulate and take responsibility for developing all members of the community.

Developments which became preconditions for the educational development of many young people – a gender-neutral curriculum, bilingual teaching, a multi-cultural teaching, comprehensive schooling, did not emerge from Whitehall, nor from isolated individual assertion but bottom-up through local discourse and public action. The task now is to reconstitute the conditions for a learning society in which all are empowered to develop and contribute their capacities.[33]

Notes and references

1. See DES, *National Curriculum From Policy to Practice* (HMSO, 1989) Section 2.1.
2. H. Thomas, 'Pupils as Vouchers', *The Times Educational Supplement* (2 November 1988).
3. See K. Jones, *Right Turn: The Conservative Revolution in Education* (Hutchinson Radius, 1989).
4. S. Sexton , *Our Schools – A Radical Policy* (Institute of Economic Affairs, 1987).
5. Hillgate Group, *Whose Schools? A Radical Manifesto* (Hillgate Group, 1987).
6. (a) The struggle over the interpretation of the policy on Grant-Maintained Schools between the Secretary of State, Kenneth Baker who believed that some schools might opt out, and the Prime Minister, Margaret Thatcher who believed that all schools should opt out (see *Times Educational Supplement*, 18 September 1987)
   (b) Officials, for example, Duncan Graham (National Curriculum Council), Eric Bolton (Her Majesty's Inspectorate), Philip Halsey (Schools Examination and Assessment Council), Professor Paul Black (Chair, Task Group on Assessment and Testing), Nick Stuart (Deputy Secretary, Department of Education and Science).
7. See S. Ranson, 'Education', in F. Terry (ed.), *Public Domain: 1991* (Public Finance Foundation, 1992) pp. 133–43; and H. Heller with P. Edwards, *Policy and Power in Education: The Rise and Fall of the LEA* (Routledge, 1992).

8. Cf. Coopers & Lybrand, *Local Management of Schools* (DES, 1988); Audit Commission, *Losing an Empire, Finding a Role: The LEA of the Future*, Occasional Paper 10 (HMSO, 1989); S. Ranson, *The Role of Local Government in Education: Assuring Quality and Accountability* (Longman,1992); P. Cordingley and M. Kogan, *In Support of Education: The Functioning of Local Government* (Jessica Page, 1993).

9. The strengthening of 'right wing' ministerial appointments, for example, of Tim Egger and Michael Fallon, and what were publicaly regarded as the political appointments of Pascal at NCC; Griffiths at SEAC).

10. Sir Ron Dearing, *The National Curriculum and Assessment: Interim Report* (School Curriculum and Assessment Authority, 1993; *Final Report* (SCAA,1994).

11. *The Times Educational Supplement* (1 October, 1993).

12. DES, *Education and Training for the 21st Century* (HMSO, 1991).

13. Reported in *The Times*, 23 November, 1992.

14. Reported in *The Times*, 23 November, 1992.

15. A. Green, 'Post-16 Qualification Reform', *Forum*, vol. 35, no. 1 (1993) pp. 13–15.

16. S. Ranson, 'Towards a Tertiary Tripartism: New Codes of Control and the 17+', in P. Broadfoot (ed.), *Selection, Certification and Control: Social Issues in Educational Assessment* (Falmer, 1984).

17. See M. Adler, A. Petch and J.Tweedie, *Parental Choice and Educational Policy* (Edinburgh University, 1989); S. Ball, 'Schooling Enterprise and the Market' (AERA Symposium paper, 1992); R. Bowe, S. Ball and A. Gold, *Reforming Education and Changing Schools* (Routledge, 1992); F. Echols, A. McPherson and D. Willms, 'Parental Choice in Scotland', *Journal of Education Policy*, vol. 5, no. 3 (1990); R. Jonathan, 'State Education Service or Prisoners' Dilemma: The "hidden hand" as a source of education policy', *Educational Philosophy and Theory*, vol. 22, no. 1 (1990) pp. 16–24; G. Walford, *Selection for Secondary Schooling*, Briefing Paper 7 (National Commission for Education, 1992).

18. Figures supplied to the Commons Select Committee by the DES: (*The Times Educational Supplement*, 12 November, 1993).

19. R. Morris, E. Reid and J. Fowler, *Education Act 93: A Critical Guide* (Association of Metropolitan Authorities, 1993).

20. See R. Morris and J. Fowler, *Beyond Clause Zero:The Education Bill 1992–93* (Association of Metropolitan Authorities, 1993).

21. House of Commons, 19 November 1993, cols. 80–1, in R. Morris *et al.*, *Education Act 93*, p. 28.

22. R. Morris, 'The New Governance of Education: New Magistracies', paper to an INLOGOV Conference, 4 July 1989; J. Stewart, 'The Rebuilding of Public Accountability', in J. Stewart, N. Lewis and D. Longley, *Accountability to the Public* (European Policy Forum for British and European Market Studies, 1992).

23. White Paper, *Choice and Diversity* (HMSO, 1992) p. 32.

24. House of Commons 26 July, 1993, col. 963, in Morris *et al.*, *Education Act 93*.
25. See F. Echols *et al.*, 'Parental Choice in Scotland'.
26. A. McPherson and C. Raab, 'Centralisation and After', *The Times Educational Supplement* (27 May 1988).
27. M. Adler *et al.*, *Parental Choice and Educational Policy*.
28. J. Chubb and T. Moe, *Politics, Markets and America's Schools* (Brookings Institute, 1990).
29. J. Chubb and T. Moe, 'Classroom Revolution' (*The Sunday Times Magazine*, 9 February 1992).
30. J. Tooley, 'The Prisoners' Dilemma and Educational Provision: A reply to Ruth Jonathan', *British Journal of Educational Studies*, vol, 40, no. 2 (1992) pp. 118–33; J. Tooley, *A Market-led Alternative for the Curriculum: Breaking the Code* (Institute of Education, 1993).
31. See note 17.
32. J. Dunn (ed.), *Democracy: The Unfinished Journey, 508 BC to AD 1993* (Oxford University Press, 1992).
33. S. Ranson, *Towards the Learning Society* (Cassell, 1994); S. Ranson and J. Stewart, *Management for the Public Domain: Enabling the Learning Society* (Macmillan, 1994).

8 Community Care and Social Services

Martin Willis

Social services departments in England and Wales were created by the Local Authority Social Services Act of 1970 and in Scotland, social work departments arose out of the Social Work (Scotland) Act of 1968. In the subsequent two decades their importance to local government grew rapidly. This expansion can be readily charted in the doubling of the proportion of local government revenue expenditure devoted to the personal social services between 1971–72 and 1990–91 in both England and Wales and Scotland (Table 8.1).

This increased expenditure is reflected in the dramatic rise in full-time-equivalent employees of social services departments in the UK from 145000 in 1971 to 250900 in 1981 and 306600 in 1991.[1] Whilst the majority of these increases occurred in the 1970s, these statistics show that social services departments continued to grow during the 1980s.

Table 8.1 Gross revenue expenditure by local authorities

	1971–72 £M	1980–81 £M	1990–91 £M
England and Wales			
Personal social services	314.4	2155.5	5450.0
Total LA expenditure	7080.7	30337.5	62678.0
PSS as % of total	4.4%	7.1%	8.7%
Scotland			
Social work services	33.2	249.6	668.8
Total LA expenditure	721.6	3536.8	7429.8
SW as % of total	4.6%	7.1%	9.0%

Source: Central Statistical Office, *Annual Abstract of Statistics* (HMSO, 1981 and 1993).

There are a number of explanations for this growth. First, every aspect of social services practice has been subject to major legislative change since 1970. The ten most notable of these Acts of Parliament can be briefly summarised as follows. Scotland has its own system of childcare and criminal jurisdiction, the former being currently the subject of a major review. Reference to childcare and criminal justice legislation in this list and elsewhere in this chapter relates primarily to England and Wales, whereas other Acts either apply directly to Scotland as well or have their Scottish equivalents.

- **Chronically Sick and Disabled Persons Act 1970**: Services for people with a disability
- **Children Act 1975 and Adoption Act 1976**: New procedures for adoption
- **Child Care Act 1980**: Provisions for voluntary care and assumption of parental rights by the local authority
- **Criminal Justice Act 1982**: Provision of Intermediate Treatment for young offenders
- **Mental Health Act 1983**: Introduction of Approved Social Workers with powers to make applications for admission to psychiatric hospitals
- **Registered Homes Act 1984**: Duty to register residential care homes
- **Disabled Persons Act 1986**: Assessment of needs of people with a disability
- **Children Act 1989**: Complete revision of law relating to children and families
- **NHS and Community Care Act 1990**: Planning, assessment, purchase and provision of services to adults in need of community care
- **Criminal Justice Act 1992**: LA responsibility extended to young people up to 18 years old

In contrast to the impact of government policy elsewhere on local authorities, the net effect of these legislative changes has been to increase the duties and responsibilities of social services departments. This outcome has been most noticeable in relation to the development of community care policies, a subject which will be considered in more depth later in this chapter.

Second, the consumer population of social services departments has increased substantially since 1970. During the 1980s, the number of people over 85 went up by more than 50 per cent and the rising proportion of frail older people over 75 years of age is set to continue well into the next century. Greater awareness of the prevalence of child abuse, physical and learning disabilities and the development of community-based mental health services have all contributed to a growth in consumer demand. Given that much of the work of social services departments is related to the impact of poverty on individuals and families, the rise in unemployment and the widening disparity between the earnings of the rich and the poor over this period have also led more people to call on social services for assistance.

Third, a series of well-publicised enquiries into failures within services for both children and adults have pushed social services into the forefront of public and political debate. Such enquiries have tended to move beyond the individual case focus of the 1970s and early 1980s (for example, Maria Colwell and Jasmine Beckford) to examine wider issues of departmental policy and inter-agency cooperation (e.g. the Staffordshire Pin-Down Enquiry; the Cleveland Report; the Warner Report and the SSI inspection of services to disabled people in Gloucestershire). The role of the strengthened Social Services Inspectorate and the Audit Commission have also been instrumental in raising the profile of social services issues.

A fourth reason for the increasing importance of social services within local government has been their centrality to the development of equal opportunities policies and practice. Consumer, professional and political pressures have combined to force an examination of social service delivery and employment policies. As a result, social services departments have been variously seen as the leading edge of equality work within local government or a hotbed of fashionable 'isms' and political correctness. Whatever else, this has contributed to their higher profile.

Finally, the Government's aim to limit the role of local government, and the consequent reduction of executive powers in the fields of education and housing, has left social services as one of the few areas in which councillors can still have a significant influence over direct spending on service provision. The once relatively calm backwater of the social services committee has moved centre stage, one possible reason for the rapid turnover of social services directors in recent years.

This development in the political importance and relative size of social services and social work departments has been accompanied by some confusing and paradoxical changes in the nature of the services provided or funded for consumers. The remainder of this chapter will explore these changes and seek to establish if any firm predictions can be made as to what the future may hold. A key difficulty in this analysis is that unlike the forced universal implementation of important changes such as compulsory competitive tendering, the right-to-buy policy and the local management of schools, government policy towards social services has given them both discretion and latitude in implementing key aspects of the two major pieces of recent social services legislation, the Children Act 1989 and the NHS and Community Care Act 1990. As Le Grand describes:

> Ministers have not asked local authorities to introduce a purchaser/provider split for care management immediately; nor have they set down any blueprint for the split or for care management itself. Local authorities are able to adopt their own approach in their own time, subject to some progress being made particularly in the area of contracting out to private agencies.[2]

The values which underlie these two Acts share common ground with other aspects of national policy towards local government during the 1980s. An emphasis on individual responsibility and minimising state involvement; enabling not providing: promoting the independent sector; separation of purchasing from provision; enhancing consumer involvement and choice; and ensuring effectiveness form the bed-rock on which these Acts were constructed.

Emphasising individual responsibility and minimising state involvement

Speaking to the WRVS in January 1981, Margaret Thatcher heralded what was said to be a dramatic change in thinking about the role of the welfare state in community care:

I believe that the volunteer movement is at the heart of all our social welfare provision. That the statutory services are the supportive ones underpining where necessary, filling the gaps and helping the helpers. We politicians and administrators must not forget that the state has a limited role. The willingness of men and women to give service is one of freedom's greatest safeguards. It ensures that caring remains free from political control. [3]

In fact, social services departments have always been minor players in the totality of community care. With an estimated 6 million people providing 'community care' for relatives and friends at an equivalent annual wage cost of between £15bn and £24bn,[4] individual caring far outstrips the funding for the personal social services. Add to this the work of thousands of large and small voluntary organisations and Thatcher's speech can be seen as a statement of present reality rather than a fundamental reversal of the role of the state in the personal social services.

A number of recent studies have provided a valuable analysis of the nature of this community care. For example, Allen *et al.* found that three-quarters of their interview sample of carers of elderly people in the community were women and nearly half were over the age of 60.[5] The length of caring was also striking with nearly half more than five years and a quarter over ten years. Given the increasing proportion of dependant elderly people relative to the working population, the emotional and economic implications of these findings for the future of community care are far-reaching. In the absence of a marked growth in social services provision, expectations on relatives to provide long hours of care will rise markedly and without a change in social attitudes, most of this increased burden will fall on women.

Community care has in fact been a central tenet of government policy ever since the creation of the welfare state. A long line of reports, White Papers and policy initiatives can be traced, all recommending more community care. From the Guillebaud Peport (1956) on the costs of the NHS, through the MoH Health and Welfare plans of the 1960s, the Seebohm Report (1969), the Good Neighbour Scheme of the mid-1970s, to the Griffiths Report on *Community Care: Agenda for Action* (1988), community care has found favour with politicians of all hues. However, the exhortations of government have only been partially matched by a shift in national and local government resources away from hospital and residential care and towards the support of people living in their own homes.

The influential Audit Commission's report *Making a Reality of Community Care* starkly concluded: [6]

> There are serious grounds for concern about the lack of progress in shifting the balance of services towards community care. Progress has been slow and uneven across the country; and the near-term prospects are not promising. In short, the community care policy is in danger of failing to achieve its potential.[6]

The evidence for this indictment was drawn from every branch of adult social services. For example, the report stated that in ten years, 25 000 psychiatric beds had gone but only 9000 extra day care places had been set up 'and no one knows what happens to many people after they are discharged'.[7]

One aspect of government policy during the 1980s was working directly against their stated preference for community care. The payment of board and lodging charges out of the social security budget to people in private and voluntary residential care or nursing homes led to a threefold increase in elderly residents of such homes between 1981 and 1991 whilst the numbers in local authority homes fell by a fifth. The outcome of this concern about the failure of community care policies and the open ended growth of government spending on residential care was the NHS and Community Care Act 1990 giving local authorities the lead responsibility for community care. A key feature of this Act is the ending of Income Support for residential care and the transfer of a cash-limited budget to social services departments, 85 per cent of which has to be spent in the independent sector. It remains to be seen whether this stimulates more home-based care or continues to be spent on private residential care. In any case, the limitations on this funding will put local authorities in the firing line of care homes associations angry at the impact of the inevitable rationing of resources on their members.

The reduction in local authority residential care for elderly people during the 1980s was more than matched by a major fall in the numbers of children in residential care. Two factors have contributed to this, a decline by a third in the total number of children in care and a proportional rise in the numbers being fostered. Both these trends are likely to be enhanced by the provisions of the Children Act 1989 with its value base that 'children are generally best looked after within the family with both parents playing a full part and without resort to legal proceedings'. [8]. The Children Act is founded on the primacy of parental responsibility with local authorities restricting their intervention as far as possible to being 'partners'. In a similar way, the NHS and Community Care Act has given a high priority to providing practical support for carers, emphasising once again the Government's intention that local authorities should promote and not undermine individual responsibility for caring for child or adult dependants. This perhaps is the greatest challenge facing social services and social work departments in the 1990s, to end what has been called the 'dependency culture' of the personal social services. The related themes of partnership, empowerment and consumer choice will be returned to later.

Enabling not providing – promoting the independent sector

In common with other local authority provision, Nicholas Ridley's vision of a minimalist enabling authority[9] has had its impact on the development of social services. Both the two recent major pieces of social services legislation and their accompanying notes of guidance have included requirements to promote the development of private and voluntary providers. The current pattern of social services provision has its roots in nineteenth century voluntary organisations. Unlike in health, education and Income Support where the welfare state radically reduced independent provision, small and large voluntary organisations have remained as significant providers though 'thinly and unevenly distributed, and where the need is greatest, they do not exist'.[10]

Over the past ten years, shifts in the pattern of provision have occurred first with the development of a number of small inner-city organisations, sometimes funded by urban aid and often serving black community groups neglected by the statutory services; second by the growth of private residential care noted above and the beginnings in some areas of private domiciliary care organisations;

and third by the development of housing association projects which specifically cater for people requiring social care. However, it has been the case that particularly for those children and adults with the greatest social care needs, social services have remained the overwhelmingly largest if not the sole provider in most areas.

The Government's policy is that this balance should change with local authorities contracting provision from the independent sector. However, apart from the requirements regarding the transferred social security monies, the Government has not compulsorily imposed tendering or contracting on social care services. The possible reasons for this, for example, the stated resistance of some of the larger voluntary organisations particularly in the field of childcare or the complexities of social services provision, are a matter of speculation. The fact has been that government policy has been implemented primarily by means of procedures, exhortation, financial direction and structure.

With regard to community care, the key procedural arrangement designed to encourage the enabling role has been the requirements for partnership and collaboration with other statutory, voluntary and private organisations in the preparation of plans for the provision of services. A DoH study of the first set of Community Care Plans[11] found that whereas there was widespread involvement of voluntary organisations in their preparation 'private providers typically did not participate in developing plans nor did they feel engaged in effective consultation'. The Government's response was to exhort local authorities to involve the private sector but how local authorities respond to this is likely to depend mainly on the politics of local councillors.

Advice and exhortation have flown freely from the Department of Health on the implementation of the Children Act and the NHS and Community Care Act. In relation to the former Act, this advice has largely been concerned with the issues of professional practice whereas for the latter it has been more overtly political especially in respect of the development of a mixed economy of care. For example the DoH 'Introduction to the Children Act' makes only passing reference to the requirement on local authorities to 'facilitate the provision by others (in particular voluntary organisations) of services which they provide under Part 111',[12] whereas the policy guidance on community care[13] devotes a whole chapter to this subject. This has been reinforced by a regular DoH newsletter on community care and a series of conferences targeted at involving the independent sector. It seems that childcare is seen by Government as primarily an arena for professional decision-making whereas adult community care is meet territory for political determination.

In addition to advice and Guidance, the government has used three other means of exhortation. The first has been to commission external consultants, particularly those with a track record in the private sector, to provide reports which spell out options for change or report on progress by local authorities in achieving the Government's objectives. For example, three approaches to defining purchaser, commissioner and provider roles were set out by the Department of Health.[14] The second has been to use the Social Services Inspectorate and the Health Service Management Executive to set outcome objectives for authorities in preparation for the implementation of the Act and to monitor their achievement. The most specific of these were a list of 'eight key tasks' (March 1992) and agreed strategies with health authorities for discharge arrangements and placing people in nursing homes (September 1992). Because of concern at the slow implementation within some authorities, the Government introduced a third means of exhortation when it established a Community Care Support Force to work with local and health authorities, particularly those adjudged to be struggling with community care implementation.

The outcome of all this advice and exhortation is yet to be determined. Initial reports and impressions suggest that change has had varied consequences and that many of the claims made by Government about the intended improvement in quality of services to consumers will largely depend on the availability of local resources and good working relationships between practitioners from social services, health, housing and voluntary organisations for their achievement. Whether the exhortation and advice has helped to stimulate either the development of new resources or good working relationships is open to question.

The Government has developed few financial means to impose its community care policies on local authorities. Until their alteration in August 1991, an unintended consequence of the Income Support regulations was that a few local authorities transferred all or part of their residential accommodation to not-for-profit companies or trusts so that people taking up residence before April 1993 would be eligible for higher rates of Income Support. This move was also justified by the need to finance registration standard improvements with private capital. An initial flurry of such privatisations has substantially decreased as the short-term financial gains were eliminated. The Government has sought to use finance to direct change on two occasions first by proposing to make the payment of a ring-fenced special transitional grant for community care conditional on receiving evidence by December 1992 of the agreements between health and local authorities discussed above and second by requiring that 85% of the grant be spent on services supplied by the independent sector. Local authorities failing to meet this condition might be asked to repay all or part of the grant. It could be argued that neither of these proposals have teeth and are unlikely in themselves to change the current pattern of delivery between local authority and independent providers.

Structure – the separation of purchasing from provision

The main plank of government policy with regard to structure is the separation of purchasing and provision for community care. Despite its importance, the achievement of this too has been pursued by advice and exhortation, with the result that local authorities have varied considerably both in their interpretation of this policy and their time scale for its implementation. The Department of Health's paper *Community Care in the Next Decade and Beyond* set out the Government's thinking which mirrors the ideology behind reforms in education, housing, health and compulsory competitive tendering. The difference in social services is that the change is not mandatory:

> In practical terms in developing the enabling role authorities will need to distinguish between aspects of work in SSDs concerned with the assessment of individuals' needs, the arrangement and purchase of services to meet them and direct service provision. It will be important that this distinction is reflected within the SSD's management structure at both the 'macro' level (involving plans to meet strategic priorities as a whole) and at the 'micro' level (where services are being arranged for individuals.[15]

Most social services departments, with their predilection for structural reorganisation, have gone some, if not all, of the way to meet the Government's objective of purchaser/provider separation. For many, this has resulted in a return to the fieldwork/residential and day-care functional split which community based social work developments of the early 1980s had aimed to eradicate. In fact, the most significant consequence of this legislation has been almost universal adoption of a specialist structural separation of services for children and adults and the demise of patch-based neighbourhood social work. Parallel with this has come the targeting of resources on those assessed as being in highest need and a further squeeze on preventative services.

The Government's argument is that a purchaser/provider separation is necessary to ensure that there is a functional distinction between the assessment of a user's needs and the provision of services to meet those needs. Thus an elderly person would be assessed in respect of the totality of their social care needs rather than their suitability for a particular local authority day care or residential unit. The logic of this is that budgetary responsibility should be devolved to the person (now entitled the 'care manager') who makes the assessment, and designs, implements and monitors the 'care package'. The DoH guidance on approaches to purchaser/provider separation[14] suggested that such 'buyer budgets' should be the objective of a three-stage process of development, whilst recognising that such a radical change might take several years to achieve.

Only a handful of local authorities have reorganised to create a purchaser/ provider split at practitioner-level with devolved budgetary responsibility. Most remain concerned that the lack of adequate information systems and practitioner level skills in budget management make such a development problematic. Historically, information systems have been designed to service strategic policy-making and the demands of government departments. A major reframing of their purposes is needed if they are to provide financial and service delivery statistics in formats which are user-friendly to team managers and practitioners. This issue is particularly acute given that the training and experience of most of these staff have provided them with almost no familiarity with information management.

A second area of concern surrounds the possible consequences of fully devolved budgets for the future of in-house provision. For example, residential homes depend on a high occupancy rate to remain efficient. This can be planned and managed where decisions about purchasing are handled by middle or senior managers. A fear is that a steady referral rate of new residents could not be guaranteed if decisions were being taken on an individual customer basis by front-line care managers. The preferred approach so far has been to separate purchasing and provision at senior or middle manager levels and to devolve only limited aspects of budgetary responsibility.

A practical example of this can be seen in relation to contracting, a central thrust of government policy.

> The Government believes that service specifications and clear understandings between commissioning authorities and service providers through agreements and contracts will improve quality and value. Budgets have never been unlimited and never will be. However, contract and service specifications are not and should not simply be a means of purchasing the cheapest care available, they must be the means of identifying and ensuring that the best quality care is obtained.[16]

If services are to be tailored to individual need, then the expectation would be that social services contracts would be concerned with individual people and their agreed care packages. However, it is not surprising that given the complexities and costs of social care contracting,[17] social services departments have concentrated on developing block contracts (sometimes known as service level agreements) for the provision of services to a number of potential users. For example, the Association of Metropolitan Authorities (AMA) report on contracts in the personal social services cites two examples of what it calls 'micro level' individual contracts which are for the provision of 18 pre-school day centre places and 2066 hours of care per year by a multi-handicap group.[18] Such contracts will necessarily be negotiated and monitored at management and not practitioner level. The pressure to take up places in block contracts may well frustrate the objective of developing flexible services within tailor-made packages of community, voluntary, independent and social services resources to meet individual user needs.

Contracting for social care is at a very early stage of development in the UK. Experience in other countries such as the USA[19] suggests that the hoped-for gains in quality and matching of services to users, needs can be lost in increased bureaucracy and commercialisation. It is difficult to see how similar drawbacks can be avoided here.

As with other local authority services, if social services do move towards a greater degree of devolved responsibility and power, this has far-reaching consequences for the role of councillors. For as long as government policy towards structure and contracting within social services lacks the legal compulsion witnessed in other services, it is probable that most councillors will seek to retain control over policy and financial decision-making. A tension will thus exist between the aim of user-led service determination and the central control of the local political process, with social services councillors still having the power and the right, by virtue of their being elected representatives of the community interest, to ensure that they decide the outcome.

Enhancing consumer involvement and choice

The Children Act and the NHS and Community Care Act both place consumer involvement at the forefront of their underlying principles. The Children Act is highly prescriptive in requiring that, before taking a decision with respect to a child whom they are looking after, a local authority must, so far as is reasonably practicable, find out the wishes and feelings of the child, his/her parents and relevant others, and give due consideration to the child's religious persuasion, racial origin and cultural and linguistic background.[20] The attendance of parents, carers and children is now common practice at case conferences and reviews, being the rule rather than the exception.

Less prescriptively but equally forcefully, consumer involvement is stressed in the Social Services Inspectorate's care management guidance:

> All users and carers should be encouraged to participate to the limit of their capacity because a passive role will only reinforce a sense of dependence. The more users and carers participate, the more they will be committed to act on the outcome of the assessment.[21]

A wide range of initiatives and projects are currently being implemented by social services and social work departments designed to analyse the effectiveness of methods of involving users and carers. However, the assumption that social services users can 'be enabled to exercise the same power as consumers of other services'[22] is always likely to be frustrated given that a prime role of local authorities is to ration limited community care resources in accordance with legislative duties and local politically determined priorities. As Kathryn Ellis concluded from her direct observation of assessment practice:

> Many practitioners seem to regard initial assessments not as an opportunity to provide information but rather as a means of managing demand. Indeed, assessment itself is seen as a resource to be rationed.[23]

Further complications arise when users feel they have to accept a service either because of pressure from relatives or a fear of the consequences if they do not comply; others have difficulty in communicating their wishes because of illness or disability or in some instances state preferences which are felt by others to be not in their best interests. One way to enable users to be involved in these circumstances is for them to be helped or represented by an independent advocate[24] but few authorities have been able to resource such a service for adults. In limited circumstances, the Children Act requires the appointment of an 'independent visitor' to visit, advise and befriend children in care.

The discussion about user participation within social services needs a realistic understanding of the inequalities in power between users, carers and professional staff. There is much that staff can do to ensure that users' and carers' views are understood and taken seriously both in relation to assessment and in evaluating the quality of service delivery. However, to suggest that users can determine the nature of services they receive is disingenuous given the rationing and social control functions of social services departments.

A key principle of recent legislation is that social care assessments should be needs-led rather than service-led. However, even if this principle holds sway in practice, an authority still has to decide which needs it regards as justifying the provision of services and whether it has the resources to meet these needs. The DoH guidance identifies these boundaries on needs by defining them as follows:

the requirements of individuals to enable them to achieve, maintain or restore an acceptable level of social independence or quality of life, *as defined by the particular care agency or authority*.[25]

This concept has caused particular difficulty as authorities have been subject to legal challenge by users arguing that once an authority has acknowledged that they have an assessed need then it is obliged to provide resources to meet this need. Because of this authorities have been advised to avoid recording individuals' needs which the authority cannot meet. Unless some way can be found round this, this has the effect of making such information unavailable to the authority for the longer-term planning of social services.

In any case, it has been argued particularly by organisations such as the British Council of Organisations for Disabled People that the concept of needs is both nebulous and paternalistic.[26] They suggest that local authorities should be asserting statements of rights which define standards that users of social services can expect and demand. Several social services departments have included such statements in the community care plans and for children's services.[27] It will be important for the impact of these statements to be monitored and evaluated to see whether they provide a firmer basis for active user involvement. If the fact that the sections of the Disabled Persons Act 1986 concerning users-and carers-rights to consultation, representation and information have not been implemented is anything to go by, it is unlikely that the Government will support legislation in this area.

Statements of rights might give users some semblance of power. However, users can only begin to act as genuine consumers of social services when they have some control over resources. It is perverse that the transfer of social security residential home funds and the ending of the Independent Living Fund have both reduced the direct power of users to choose how social care resources are spent. Social services departments are legally prohibited from making direct cash payments to users for the purchase of their own care services as occurs in brokerage schemes in other countries. There is considerable pressure on the Government to change this law which is the greatest barrier to the promotion of real consumer choice.

In the meantime, the Government has given users a legal right to choose their residential care or nursing home but such choice is likely to be restricted to places in homes that the local authority decides are of the right quality and that it can afford. The exercise of user involvement and choice within social services will continue to depend on the good professional practice of staff rather than the power of consumer self-determination.

Ensuring effectiveness

As with all other aspects of the public sector, resource constraints and government policy have put demonstrating effectiveness high on the agenda of social services and social work departments. The personal nature of social services necessarily means that considerations of quality and value for money are beset with definitional problems. Three main mechanisms have been introduced by Government to enable the evaluation of effectiveness.

First has been the increased role of inspection both of and by social services departments. The Social Services Inspectorate and Audit Commission have both been given extensive powers to review, monitor and inspect social services provision. In addition, social services departments have been given responsibilities under the Registered Homes Act 1984, The Children Act 1989 and the NHS and Community Act 1990 to set up free-standing inspection units to check and promote the quality of social services in public, private and voluntary residential and other care.

The second method has been a series of DoH/SSI publications entitled *Caring for Quality* with the objective of setting standards for the evaluation of practice. These detailed documents have concentrated on adult residential and day-care services and it is to be expected that they will be extended to other aspects of the personal social services. A cruder and more limited set of performance standards for social services has been developed by the Audit Commission as part of their statutory work on the Citizen's Charter.[28] Finally, the Government has legislated that social services departments must establish complaints procedures for both children's and adults, services to allow access to a statutory procedure for anyone who wants to make representations.

An essential component of any evaluation of effectiveness is the question equity of access to services. Social services departments have been subject to considerable pressure from consumer groups to ensure that their services are anti-discriminatory with regard to race, gender, disability, sexuality and other forms of oppression. In many instances, analysis has demonstrated that significant groups in the population have been denied access, making the quality of service to them zero. The Children Act requires social services to take issues of race and culture into account in assessments and decision-making and for most social services departments, developing practical ways of enabling equal access to all services is becoming a central feature of their work to ensure the effectiveness of service delivery.

Social services towards the twenty-first century

The pace of change within the personal social services over the past ten years has been immense. Most managers and practitioners welcome the growth in importance of social services and regard the ideology of user empowerment, community care, needs-led provision and quality as being supportive of their professional values. What they would now like is a period of stability both in relation to legislation, resourcing and structures to implement the changes outlined in this chapter. It is improbable that this will happen.

First, the reorganisation of county councils will not only entail the need to restructure social services departments but to reestablish the network of inter-agency collaborative arrangements upon which children's and adults' services are founded. Second, the uncertainties of future resource allocation to social services particularly to meet new responsibilities with regard to community care will mean that departments are constantly engaged in finding ways of further rationing services. Alvin Schorr in 'an outside view' states this more trenchantly:

> It is the conclusion here that the PSS [Personal Social Services] must now be given room and resources for collecting themselves to meet the challenges that have been set for them. Restraint, diversion and resources are the recommendations offered. Failing these, PSS will probably decline into a state of disorganisation from which recovery will be all but impossible.[29]

Third, the Conservative Government is likely to seek ways to impose their desire for a mixed economy of welfare on the personal social services if their exhortation continues to be met with what is adjudged to be slow progress. Fourth, public expectations of social services will continue to rise particularly if relative poverty increases as a result of unemployment and government policies further restricting people's eligibility to social security benefits.

The Audit Commission concludes that three elements are required in the 'community revolution' if local social services authorities are going to be successful in implementing the community care changes: 'gaining the commitment of members and staff; developing systems to support strategic and operational aspects of implementation and achieving good collaboration with other agencies.'[30] Most social services managers would want to add a fourth – setting and maintaining realistic expectations on service delivery and providing the necessary resources for their achievement. Without this, Alvin Schorr's prediction could become fact.

Notes and references

1. CSO, *Social Trends* (HMSO, 1976 and 1993)
2. J. Le Grand, 'Quasi-Markets and Community Care', in N. Thomas *et al., Rowntree Symposium Papers*, ch 5 (forthcoming).
3. Quoted in M. Brenton, *The Voluntary Sector in British Social Services* (Longman, 1985).
4. M. Henwood, *Family Care in Focus*, Family Policy Bulletin No. 6. (Family Policy Studies Centre, 1991).
5. I. Allen *et al., Elderly People: Choice, Participation and Satisfaction* (Policy Studies Institute,1992) p. 21.
6. Audit Commission, *Making a Reality of Community Care* (HMSO, 1986) p. 13.
7. Ibid. p. 2.
8. DoH, *An Introduction to the Children Act 1989* (HMSO, 1989) p. 1.
9. N. Ridley, *The Local Right – Enabling not Providing* (Centre for Policy Studies, 1988).
10. M. Brenton, *The Voluntary Sector in British Social Services*, p. 79.
11. DoH, *Implementing Community Care: Improving Independent Sector Involvement in Community Care Planning* (DoH, 1992) p. iii.
12. DoH, *An Introduction to the Children Act 1989*, p. 45.
13. DoH, *Community Care in the Next Decade and Beyond* (HMSO, 1990).
14. DoH, *Implementing Community Care: Purchaser, Commissioner and Provider Roles* (HMSO, 1991).

15. DoH (1990), *Community Care in the Next Decade and Beyond*, pp. 37–38.
16. Ibid., p. 6.
17. See for example R. Common and N. Flynn, *Contracting for Care* (Rowntree, 1992).
18. AMA, *Quality and Contracts in the Personal Social Services* (AMA, 1991).
19. R. Gutch, *Contracting Lessons from the US* (NCVO, 1992).
20. DoH *An Introduction to the Children Act 1989*, p. 52.
21. SSI/SSWG, *Care Management: Assessment Practitioner's Guide* (HMSO, 1991) p. 51.
22. SSI/SSWG, *Care Management: Assessment Manager's Guide* (HMSO, 1991) p. 11.
23. K. Ellis, *Squaring the Circle, User and Carer Participation in Needs Assessment* (Rowntree, 1993).
24. SSI/SSWG, *Care Management: Assessment Manager's Guide*, pp. 55–7.
25. Ibid., p. 14, with emphasis added.
26. M. Oliver, 'Discrimination, Disability and Welfare: From Needs to Rights' (Conference paper, 1992).
27. For a fuller discussion of the distinctions between service-led, needs-led and rights-led approaches see M. Willis, *Older People and Equal Citizenship: An Agenda for Local Authorities* (LGMB, 1993).
28. Audit Commission, *The Publication of Information (Standards of Performance) Direction 1992* (Audit Commission, 1992). Two example of these standards are 'The number of requests for bath board and/or bath seat' and 'The sum of the number of bath boards and bath seats provided'. These have been rightly criticised as being purely quantitative with no indication as to the appropriateness of the provision in relation to users' needs.
29. A. Schorr, *The Personal Social Services: An Outside View* (Rowntree, 1992).
30. Audit Commission, *The Community Revolution, Personal Social Services and Community Care* (HMSO, 1993).

9 The Reform of Social Housing

Kenneth M. Spencer

Local government in Britain has played a very major and distinctive role in the provision of social housing. Until the mid-1980s this housing role continued to expand. There was a general consensus that local authorities were the proper body to carry out this task. In the 1980s this consensus was broken, though it was already being seriously challenged by the Labour Government in the later 1970s because of escalating public investment costs.

A great deal had been achieved in terms of new building, slum clearance, housing renovation, the provision of suburban dwellings and considerable improvement in the quality of the social housing stock. By 1961 there were 4.5 million local authority-owned dwellings in the United Kingdom, rising rapidly to 6.8 million by 1980. This period witnessed a growth in the proportion of the housing stock owned by local authorities from 26 per cent to 32 per cent. 'Only in this country do public authorities acquire the land, build the dwellings, receive the subsidies, allocate the completed accommodation and collect the rents. No other market economy has so much publicly owned housing.'[1] Perhaps public housing's very success proved its downfall when new political values oriented towards market forces, tightened public expenditure control, and a reduction in the role of governmental provision were powerfully combined in the Conservative governments of the 1980s and 1990s.

By 1991 there had been a reduction to just under 5 million local authority-owned dwellings. The bulk of the reduction was a result of the 'right to buy' legislation of 1980 which offered discounts to sitting tenants wishing to buy their council home (1.4 million houses were sold in this way between 1980 and 1991). New construction of council housing decreased dramatically. Very little new housing has been added to the council stock since the 1980s. From around 130 000 new council home completions in 1975 the number had fallen to 33 000 by 1985, since when a further decline to about 13 000

145

completions a year had occurred by 1991. The UK. in 1991–92 had the lowest ratio of new-built dwellings in the whole of the EC at 3.2 dwellings per 1000 inhabitants.

Local authorities often faced problems in their housing role, including paternalism towards tenants, discrimination in allocations, poor design and layout, and poor management systems. Until the 1980s housing duties as laid down by Parliament and placed upon local authorities were expressed in 'vague (and unenforceable) terms. There is certainly no duty upon a local authority to provide housing, though there is a long list of needs which it has a duty to consider.'[2] Local authorities had much discretion in meeting local housing needs. It was possible to argue in 1978 that 'central government faces real difficulties when it attempts to ensure that the policies which it favours are carried out'.[3]

The Conservative governments of the 1980s and 1990s have taken very real control of the local authority housing role, through much stronger directive legislation and through greater control of individual local authorities' housing accounts. In a decade we have witnessed a complete reversal of the power relationship in public housing between local government and central government. Power increasingly is held by the centre at the cost of local decision-making. The key impetus has been the Government's drastic measures to constrain public sector spending on council housing. During the period 1979–89 public spending on council housing in England fell by 80 per cent in real terms. Since then reductions have continued. Of social housing expenditure an increasing proportion is being channelled through the Housing Corporation to housing associations. Indeed in 1989–90 housing association new homes construction exceeded, for the first time, those built by local authorities. It is clear that the Government sees housing associations as the main source of publicly subsidised housing and is directing finance accordingly. Though even here it is insisting on much higher levels of private finance being drawn in by housing associations themselves.

A number of reports in the 1980s and 1990s have been critical of the local authority housing service, amongst the most significant being that of the Audit Commission in 1986.[4] However, the report did point out that public sector housing was significantly under-funded so that the problem was not simply one of the quality of management of the housing stock vested in local authorities. Indeed a 1989 report sponsored by the Department of the Environment suggested that local authorities were no less efficient than housing associations, despite the latter's higher staffing ratios.[5]

An Audit Commission report of 1992 which dealt with local housing strategies pointed to a current shortage of some 12000 social housing units a year as contributing significantly to the housing problems of local authorities.[6] A further analysis undertaken for the Housing Corporation indicated that the minimum need for new social housing units was 100000 per year.[7]

Through Priority Estates Projects, Design Improvement on Council Estates, Estate Action and Housing Action Trusts, central government has been targeting resources to managing run-down council estates. As part of wider government initiatives broader City Challenge schemes contain a social housing element while the work of the new English Partnerships Agency is also envisaged as contributing to the alleviation of social housing problems.

The rest of this chapter considers first the driving forces behind the Conservative Governments' housing reforms. It then outlines the reforms themselves and focuses upon tenants' choice, rent increases, housing revenue finance, capital finance for housing, housing associations and finally competition in housing management.

Pressures for change

The 1980s witnessed the development of an increasingly comprehensive New Right ideology about competition, markets and choice as applied to public policy. Much of the change in social housing runs in parallel with these wider philosophies. At the same time individual as opposed to collective choice is emphasised, thus new rights are designated with the aim of increasing the options open to some people. This emphasis on competition, markets and choice also incorporates ideas of growing consumer influence over bureaucracy. Such an alteration of the balance of power between consumers and bureaucracies is a means to strengthening consumer power in public agencies, thus pressing such bureaucracies to behave more in a market-led fashion.[8]

Another key driving force to reform has been central government's strong desire to keep local authorities in check and to tie local authority housing policy much more closely to that determined by central government. Much legislation is therefore aimed at curbing independent local discretion which could detract from the achievement of the Government's political aims. Thus national agendas dominate local ones to a greater degree than previously.

Further, central government has been pressing the role of local government as 'enabler' and 'networker' rather than as a 'sole provider' of services. Pressures are increasing for local authorities to work with the private sector and with the voluntary or independent sector. It is, nonetheless, important to recognise that enabling and providing roles are not necessarily mutually exclusive, nor do market forces seem able to solve social housing problems.

The Government sees an on-going dominance and enhancing of the status of owner-occupation in housing as a key goal of its philosophy of market-led forces. Thus in a property-owning democracy it is up to each individual to make decisions to resolve their own housing needs. As a result of this there has been the strong shift of council housing into owner-occupation through the 'right to buy' legislation. At the same time other policies associated with the encouragement of owner-occupation have continued, of which the most important is mortgage tax relief, though this may be significantly reduced or abandoned given the low level of mortgage interest rates combined with a housing market recession.

Housing policy has also provided a key ground for the Conservative Government to launch a major offensive on key areas of Labour support on the large council estates. Right to buy was a first major inroad, which was supported by a right to repair which largely failed to achieve its goals. The new offensive is by the right to select a new landlord if a tenant is dissatisfied with his or her local authority landlord, together with rights to compensation, management, the conversion of rents to mortgages and the right of council flat-dwellers to buy their leases as well as their flats. This is being followed by compulsory competition for housing management services.

The Government's housing reform programme

The 1987 White Paper *Housing: The Government's Proposals*[9] established a new direction for the local authority housing service.

It set out the Government's proposals for action which were put into place by the Housing Act of 1988 and the Local Government and Housing Act 1989.

The White Paper set out four key aims for the reform of housing policy:

- To reverse the decline of rented housing and improve its quality
- To give council tenants the right to transfer to other landlords if they choose to do so
- To target money more accurately on the most acute problems
- To continue to encourage the growth of home ownership

The Government adopted four strategies as a basis for its legislation. These were, first, to spread home ownership as widely as possible by encouraging higher council rents, by ensuring right to a mortgage for council tenants, pressing on with right to buy, ensuring adequate housing land through the planning system and assisting owners with limited means to keep their property in good condition. Second, it was intended to revive renting by making the letting of private property an economic proposition, and by helping housing associations to restructure financially in order to utilise a higher degree of private finance. At the same time measures were to be taken to ensure that tenants on low incomes obtained adequate housing benefit. Third, the Government wished to change the role of local housing authorities so that their role as landlord and provider diminished as alternative forms of tenure and tenant choice increased. This meant giving tenants greater rights to a say in their own future. Fourth, scarce public money would be used more effectively and a new business-like management of the stock would be adopted by local authorities through the development of a new financial regime. Housing Action Trusts (HATs) were to be introduced on some of the most intractable of local authority housing estates.

The subsequent legislation of 1988 and 1989 covered nine points:

1. A changed financial system for housing associations to inject greater private funding.
2. A changed system of financing for local authority housing in order to improve efficiency in revenue and capital budgets.
3. Private lettings, outside the control of the Rent Acts, were introduced. These included new shorthold lettings, where the

tenant had no security beyond the tenancy period, and new assured tenancies, where rents were to be freely negotiated but the tenant had security of tenure. Rent Act fair rents were to be phased out.

4. Tax inducements to create more private sector housing investment, especially for lower-income groups who would face higher rent levels (assured tenancies) in order to provide an incentive for private investment, e.g. through the Business Enterprise Scheme.[10]

5. Power to establish local estate Housing Action Trusts to take over run-down estates from local authority ownership. The purpose was to improve the estate and subsequently hand it over to various permutations of owner-occupiers, private landlords, housing associations and tenant cooperatives.

6. Council tenants' rights to form tenant cooperatives to both own and manage their own estates or flat block.

7. Council tenants were given a choice of landlord through rights, both individually and collectively, to transfer to a socially 'approved' landlord of the tenant's preference. Such landlords were to be approved and monitored by the Housing Corporation, Housing for Wales and Scottish Homes. The right was for each individual household in council houses to exercise; but for tenants in blocks of flats this right was based on a majority decision with a series of sub-lettings for those not wanting the majority landlord. Certain dwellings were exempted.

8. The subsidy from the General Rate Fund to the Housing Revenue Account was abolished. This stopped local authorities from subsidising rents through rates. It dramatically increased costs for many urban authorities where heavy subsidies had been made. It will also not be possible to subsidise the General Rate Fund from the Housing Revenue Account without the permission of the Secretary of State. This will stop the practice of a number of local authorities which have used surpluses on that account to subsidise future rate, poll tax or council tax increases.

9. Improvement grant and housing repair schemes were revised to target resources to low household income. Renewal areas replaced General Improvement Areas and Housing Action Areas.

The legislation to enact these changes and give further impetus to the reformed housing programme was contained in the Housing Act of 1988, with the exception of points 2, 8, and 9 above which were dealt with in the Local Government and Housing Act of 1989.

Subsequent legislation and parliamentary guidance has continued to press the key themes of the reform process. The voluntary transfer of council housing stock to new or existing housing associations has quickened pace, partly because for some small local authorities it is a means of avoiding the likely problems associated with the extension of compulsory competitive tendering legislation in the 1988 Local Government Act to white-collar activities and particularly to housing management. The CCT process in housing management has begun and is discussed later in this chapter.

Changes in the social security rules applying to young people have made finding accommodation more difficult for this group. Combined with significant rent increases and lack of new accommodation, this has led to a rapid growth in homelessness. This is especially so in the larger cities and London in particular where the London Research Centre showed that the number of homeless in temporary accommodation in London has risen by 25 per cent in the year to June 1992.[11] Similarly a study of the Government's Rough Sleepers Initiative, designed to tackle this problem, showed London had about 40000 homeless households and that the policies of the Department of the Environment were being frustrated by other governmental department policies, e.g. Department of Social Security, and by housing benefit rules.[12]

Pressure on local authorities' housing stock is growing from legislation concerned with care in the community as more people move out of residential care in hospitals and institutions. The White Paper directed at housing authorities ignores the resourcing issue.[13] There is also mounting pressure as a result of the Children Act – where a family's housing circumstances may well be a central issue.

The Leasehold Reform, Housing and Urban Development Act of 1993 boosts a number of the initiatives taken in 1988–9. It gives tenants new rights to demand repairs and compensation from landlords (including council tenants), it gives a right to consultation and the right to manage their own estates. In addition it allows tenants to convert their council rents to mortgages and gives tenants of flats the right to buy their leases. Both these latter initiatives are attempts to bolster council house sales further (at a time of housing market recession) and also to encourage tenant self-management groups.

Tenants' choice

The Government's legislation on tenants' choice includes right to repair, right to select a new landlord, annual reports from the housing authority, proper complaints procedures, the statutory Tenant's Charter and the 'right to buy' legislation in the Housing Act 1980, later extended in 1984, 1986 and 1993. All this is seen as exerting further pressure on council landlords to 'improve the quality and responsiveness of their housing management'.[14] Tenants' choice is clearly intended to complement the right to buy. 'The effect of this will be to open up the closed world of the local authority housing estates to competition and to the influence of the best housing management practices of other landlords'.[15] The purpose is to begin to break the virtual council monopoly of rented housing in some areas.

New independent landlords have to obtain prior approval as social landlords under the conditions of the Housing Corporation, if they wish to take over council housing stock and a vote of tenants so decides.

In maisonettes or blocks of flats tenants' choice is exercised collectively. In the case of houses this can be done collectively by estates, or in groups, but the right also applies to individual households. No council tenants will have to change landlords under tenants' choice unless they choose to do so. The Government also argues that the spur of competition provided by this new right should promote better services and better value for tenants, even where they do not exercise their new rights. Nationally, some 70 to 80 per cent of council tenants say they are satisfied with their existing local authority landlord.

There is ample evidence that local authority housing management is undergoing fundamental reappraisal and review partly because it has been recognised as long overdue but also partly because of tenants' choice. As has been pointed out by the Association of District Councils, 'Housing authorities have every reason to give a good account of themselves and there have been encouraging signs over the past year of tenants' desire to stick with their council landlords. This has increased the morale of those providing the service and has confirmed that local authorities have a unique advantage as they are publicly accountable.[16] This statement accompanied the publication of a guide to housing authorities urging them to examine their policies, alter them where necessary, and go out to fight and win in the tenants' choice stakes.[17]

Some councils have attempted voluntary transfers of their housing stock using voting procedures which parallel those in the 1988 Housing Act. At least 50 per cent of all eligible voters have to vote 'no' in order to stop a transfer.[18]

Chiltern was the first district council to transfer in this way when some 5000 units were transferred to Chiltern Hundreds Housing Association, newly formed and staffed by the council's staff. By mid-1991 about 100 000 units had transferred in this way including units in Bromley, Rochester, Newbury, Sevenoaks and Christchurch. In many cases plans have been abandoned after unfavourable tenant votes, e.g. Salisbury, Rochford, Torbay.[19] It was the existing local authority housing staff who created and worked for the new housing associations. Thus the alternative landlord has the same staff but a different legal status independent of the district council. Some staff opt out to escape increasingly restrictive housing legislation and also possibly the advent of CCT.

Housing Action Trusts (HAT) were created by the 1988 Housing Act. The proposals set out by Government[20] were clearly not workable. There was opposition, costs were higher than expected and the intended programme was dramatically reduced. Votes were introduced so tenants could choose rather than have a scheme enforced upon them. There are now a number of HATs running but tenants have often wished to retain the right to transfer back to the local authority as landlord once the capital programme of improvements is completed. Tenants have actively become involved in discussions about the sorts of improvements required to their HAT estates. The Government had to clearly modify its original ideas in the light of pressure from the tenants themselves.

Many tenants are clearly wary of potential new landlords. With the uncertainties involved, moves to opt out may proceed relatively slowly, at least initially. Much will depend upon how far local authority housing departments develop a new tenant-oriented system of quality housing management. The onus is clearly upon local authorities to improve their services and their management performance. Those least able to do so may lose higher proportions of their tenants to other landlords.

A tenants' choice scenario of 2 per cent per year opting out would equal the rate of right-to-buy sales each year. Nationally, on this scenario the five million council dwellings of the United Kingdom in 1991 could reduce to about four million dwellings remaining in council ownership by about 1995.

The Audit Commission envisaged a scenario of higher sales and higher levels of opting out so that only 50 per cent of the stock in 1986 would remain by about 1994.[21] It is clearly wrong. Reform has been slower to bite.

Rent increases

The introduction of assured tenancies for new lettings of rented accommodation apply to new council lettings as well as to housing associations and private landlords. Clearly the pressure is to push rents higher. Rents are discussed in terms of 'affordable rents' which are not precisely defined. However, the general view is that rents will double or more in real terms as a result of various measures in the Government's housing reform programme. The pressures for higher rents come from several sources in addition to the shift to assured tenancies. These are the need to finance the housing service adequately and especially to improve local repair and maintenance standards, the pressure to differentiate local authority rents and make popular homes dearer, the pressure to move towards market rents, the introduction of the new housing revenue financial regime (see later) and the need to increase council house rents so that competition can be placed on a 'fair footing' ahead of the introduction of CCT.

The results of all this will be more tenants deciding to buy, most continuing tenants paying significant extra rental, new tenants paying much higher assured rents, possibly higher levels of rent arrears amongst some low-income-band groups, and ceilings introduced on eligible rental costs for housing benefit payments. Indeed such informal ceiling benefits often dictate rent levels themselves in the private sector. Housing benefit payments then have risen though central government intends local authorities to increasingly take up the costs of these extra benefits through surpluses on Housing Revenue Accounts. Between 1989 and the end of 1991 local authority rents had risen by 47 per cent, some 12 per cent over the Government's guidelines. This was generally to keep local authority spending on management and maintenance at levels above government allowances, which were regarded as too low.[22] These social renting measures are likely to detract from the Government's declared aim of enabling a higher degree of national population mobility.[23] The result is likely to be that council tenants will stay put, as job mobility would lead them into the higher assured tenancy rent levels.

Housing revenue finance

The 1989 Act (Part VI) provides for stringent controls by central government over the statutory Housing Revenue Account (HRA) of housing authorities. The Government's considerations were set out in its consultation paper.[24] The key reasons for change were basically twofold: first, to regain control by central government over the behaviour of local housing authorities (made more difficult as many had fallen outside the scope of housing subsidy under the 1985 Housing Act); and, second, to find a new source to finance the spiralling cost of housing benefit. The legislation brought all housing local authorities back into central government subsidy and hence control. Over time it will transfer some of the financing of housing benefits from the Government to local authority rent-payers.

This housing revenue reform was operative from 1 April 1990, but a transition period of three years was introduced to minimise the sharp impact of an approximate doubling or more of rents. The Housing Revenue Account (HRA) became an independent trading account through a system of ring-fencing. This means that Rate Fund contributions will not be allowed to be paid into the HRA after 1990, nor will the HRA be able to transfer surplus to the General Fund unless specified by the Secretary of State. A new HRA subsidy was payable to local housing authorities. This replaced subsidy payable under the Housing Act 1985, and that part of rent rebate subsidy payable to them under the Social Security Act 1985 (which relates to rent rebates required to be granted to tenants of HRA dwellings). The decisions on subsidy levels are based on a government formula, which can be varied by the Secretary of State for the Environment, and which includes regional rent levels, efficiency and effectiveness measures, e.g. levels of rent arrears, percentage of empty property. Thus more inefficient housing authorities will be more heavily penalised through loss of subsidy – which in turn will push up rents even more.

The legislation pushes rents to reflect property values more closely and, it is acknowledged, in the longer term to achieve market rents for council housing. This erodes the basis of council house financing since 1919. Again this is likely to lead to yet more pressure on tenants to buy their council home.

The pressure is to increase council rents, to develop the HRA as an essentially trading account, and to take tighter control of local authority financial decisions about their housing. At the same time it will be an incentive for improved management performance by the local authority housing department, and ultimately by the local authority as a whole, because other local authority departmental charges to the HRA are likely to be increasingly challenged by those responsible for the local authority housing service. The introduction of service level agreements and competition also lead to a challenging of overheads.

Over time surpluses on the HRAs are to be used to offset increased levels of housing benefits to match rising rents. Thus better-off tenants will ultimately contribute towards the rebates of poorer tenants.

The housing revenue reforms have had a very significant impact on local authority housing services. It led the Institute of Housing[25] in its response to the consultation papers on capital and revenue financing for housing to state that the Government had to be clearer about defining 'affordable rents', and that the adequacy of the housing benefit scheme, take-up and the poverty trap needed to be addressed before rent increases on the scale envisaged would be acceptable.

In relation to the new housing capital control system the Institute felt this would result in three things. First, it would lead to a reduced local authority ability to meet housing need. Second, the new system would offer little improvement over the existing system in relation to the need for long-term planning. Third, it would place considerable pressure on local authorities' ability to provide affordable accommodation. However, as already noted, the emphasis on enabling rather than providing meant these comments fell by the wayside.

The Association of Metropolitan Authorities[26] in its response to the housing revenue consultation paper stressed that the legislation would have a more drastic effect on local authority housing services and public sector rent levels than any other previous recent legislation. The 1989 Local Government and Housing Act was a boost towards greater home ownership on the part of existing council tenants.

These financial pressures have significantly assisted the Government in getting to grips with enhancing a number of its policy objectives, first through a period in 1987–89 of escalating home prices and then through a period of housing market recession accompanied by falling interest rates. The complexities of the system are intricate[27] and the debate about equity as between owner-occupiers, private renters and social housing renters (whether housing association or local authority) continues.[28]

Capital finance for housing

In the 1989 Act (Part IV), central government adopted powers to reform the local authority capital control system. This was against a background of decreasing capital expenditure by local authorities on housing provision – given their new enabling rather than providing role, and given the Government's own emphasis on enhancing the role of the Housing Corporation (including Housing for Wales, which took over from the Housing Corporation in Wales in 1989, and Scottish Homes in the case of Scotland), and on drawing upon open money markets.

The Government created new mechanisms for dealing with high levels of local authority capital receipts (e.g. about £3 billion from council house sales alone in 1989–90) and to close legal loopholes. The new system switched to control over borrowing rather than over spending. The two prime aims were, first, to control conventional borrowing and creative accounting and, second, to reduce local authority debt. The new capital finance regime began on 1 April 1990. Annual credit approvals for borrowing were notified to each local authority (by service areas of expenditure for England but not for Wales). The Housing Investment Programme (HIP) system is thus subject to basic credit approvals and special credit approvals for housing capital expenditure. There is a three-year rolling programme of credit approvals – allowing a degree of forward planning. As for capital receipts, the local authority under the pre-1990 system could spend 20 per cent a year of income, with 80 per cent rolled over so that the receipt fund (and the value of a 20 per cent proportion) increased in size on the basic sums unspent. After 1990 25 per cent had to be spent in the year the receipts were accumulated, but there is no spillover allowed between different financial years. The other 75 per cent of capital receipts from housing must be spent on redeeming debt. Thus housing debt is decreasing significantly but housing needs are also increasing for lack of investment.

Debt payments are brought forward by increasing the burden of debt charges in the early years through the 1990 system of payment by equal annual instalments of principal (EIP). Under this system a higher proportion of the principal borrowed has to be paid back earlier: thus reducing resource flexibility by lessening the amount of housing debt which can be pushed further into the future for repayment. Basically all this tightens central government's control over local authority capital spending. An immediate impact of these changes was for local authorities to rush into spending their maximum capital receipts allowance before 1 April 1990.

Housing associations

The reform programme gives enhanced status to the housing association movement. Such associations owned around 5 per cent of the housing stock in 1989. The Government sees them as the new main engine of publicly subsidised housing in Britain, and argues that by applying pressure on them to seek and obtain private sector funding, the available public money will extend even further in terms of the production of new social housing units. The purpose of such mixed funding is to produce homes at the elusive 'affordable rent'. The average grant for mixed funding schemes nationally rose from 60 per cent in 1988–89 to 75 per cent in 1989–90, though regional allocations vary around the national average. Since then it has fallen back to about 60 per cent and is set to decline further as associations use asset bases to secure loans.

Government's proposed gross expenditure plans for housing associations in England and Wales demonstrate this commitment with a rise from spending of £580 million in 1986–87, to £815 million by 1989–90, and £1328 million by 1991–92. The Housing Corporation grows in power and influence as a result of this and its approval and monitoring role of new social landlords. Directives from the Housing Corporation have, amongst other things, suggested that associations operating in relatively expensive areas need to consider whether they could achieve the same objective in surrounding districts at lower cost. It assists in meeting ministerial priorities. It has argued that regional directors will need to protect the more vulnerable elements of the development programme, including small, new, ethnic minority and cooperative housing associations expecting to undertake special needs schemes and rehabilitation in the inner cities. It is concerned about the propriety and accountability of housing associations and has raised the issue of specialist types of association, e.g. development only, management only, and both development and management. It has encouraged the merger of housing associations to form larger, more financially viable and balanced associations. It may well be under pressure to 'encourage' housing associations to tender under compulsory competitive tendering (CCT) in local authority housing management. Many associations are cautious on this valuing their existing links and networks – which they feel could be placed in jeopardy by CCT. Some, however, are likely to seek opportunities to take on a larger share of the local authority housing stock both in terms of ownership and, under CCT, management.

The pressures on their rents remain the same as those within the local authority, as assured tenancies begin to operate for new housing association tenancy agreements. People could be living in very similar dwellings but be paying vastly different rents. This is because new tenants would be paying assured rents, whereas existing tenants would continue to pay their rents under the previous system of fair rent registration.

Given the new pressures of financing for housing associations, some are facing tough times in obtaining private finance, including tougher loan conditions. So much so that in a number of cases there have been serious threats to financial viability or worse.[29] The housing association movement has been largely captured as an additional arm of central government policy shifts. CCT or something similar could be introduced within the associations themselves.

At the same time closer scrutiny reveals management and operational shortcomings, as for example in relation to the nominations process of housing associations.[30]

Compulsory competitive tendering for local authority housing management

In 1991 the Citizen's Charter White Paper stated: 'Compulsory competitive tendering would be introduced into housing management.'[31] Much of the reasoning behind this was to bring in more choice and competition so that tenants would see an improvement in the quality of housing management. It is, of course, also influenced by the pressure to reduce public spending, keep costs down, and transfer local authority provision to others.

A study had been commissioned by Government in 1991 to examine issues about the introduction of competitive tendering in housing management. This report highlighted a number of issues of concern but could see no objections to its introduction. Its conclusion was: 'The evidence to date suggests there is a *prima facie* case for considering extending CCT to housing management.'[32] A subsequent government consultation paper identified several key themes which CCT would achieve.[33] They were, first, to enhance good management practice already in existence, second, to raise standards and provide tenants with better services in future, third, to open up management opportunities to non-local government providers and, fourth, to achieve cost savings as a result of CCT. Such objectives can be contradictory.

The legislative framework springs from the Local Government Acts of 1988 and 1992 in particular. The manual service base of CCT in 1988 is being extended to white-collar services and housing management is one such service. This shift to competition is thus part of a wider governmental policy objective (see Chapter 3). However it will be necessary for the government to amend certain housing legislation, especially elements of the consolidating 1985 Housing Act, in order to proceed. Legislation is before Parliament.

The Government hopes to speed up the original housing management CCT timetable so that this can all be completed by

1996. Pilot schemes are already running in several housing authorities which should be letting contracts for April 1994, whether to successful in-house bids or not.

CCT will apply to the housing management function, now defined by Government as: rent and service charge collection; allocation of properties and arranging lettings; management of vacant properties; management of repairs and maintenance; management of caretaking and cleaning; advice to tenants and dealing with complaints. This will be the minimum list of housing management functions under CCT. Local authorities may add other functions if they wish. Services will have to be specified and terms and conditions of service drawn up. Many authorities are identifying issues of performance targets, quality of service to tenants and costing mechanisms as key elements of their preparatory work. The mainstream of contracts should be let by 1995 with others, parts of larger housing stock authorities, being let by 1996.

There are other important points to highlight about CCT. It is argued in government papers that the retention of a comprehensive housing service is vital. Comprehensiveness might remain but whether it will be as comprehensible to tenants remains to be seen.

The local authority landlord function will remain, hence policy decisions, e.g. rent levels, repair policy, budget formation, capital investment, housing strategy, housing benefits, will remain within the discretion of local councils. In some cases it will be necessary to tie current contracts, e.g. housing repairs, grass cutting, into the new contracts for housing management.

There is added complexity because of the Local Government Review programme and therefore questions about which authority, new or existing, will be responsible for landlord functions. At the same time other white-collar CCT has a very direct impact on housing services and costs and vice versa. This is significant because of the scale of housing services.

The role of tenants within CCT will allow consultation at the tender specification stage and most contracts will have tenant satisfaction surveys built into them. However tenants will not have the right to select the successful tender bid. This will be done in accordance with existing CCT legislation. It has been decided that the units for contracting-out purposes will be estates where possible and that these should be blocks of stock of a size attractive to potential bidders (up to about 5000 to 7000 dwellings). Much will depend on the geography and scale of existing estates, or geographical spread in sparcer rural areas.

Pilot authorities for housing CCT include Brent, Derby, East Staffordshire, Mid-Suffolk, Newham, Rochdale and Westminster. Clearly preparation for CCT is a time-consuming activity. Only time will tell whether there is a significant market of housing management bidders, e.g. housing associations, private companies, including those from countries in Europe with experience in this field (The Netherlands, Germany, France).

One thing is already clear; approaching CCT has led to much greater thinking about the nature and quality of the housing management function as well as about its cost. It has also often enhanced tenant involvement. This of itself is an important mechanism for policy review and service improvement.

Conclusions

Whether the Government will achieve its housing aims through this reform programme remains open to question. Most likely there will be gradual rather than revolutionary change. Tenants are not likely to exercise the right to choose a new landlord on a significant scale if many of the opinion polls are correct. The outcome over the next five years or so depends on several factors. These include, first, the extent and speed with which new financial resources from the private sector will be drawn into the provision of housing for low-income groups. Despite assured rents the record here does not suggest massive private investment waiting to come in. Second, the future pace of council house sales will be important to the local housing authority as it will reduce its capacity to cope with all but the most acute housing need cases, i.e. homelessness. Third is the rate at which tenants decide to opt for other landlords, which in turn will be related to the speed with which local authorities can deliver better services and keep rents within competitive levels, *vis-à-vis* rents of other social landlords. Fourth, the future varying pattern of house prices will have an effect, especially on dwellings towards the bottom end of the market for first-time buyers. Fifth will be the degree to which housing issues become of greater significance on the national agenda of political concern. Sixth is the impact CCT will have on tenants perceptions of housing management service delivery. Clearly a different government may well have new philosophies about social housing and a local authority role – however many of the strands of policy developed thus far may survive such a change.

If private sector investment is not forthcoming, and there is little sign of this so far, then greater social housing through housing associations and local authorities will be needed. If there is a breakdown of housing provision for certain groups of the population e.g. new first-time buyers, the elderly, the homeless, young people seeking hostel accommodation – then it is more likely that housing issues will once again rise within the political agenda creating wider debate about the future of social housing in Britain. Much will depend upon the degree of responsiveness by local authority housing staff and others as to whether tenants opt for other landlords, including self- management, or not.

Finally, it is evident that much of the existing council housing stock will remain with local housing authorities well into the later 1990s. The local housing authority will thus retain a significant role. It will need a capacity to develop its services to match new expectations and new demands. Much will depend on enhancing the management ingenuity and capability of both local politicians and housing service professionals. Central government has challenged local housing authorities. Many have the capacity to respond effectively to that challenge and to steer themselves through the new complex changes in the best interests of the housing needs of their local communities. Inevitably this will lead to greater diversification of organisational structures and modes of operation between local housing authorities. Perhaps that is a good sign for the future well-being of a responsive local housing authority and for local government more generally.

Notes and references

1. D. Donnison and C. Ungerson, *Housing Policy* (Penguin, 1982) p. 63.
2. J. B. Cullingworth, *Essays on Housing Policy: The British Scene* (Allen & Unwin, 1979) p. 8.
3. Ibid., p. 14.
4. Audit Commission, *Managing the Crisis in Council Housing* (HMSO, 1986).

5. Department of the Environment, D. MacLellan *et al.*, *The Nature and Effectiveness of Housing Management in England* (HMSO, 1989).
6. Audit Commission, *Developing Local Authority Housing Strategies* (HMSO, 1992).
7. C. W. Whitehead and M. Kleinman, *A Review of Housing Need Assessment* (Housing Corporation, 1992).
8. K. Walsh and K. Spencer, *The Quality of Service in Housing Management* (Institute of Local Government Studies, 1990).
9. HM Government, White Paper, *Housing: The Government's Proposals* (HMSO, 1987).
10. D. Coleman, 'The New Housing Policy – A Critique', *Housing Studies,* vol. 4, no. 1 (1989) pp. 44–57.
11. London Research Centre, *Housing Update No. 6* (LRC, 1992).
12. Centrepoint, *No Way Back* (Centrepoint, 1992).
13. Department of the Environment, Welsh Office, Department of Health, *Housing and Community Care*, Circular 10/92 (HMSO,1992).
14. Department of the Environment, *Tenants' Choice: the Government's Proposals for Legislation* (DoE, 1987) para. 3.
15. Ibid., para. 5.
16. Association of District Councils, *ADC News,* 15 November (ADC, 1988).
17. Association of District Councils, *The Challenge of Tenants' Choice* (ADC, 1988).
18. C. Game, 'What's a Majority', *Public Service and Local Government* (January 1989) p. 38.
19. M. P. Kleinman, 'Large Scale Transfers of Council Housing to New Landlords', *Housing Studies,* vol. 8, no. 3 (1993) pp. 163–78.
20. Department of the Environment, *Housing Action Trusts* (DoE, 1987).
21. H. J. Davies, 'Local Government under Siege', *Public Administration,* vol. 66, no. 1 (1988) pp. 91–101.
22. P. Malpass *et al.*, *Housing Policy in Action – the New Financial Regime for Council Housing* (SAUS, 1992).
23. J. Salt, 'Labour Migration and Housing in the UK: An Overview', in C. Hamnett and J. Alden (eds), *Labour Markets and Housing* (Hutchinson, 1989).
24. Department of the Environment/Welsh Office, *New Financial Regime for Local Authority Housing in England and Wales* (DoE/WO, 1988).
25. Institute of Housing, *Response to DoE/WO Consultancy Papers on Housing Revenue and Housing Capital* (1988).
26. Association of Metropolitan Authorities, *A New Financial Regime for Local Authority Housing in England and Wales. The AMA Response* (AMA, 1988).
27. P. Malpass *et al.*, *Housing Policy in Action.*
28. D. MacLennan and K. Gibb, *Housing Finance and Subsidies in Britain* (Avebury, 1993).
29. M. Pryke and C. Whitehead, *Private Finance in the Provision of Social Housing*, Housing Research Findings No. 73 (Joseph Rowntree Foundation, 1992).

30 Department of the Environment, *Access, Allocations and Nominations: the Role of Housing Associations* (HMSO, 1992).

31. Prime Minister's Office, White Paper, *Citizen's Charter* (HMSO, 1991)

32. Department of the Environment/Scottish Office/Welsh Office, *The Scope for Competitive Tendering in Housing Management* (HMSO, 1991) p. 73.

33. Department of the Environment/Welsh Office, *Competing for Quality in Housing – Competition in the Provision of Housing Management – A Consultation Paper* (DoE/WO, 1992).

10   Urban and Economic Development

Alan Harding and Peter Garside

The context: the public sector, urban policy and economic development

This chapter deals with two public policy fields: the *urban* (or 'inner city') *policies* of national governments, especially the role of local government within them, and the *economic development policies* of local authorities. Both remain fairly insignificant in public expenditure terms, but they have become steadily more important over the past twenty years and have attracted academic attention out of all proportion to their size. They are examined together because they are clearly interrelated. The primary goal of national urban policy since the late 1970s has been the economic regeneration of selected areas and many local authorities have relied significantly on national programmes to support their local development efforts. The two are not synonymous though. They are products of two different policy-making systems and, until a recent and somewhat uneasy 'truce', there have been significant tensions between them.

At the national level, we must distinguish between explicit and incidental urban policies. The actions of most government departments have implications for the urban environment, the quality of urban life or the operation of urban property and labour markets, even though their cumulative effects would be virtually impossible to quantify. Very few expenditure or policy decisions consider the likely spatial effects, though, so different urban areas are *incidentally* rewarded or punished by mainstream policies. Rather than attempt to anticipate the differential and incidental urban effects of mainstream programmes when making policy decisions, British governments have developed somewhat under-specified but nonetheless *explicit* urban policies that are separated

166

from the wider range of national policies that impinge, positively or negatively, upon urban areas.

There has been just one government statement of any consequence on urban policy in the last decade.[1] This set out a number of general, unquantified policy aims[2] of the 'motherhood and apple pie' variety. It also listed over thirty programmes – covering economic development, education, training, planning, infrastructure provision, land reclamation, crime, housing and the environment – that had an ostensible urban focus. Most were specific initiatives targeted solely on urban priority areas.[33] Others, operating inside and outside priority areas, were considered part of urban policy – sometimes dubiously – largely because the Government was committed to making a policy statement and was keen to create the impression that it was making substantial efforts in urban areas. Clearly, even the governments responsible for urban policy find difficulty in saying exactly what is and is not included in it and precisely what it is trying to achieve. The only practical working definition is that urban policy is simply the sum of the limited range of special programmes targeted, wholly or in part, on selected urban areas. The arbitrariness and vagueness of urban policy has led some to argue that it is 'an example of creating solutions to a problem that has never been clearly defined'.[4]

The key urban policy players at national government level are the Department of the Environment (DoE) and the Scottish and Welsh Offices. They bear primary responsibility for operationalising the Government's approach to urban areas, through devising appropriate programmes (in the case of the DoE) or setting guidelines for the operations of the agencies that have urban policy responsibilities (the Welsh Development Agency and Scottish Enterprise along with its network of Local Enterprise Companies).[5] The urban policy initiatives of Conservative Governments[6] during the 1980s had a number of basic characteristics.

- it was assumed that lasting economic, social and environmental regeneration could only result from the action of the private sector
- it was further assumed that the proper role of government was therefore to make urban areas more attractive to the business community and that benefits – jobs in particular – would 'trickle down' automatically to local residents

- special urban programmes prioritised economic regeneration and employment, particularly through adaptation of the physical environment by means of capital expenditure
- there was a proliferation of independent initiatives, each with their own limited financial resources, expenditure rules and delivery procedures
- initiatives tended to be short-lived and were often developed in response to particular 'shocks' such as the urban riots of 1981 and 1985 programme expenditures were increasingly allocated according to an area's perceived 'potential' rather than its 'need'[7]
- new implementation agencies were created in which private business figures and regional government officials played a more important role than local authorities[8]

Local authorities whose territories were designated under national urban policy had an ambiguous stance toward national programmes for much of the 1980s. On the one hand, those programmes that were channelled through local government offered an important resource that could support local economic strategies, albeit only within parameters set by central government. On the other, the role of local government in urban policy was clearly being down-graded. Programmes formulated and delivered by the officials of government departments or by private sector-led, quasi-public agencies appointed by Government were obviously less amenable to local government influence.[9] Because they involved the injection of non-local resources, few local authorities were prepared to obstruct their implementation in practice but they undeniably created a new economic development 'policy infrastructure' beyond local government.

The centralisation of urban policy[10] would have had few implications for local authorities if national and local government had shared a common urban development agenda or if authorities had been able to marshal substantial independent resources in support of their own economic development efforts. Neither was the case. Until 1989 local authorities had no statutory powers in the economic development field. Whilst that did not mean they had no influence within local economies, it meant economic strategies depended on the creative use of other statutory powers and the market power of the authority. During the earlier part of the decade, many urban authorities had undertaken a number of local economic experiments.[11] They used specific and general[12] powers, along with their 'clout' as employers, contractors and purchasers, to follow an agenda which was partially antagonistic to that of central government. In particular, they put less emphasis on physical restructuring and inward investment and more on 'people-based' policies which prioritised local labour recruitment, equal opportunities, trade union organisation and anti-poverty campaigns. They also used various means of supporting the private sector as levers with which to influence company policies with regard to employment, product development and investment.

In the hostile climate of central–local government relations of the time, however, these Labour authorities found that as soon as they discovered legislative loopholes through which to develop alternative strategies, they were closed down by central government.[13] The Conservatives' national election victory in 1987 was a watershed for Labour local authorities[14] and triggered a change of approach to both national urban programmes and local economic development policy. Faced with another Government that continued to limit the urban policy role of local authorities and tighten central control over the dwindling number of programmes implemented through local government, Labour authorities, sometimes reluctantly, embraced the 'new pragmatism'.

Thereafter, Labour authorities accepted that they were only one part of a local economic development infrastructure which they did not have the capacity or authority to lead. Local economic policies increasingly concentrated on pragmatic goals, such as:

- attracting the maximum possible levels of investment from other levels of government (including the European Commission), irrespective of the control the local authority had over their use
- encouraging partnerships with other local agencies to improve the co–ordination of disparate programmes, pool scarce resources and use local authority intelligence to influence the priorities of other agencies at the margin
- encouraging partnerships with the private sector[15]

A somewhat schizophrenic approach. Urban development was pursued through attempts to capitalise on market trends and a 'needs-based' approach was pursued through initiatives in, for example, special needs training and community enterprise development but few links were made between them. The cost of this approach to local authorities was a diminution of the 'social agenda' that many had tried to incorporate into economic development plans. But it helped preserve an economic development role for local government – albeit an enabling and coordinating, not an implementing one – and began to reduce the hostility of central–local government relations in the urban policy field.

By 1989, the Government felt comfortable enough with the new pragmatism in local government to offer local authorities a formal, if restricted, role in economic development for the first time. The Local Government and Housing Act 1989 (Part III) replaced local authorities' general power of competence and empowered them to participate in or encourage the setting up or expansion of any commercial, industrial or public undertaking as long as it lay within the authority's area and was likely to increase or protect employment opportunities for local residents.[16] Local authorities were obliged to publish, and consult upon, annual costed economic development plans. The Secretary of State for the Environment retained wide powers to intervene should he/she have objections to an individual authority's approach.

Recent national policy developments

Recent years have seen continuity *and* change in national urban policy. By the late 1980s, British cities invariably contained within their boundaries a profusion of discrete, experimental initiatives, each supported by different sets of national and local interests and drawing upon a range of constrained funding sources. After the change in Conservative Party leadership late in 1990, signs of a more consensual and broader-based approach emerged, albeit alongside initiatives which shared the characteristics of the 1980s. Programme resources remain limited and are clearly vulnerable to public expenditure cuts in times of recession (see Table 10.1). But the Government reacted to criticisms of its preponderance for single-purpose, unelected agencies and physical development programmes, particularly the fact that this combination appeared to:

- provide limited benefits to local communities, especially disadvantaged residents with fewest prospects for entering the labour market[17]

Table 10.1 DoE urban expenditure (£ million)

Inner cities	1987–88 outturn	1988–89 outturn	1989–90 outturn	1990–91 outturn	1991–92 outturn	1992–93 outturn	1993–94 outturn
City Challenge	–	–	–	–	–	63.5	213.5
Urban Programme	245.7	224.3	222.7	225.8	237.5	243.1	175.6
City Grants	26.8	27.8	39.1	45.4	40.8	59.6	71.0
Derelict Land Grants	76.7	67.9	54.2	61.7	77.3	94.6	93.0
English Partnerships	–	–	–	–	–	–	2.0
UDCs and DLR*	160.2	255.0	476.7	607.2	601.8	514.5	337.4
Olympic bid	–	–	–	–	0.8	13.1	35.0
Task Forces	5.2	22.9	19.9	20.9	20.5	23.0	18.0
City Action Teams	–	–	4.0	7.7	8.4	4.4	3.4
Special grants	–	–	–	–	–	–	1.3
Other urban	–	–	–	–	–	–	2.2
CFERs†	–0.1	–	–1.6	–4.4	–7.2	–1.9	–
Total	514.4	597.9	814.9	964.8	979.8	1013.9	952.3

* Docklands Light Railway (London).
† Consolidated Fund Extra Receipts.

- do little to involve local residents in regeneration efforts
- complicate an already complex and fragmented policy-making environment and militate against more comprehensive, holistic approaches[18]

The DoE remains firmly in the lead in urban policy and is the source of most programme innovation. Other government departments restrict their efforts either to supplementing those elements of nation-wide programmes they deliver in urban areas in an attempt to make them more sensitive and effective or offering slightly more advantageous terms for programme recipients based in urban priority areas. The main new policy tool developed within the DoE under the Major administration is City Challenge,[19] whose main features are summarised below.

How does City Challenge work?

- **What is City Challenge aiming to achieve**   To transform specific run-down inner city areas and significantly to improve the quality of life for local residents
- **What resources are involved?**   Core funding of £7.5m per year for each City Challenge authority + complementary funding from other mainline public sector programmes + private sector investment levered in
- **How long does City Challenge last?**   Five years
- **Where does the core funding come from?**   'Top sliced' from seven pre-existing grant regimes (i.e. no new money). The 5 that are channelled through the local authority (Urban Programme, Estates Action, Derelict Land Grant, private sector housing renewal, CAT special budget) were unified for 1993–94. The others are City Grant and Housing Corporation grants
- **How are City Challenges designated?**   By annual competition. eleven were chosen from an invited list of 15 local authorities for 1992–93 starts. For 1993–94, all 57 Urban Programme authorities were entitled to bid. Twenty were chosen. The competition for 1994–95 was cancelled by the DoE
- **Who chooses the areas?**   The relevant local authority and its chosen partners

- **And the priorities?** Same again. There are no prescriptions from Government, though all projects must be suitable for financing through the chosen grant source. The DoE is the final arbiter on the 5-year plans and the annual implementation plan
- **How is City Challenge delivered?** Through an implementing agency, based on a partnership between the local authority, the private sector and the community. It is expected to be independent from the local authority, able to make rapid and effective decisions and to ensure that all partners endorse key decisions
- **Who works for the implementing agency?** Newly appointed staff plus secondees from the local authority, other public agencies, the private sector. Staff sizes are small
- **How are the partners chosen?** By the local authority
- **What about other parts of the public sector?** Coordination of Government inputs is organised through DoE regional offices or City Action Teams. Coordination of local authority departments is generally through a new subcommittee with delegated powers plus a dedicated officer team

City Challenge implicitly recognises that coherent and integrated policy-making had become virtually impossible amidst the 'patchwork quilt' of competing urban initiatives. The rationale behind the programme is that no single organisation or set of interests has a monopoly of knowledge about, or resources to deal with, complex urban problems. City Challenge effectively aims to:

- unite a wide range of statutory and non-statutory interests behind a consensual vision for particular urban areas
- provide appropriate incentives for these interests to deliver the elements of the programme that fall within their respective capacities or fields of responsibility
- change the behaviour and priorities of the various 'players' such that strategic development aims are realised in an integrated and cooperative fashion

Depending on the City Challenge, this means drawing a multitude of local and national, public and private actors[20] into new policy-making and programme delivery processes. In contrast to 1980s initiatives, local authorities are key players. They are expected to exercise civic leadership in encouraging inter-agency cooperation and innovation. Generally, formal partnership boards have been established with membership drawn from the local authority, the business community and the voluntary sector. City Challenge programmes, agreed by DoE regional offices through an annual round of bids, are less dominated by commercial, physical regeneration schemes. They are tailored to local circumstances and range across initiatives as varied as social housing, public and private transport infrastructure, technology transfer, arts and cultural industries, childcare, crime prevention, primary health care, school–industry compacts, improvements to public space, training for disadvantaged groups and capacity-building for community groups.

At the time of writing, the first round of City Challenges are just 18 months into their programmes so final judgements cannot be made. Independent observers are nonetheless asking a number of pertinent questions about the operation and impact of the programme.[21] These can be summarised as follows:

Government commitment
- The third round of City Challenge, starting in 1994–95, was cancelled due to public expenditure constraints and there are no firm plans to reactivate it
- DoE regional offices seem to be unclear whether their role in City Challenge is as partner or refereee
- The DoE seems more concerned with monitoring paper outputs than with ensuring that the Government's contribution to City Challenge is effective
- Whilst there is some flexibility within and between grant regimes, there is no recognition of the different needs and potentials of different Challenge areas, nor of the possible benefit of varying the pace of the programme between years
- Non-DoE departments have failed to deliver key projects that were included in some Challenge plans and no obvious sanctions exist to change their behaviour

Local authority commitment
- Just as it is proving difficult to get all government departments 'onside', so it is with local authority departments that have few stakes in City Challenge

- Big city authorities in particular find it politically difficult to favour City Challenge areas with mainline funds because (a) these funds are increasingly scarce, (b) City Challenge funds already far exceed those focused on other areas and (c) there are other deprived areas in need of resources

Private sector and community representation and effectiveness
- Simply having business and community representatives on a partnership board does not guarantee meaningful involvement
- The representatives are not necessarily representative (!) and may not have the confidence and support of their ostensible constituency
- The presence of community representatives does not mean they are equal partners: they often lack the skills, confidence or resources to challenge the other partners

Partnership issues
- The new partnership-based delivery bodies, because they only control administrative budgets and not the distribution of grants, are not as independent as City Challenge publicity material suggests
- The partnerships lack material incentives and sanctions to influence the behaviour of other agencies and must rely on unpredictable levels of goodwill
- The speed at which City Challenge has to run places heavy demands on all parties and can mean that the programme is bureaucratically driven

Some of the features of City Challenge underlay other initiatives. The concern with *inter-authority competition*, for example, was taken up for the temporary Urban Partnership Fund (UPF). In an uncharacteristic display of Keynesianism, the Government allowed local authorities to keep all capital receipts generated between November 1992 and January 1994 for capital spending that could boost the construction industries. To focus the spending of receipts, matching funding was created through the UPF. There was a national competition for local authorities in the 57 urban priority areas for one-off allocations, for 1993–94, to support projects that used capital receipts and UPF funding to:

- lever in private sector contributions
- complement projects financed under other national urban programmes or ones that remained unfinanced because they were part of unsuccessful City Challenge bids or relied on grant regimes that were being cut.

Another City Challenge feature – the pooling of grant regimes – underlay the creation of English Partnerships (EP)[22] EP was set up in summer 1993 and became fully operational in January 1994 when it took over the national administration of at least three budgets: Derelict Land Grant, City Grant and that of English Estates (the Department of Industry's agency for providing business space). EP is a halfway house between a national development agency (on the Welsh model) and an Urban Development Corporation. It can deploy resources anywhere in England and will rely on project ideas and bids from the public and private sectors. Whether it will act in close partnership with local authorities very much depends on the organisational culture EP develops for itself but there is no statutory requirement for it to do so.

The budgets of City Challenge, EP and Urban Development Corporations will be protected under the new system but the net effect of all the recent changes has been a significant redeployment of, not an increase in, national urban programme resources. The 'losers' in this redistribution (see Table 10.1) have been the Urban Development Corporations – the 1980s flagships – and the Urban Programme (UP). Eleven UDCs in England and Wales are due to be wound up during the 1990s. Only two – Birmingham Heartlands and Plymouth – have been designated in the last five years. It seems that UDCs, like Enterprise Zones before them, may be used for political 'firefighting' in future but are no longer the most prized national policy instrument. The UP, on the other hand, has been an important resource for local authorities but one that the DoE has found difficulty in controlling and in defending to a suspicious Treasury. From 1993–94, Urban Programme funding will only honour existing commitments. The termination of the UP, around 1996–97, will phase out the last grant regime to which local authorities are automatically entitled. It will reduce local authority's freedom of manoeuvre and is likely to have particularly drastic effects on the wide range of voluntary organisations that came to depend on it.

Local authority reactions to the new policy environment: the North West case

It would be impossible to show how *all* local authorities have adapted their economic development plans to the new urban policy environment. Instead, we concentrate on a sample of authorities in the North West of England.[23] The North West comprises four subregions whose recent economic fortunes show significant variation. The levels of unemployment in the subregions in 1993 were 8.8 per cent for Cheshire, 9.3 per cent for Lancashire, 10.9 per cent for Greater Manchester and 15.5 per cent for Merseyside. There are even greater differences between districts. This is reflected in the patter of urban policy assistance to the region. Cheshire has just one UP authority. In contrast, all five districts in Merseyside are UP authorities and the subregion also contains three City Challenges (Liverpool, Wirral and Sefton) and the Merseyside Development Corporation. It has long had Development Area status under national regional policy and it will shortly be the first area in Britain accorded Objective One status under the European Commission's regional policy. Between these two extremes are Greater Manchester (two City Challenge areas, two UDCs, five UP authorities, partial designation under regional policy) and Lancashire (two City Challenges, four UP authorities).

The most striking feature of the fifteen North West local authority economic development plans we examined was the similarity in strategic aims, objectives and procedures. Authorities covering areas as different in size and socioeconomic composition as Liverpool and Tameside, for example, pursue almost identical objectives based on attracting all available national resources, particularly to promote employment-creation, and trying to ensure that the benefits of programmes run by other agencies accrue to local people.[24] The statutory requirement on local authorities to consult on their plans – and to appear 'friendly' to a wide range of interests – might partially explain the apparent conversion of approaches.[25] But it primarily reflects constraints in the resources local authorities are able to mobilise. Authorities have abandoned ambitions to provide alternative, municipally led models of regeneration that might attract national government support and have instead taken on enabling, coordinating and lobbying functions in which:

- they play whatever role they are allowed in national initiatives
- the resources they control directly are used to plug perceived gaps, lever in extra resources and help promote a positive image of the area beyond its boundaries

Smaller authorities that receive few national resources are particularly affected by the Government's withdrawal of non-competitive funding schemes. The Commercial and Industrial Improvement Areas which were central to Hyndburn's efforts, for example, are now under threat from the run-down of the Urban Programme and it seems that UPF resources will not fill the gap, even in the short term. Local trusts and voluntary agencies that relied upon UP funds are now tend to eke out an existence from a precarious cocktail of funding from non-statutory sources (e.g. charities). Smaller authorities are increasingly withdrawing from the direct provision of finance or services and rely more on their powers of persuasion and their intelligence resources to galvanise and coordinate the efforts of others. The borough of Stockport, for example, whose development prospects are relatively bright thanks to its proximity to Manchester Airport, clearly advertises itself as a 'No Grant' authority. The majority of its services to business revolve around providing information (Business Information Desk, Stockport Business Venture) or coordinating other agencies who offer business support (Stockport Business Package).

Constrained resources mean that local authorities increasingly operate in partnership with other interests. These arrangements appear to work well where the main commodity involved is information and the local authority acts as a broker. Local authorities are important players in low-cost information networks in a number of fields, for example in increasing awareness of available support packages amongst local business communities (Lancaster and District Business Support Network), providing a more general interface between public and private organisations (Hyndburn Consultation Group) and international marketing (Stockport International Liaison Office). The performance of partnerships is more patchy in other fields. In the field of financial support for businesses, for example, some successful, small-scale, venture capital partnerships have emerged. The joint work of the metropolitan borough of Wigan and British Coal Enterprise through Wigan Metropolitan Development Company is one

example. Not all areas are covered by quasi-public sector finance
companies, though, and other initiatives in the financial field (e.g.
Greater Manchester Development Ltd) have had to close their
operations.

In the property field, many authorities have established good
relations with the quasi-public sector provider of business space,
English Estates. More ambitious property development partnerships
have also emerged. Ravenshead Renaissance in St Helens, for
example, is a partnership between landowners (major industrial
interests), the local authority, the Merseyside Task Force and
investors/developers that is restructuring an area of ex-industrial
land close to the town centre for new service and housing uses. For
every successful property partnership like this, however, there are
others struggling to cope with the recessionary climate and the
extreme caution of developers. The City Challenge programme in
Liverpool, for example, is heavily reliant on property schemes and
the benefits they can generate for surrounding communities. No
substantial private sector partners have yet committed themselves to
Liverpool's 'flagships', though, and the work completed thus far is
heavily reliant on public sector investment. Much the same goes for
the housing-led Hulme City Challenge. Here, a partnership between
the Housing Corporation, housing associations, ex-council tenants
and the local authority has produced impressive developments in the
social housing field. But both private housebuilders and retail
developers are wary of taking market risks – in the midst of a
recession – in an area that has had virtually no private investment
since the war.

Because so much of the finance for local development efforts is
locked up in discretionary funding packages, local authorities are
now heavily engaged in lobbying higher levels of Government. Not
all of this is focused on the 'beauty competitions' that can win urban
policy resources, such as the City Challenge bidding process. Many
authorities use public–private partnership groups to advance a
private, 'non-political' case to Government for mainstream funding[2]
in the hope that schemes backed by the business community will be
seen as opportunity-led and not simply as more special pleading by
the public sector. Attracting European structural funds[3] is also
becoming more important. Both Merseyside and Greater Manchester have had substantial EC regional funding through the
Integrated Development Operations (IDO) programme. IDOs have

the added advantage of requiring collaboration between neighbouring local authorities rather than encouraging inter-authority competition, as do national government programmes. A large proportion of development plans in St Helens, for example, is based upon European funds.[4]

Lobbying for EC funding is, in fact, but one aspect of the growing 'Europeanisation' of local government. A number of authorities have European liaison units that seek out and try to access EC funds, often through direct bargaining with Commission officials. Liverpool City Council, for example, was central to the coordinated lobbying operation that got the city redesignated under EC regional policy. Most authorities have also made some attempt to ensure that local firms are aware of relevant EC programmes and, more generally, of the business opportunities and threats posed by the single European market. In Manchester, the process has gone even further. The local authority is determinedly promoting Manchester as a major European city and is taking a more active part in the Eurocities network that links together local authorities across EC national boundaries. A number of interest groups in the city, encouraged by the local authority, are clearly trying to bypass regional and national audiences and play on an international stage.

Manchester is probably the North West's model city in terms of the new politics of local economic development. The city's high profile bid to attract the 2000 Olympics, for example, served a number of objectives, many of which were achieved despite Sydney's ultimate designation. Amongst other things, it:

- drew contributions, in cash and kind, from the private sector and provided a central and consensual civic theme around which a powerful coalition of city interests was cemented together, thus improving public–private sector relations
- got substantial national discretionary resources injected into the city which it would not otherwise have received whilst simultaneously improving the council's political standing with the Conservative Government
- triggered the development of top sports facilities and infrastrutural projects which begin the transformation of ex-industrial land in inner eastern Manchester, a priority area for regeneration
- presented a positive image of the city to an international audience

Tho Manchester case points up the one key difference between authorities in the North West: the level of ambition and competitiveness. Authorities in the larger urban centres are slowly developing a very aggressive, competitive approach based on ambitions about the *international*, rather than national or regional, economic roles they hope to develop. Only authorities such as those in Manchester and Liverpool, or the high-growth centres like Chester, can countenance playing this sort of high-stakes game in the hope that it will generate inward investment. In comparison, smaller authorities such as Hyndburn and Bury, though their powers are similar, have little choice but to focus their efforts on encouraging indigenous growth.

Local governance, urban policy and economic development

What, then, of the future of local authority economic policies and the local government role within urban policy? If we roll forward the trends outlined above, we can anticipate a policy making environment in the latter half of the decade which will be characterised by:

- constrained resources
- a high degree of fragmentation between local service providers
- a very limited *executive* role for local government
- a broader national policy agenda, going beyond purely physical change, but inadequately linked to the mainline programmes that impinge more heavily on patterns of urban change
- a system of support from central government which favours discretionary payments, competitive bidding and rewards for areas that display a high degree of public entrepreneurialism and 'partnership' and can, with limited help, attract market interest
- a growing role for the European Commission
- growing cross-national links between the larger and more ambitious urban authorities

The local authority remains the one player in an increasingly complex system of local governance with a local mandate and general responsibilities for the social and economic well-being of an area's inhabitants. The challenge for local government, in a period which should see less conflict with central government, will be to exercise leadership within this new system despite not having any formal authority to do so and whilst being unable to reward or discipline any of the other agencies or interests whose efforts are needed to promote change. Whatever successes local authorities are able to achieve in the way of promoting coherent strategies and inter-agency and public–private agreements, they will have to be built on local knowledge, bargaining capacity and the ability to present issues in such a way as to get others to cooperate out of self-interest. The development of City Challenge will no doubt reveal a number of possibilities for this delicate local authority balancing act, as well as any number of dead ends.

Even if local authorities are able to play their leadership-come-enabling role well, it will only overcome one aspect of policy fragmentation. The distribution of urban policy resources is focused at the district (even subdistrict) scale, so it would take enormous self-discipline and substantial mutual bargaining on the part of local authorities to encourage the coordination of effort on the sort of geographical scale that makes more economic sense than local authority boundaries.[28] Although there are limited signs of increased inter-authority collaboration,[29] the record of voluntary cooperation across local administrative boundaries is not good. Neither do UK governments show much interest in promoting regional or subregional solutions to urban problems.[30] It is therefore likely that local authorities will compete more and more aggressively with each other for public and private resources.

Indeed, inter-urban competition is likely to be one of the key themes of the 1990s. It will be in constant tension with another, that of urban social cohesion. The reasons for this are not *primarily* domestic, although the depth of public sector fragmentation created by Conservative reforms certainly heightens competition between different geographical areas and agencies. They are linked to wider shifts in the global economy, the changing roles and functions of national governments and the nature of modern labour markets.[31] The more critical British commentators often assume that the 'urban crisis' at home is worse than elsewhere and that successive Conservative governments, compared to their counterparts in other countries, have 'failed the cities'. The implication is that there are a number of obvious things that can be done to improve matters. If we look to the international experience, though, the reality is a little less comfortable.

National governments and subnational authorities across the advanced (post-) industrial nations have also been engaged in a desperate search for inexpensive solutions to urban problems in the past decade.[32] As in Britain, the most common response has focused on unlocking the economic potential of key urban areas. Some national governments have gone about this task in a more structured way. They have clearly identified the economic importance of cities to national economies that are increasingly difficult to influence through traditional macro-economic policy instruments. Subnational elected authorities have also usually been given more policy responsibilities than those in Britain. The fact remains, though, that policy-makers, like academic commentators, struggle to identify any causal link between the structures and patterns of decision-making for urban areas and economic success. No-one is very confident that they have got the 'institutional fix' right and experimentation remains the order of the day.[33]

Neither is there any simple correlation between urban–regional economic buoyancy and the life chances of city residents. The evidence of the past decade suggests that the changing nature of the labour market has substantially weakened the link between economic growth and the overall quality of urban life. Capital-intensive restructuring in manufacturing has destroyed large numbers of low-to-medium skilled jobs and only partially replaced them with higher-skilled occupations. Steady growth in services, meanwhile, has created employment at both ends of the skill spectrum. The net result has been a more polarised labour market. With many of the better employment opportunities taken by commuters, a growing number of less-skilled urban residents – even in ostensibly booming cities – have been consigned to unemployment or low-paid, insecure work. In short, we live in an age of divided cities. Once again, this concerns policy-makers within and beyond Britain but no one has come up with any magic formula to link the benefits of economic growth – if it can be achieved at all – with the needs of the ostensible targets of urban policies: the urban disadvantaged.

The tension between growth and social equity is likely to dominate the urban agenda of the 1990s in Britain and elsewhere. On the one hand, inter-urban competition, increasingly played out at the international level, will continue to drive urban policy to prioritise economic development, creating a series of dilemmas for policy-makers. National governments will have to decide:

- how important urban areas are to international economic competitiveness
- if and how they wish to reorganise or encourage subnational levels of government to support economic restructuring
- how far their interventions should be targeted spatially, rather than being the incidental spin-offs of decisions made on functional lines

Subnational authorities will need to decide:

- how to use their powers and influence within the wider system of local governance to achieve at least some of their aims through co-operation with other agencies and interests
- how far to compete and how far to collaborate with other localities, from neighbouring authorities to ones with similar characteristics in other countries

The dilemma is that it will be difficult to sustain widespread support for urban development initiatives, and they may ultimately be self-defeating even in purely economic terms, if they continue to be associated with labour market polarisation and social exclusion. The evidence from Britain suggests that national and local governments are now much closer to agreeing the validity of such questions, and even to providing some very tentative answers that they can both support, than they were ten years ago. It would be a huge surprise, though, if the same questions were not still being raised at the end of the decade.

Notes and references

1. *Action for Cities* (HMSO, 1988). The companion piece in Scotland was *New Life for Urban Scotland* (HMSO, 1988).
2. They were to: encourage enterprise and new businesses, and help existing businesses grow stronger; improve people's job prospects, their motivation and skills; make areas attractive to residents and businesses; and make inner-city areas safe and attractive places to live and work.
3. In England, the resources of national urban programmes are almost entirely concentrated within 57 designated local authority districts. The selection of priority areas has been more fluid in Scotland and Wales. They tend to be negotiated respectively between the Scottish Office,

Scottish Enterprise (and its network of Local Enterprise Companies) and Scottish local authorities or the Welsh Office, the Welsh Development Agency and Welsh local authorities

4. Rhodes, R. A. W. *Beyond Westminster and Whitehall: The Sub-central Government of Britain* (Unwin Hyman, 1988), p359.

5. Scottish Enterprise, formed in 1992, is an amalgamation of the former Scottish Development Agency – which had urban development responsibilities in the industrial and environmental fields – and the Training Agency's functions in Scotland. The bulk of its training and economic development functions are performed by 13 Local Enterprise Companies whose boards are dominated by business leaders. In England and Wales, training programmes remain separate from economic development ones. They are delivered by local Training and Enterprise Councils: again business-dominated boards which contract with the Government to deliver national training programmes.

6. For greater detail, see N. Deakin and J. Edwards, *The Enterprise Culture and the Inner City* (Routledge, 1993), T. Barnekov, R. Boyle and D. Rich, *Privatism and Urban Policy in Britain and the United States* (Oxford University Press, 1989); T. Brindley, Y. Rydin and G. Stoker, *Remaking Planning: The Politics of Urban Change in the Thatcher Years.* (Unwin Hyman, 1989); M. Campbell (ed.), *Local Economic Policy* (Cassell, 1990); A. Thornley, *Urban Planning Under Thatcherism: The Challenge of the Market* (Routledge, 1991).

7. The growing number of programmes that subsidise private property developments (City Grant, much of Derelict Land Grant, etc.) are demand-led and thus discriminate in favour of areas with economic potential.

8. The boards of Urban Development Corporations and Training and Enterprise Councils are business-dominated. Task Forces and City Action Teams are staffed by regional government officials.

9. See, for example, R. Batey, 'London Docklands: An Analysis of Power Relations between UDCs and Local Government', *Public Administration*, vol. 67, no. 2, 1989.

10. See A. Harding, 'Central Control in British Urban Development Programmes', in C. Crouch and D. Marquand (eds), *The New Centralism: Britain out of Step in Europe?* (Blackwell, 1989).

11. See the chapters by D. S. King and A. Harding in D. S. King and J. Pierre (eds), *Challenges to Local Government* (Sage, 1990); M. Mackintosh and H. Wainwright (eds) *A Taste of Power: The Politics of Local Economics* (Verso, 1989); J. Gyford, *The Politics of Local Socialism* (Allen & Unwin, 1985).

12. The general power, allowing a local authority to spend the product of a 2p rate in the interests of its area or inhabitants, was contained in Section 137 of the 1972 Local Government Act (Section 68 of the equivalent legislation in Scotland).

13. The leaders in the development of alternative municipal economic strategies – the Greater London Council and the six metropolitan

county councils – were even abolished in 1986. For more detail on central-local government relations in this field, see A. Harding, 'Spatially Specific Urban Economic Development Programmes in Britain since 1979', *West European Politics*, vol. 11, no. 1, 1988.

14. See S. Lansley, S. Goss and C. Wolmar, *Councils in Conflict: The Rise and Fall of the Municipal Left* (Macmillan, 1989).

15. The development of public–private partnerships was also helped by the greater degree of private sector self-organisation in cities encouraged by business groups like Business in the Community and the CBI (see B. D. Jacobs, *Fractured Cities: Capitalism, Community and Empowerment in Britain and America* (Routledge, 1992)) and by higher levels of property development of the later 1980s. On the politics of public–private partnerships, see A. Harding, 'The Rise of Urban Growth Coalitions, U.K.-style?', *Government and Policy*, vol. 9, no. 3, 1991; P. Cooke, 'Municipal Enterprise, Growth Coalitions and Social Justice', *Local Economy*, vol. 3, no. 3, 1988; M. G. Lloyd and D. A. Newlands, 'The "Growth Coalition" and Urban Economic Development', *Local Economy*, vol. 3, no. 1 (1988).

16. This could be achieved – in partnership with other agencies where appropriate – through the provision of property, grants, loans, guarantees, indemnities and the acquisition of share or loan capital.

17. The House of Commons Employment Committee, Session 1987–88, *Third Report on the Employment Effects of Urban Development Corporations, HC327-I*, for example, criticised UDCs for failing to link new employment to the labour market needs and aspirations of local residents.

18. See, for example, R. Imrie and H. Thomas, 'The Limits of Property-led Regeneration', *Environment and Planning C: Government and Policy*, vol. 11, no. 2, 1993

19. For general discussions, see M. Parkinson, 'City Challenge: A New Strategy for Britain's Cities?', *Policy Studies*, vol. 14, no. 2 (1993); L. De Groot, 'City Challenge: Competing in the Urban Regeneration Game', *Local Economy*, vol. 7, no. 3 (1992).

20. Government and local authority departments, Task Forces, Urban Development Corporations, Training and Enterprise Councils, City Action Teams, statutory undertakers and quangos, the Housing Corporation, housing associations, Chambers of Commerce, private developers and financiers, voluntary groups, residents associations etc.

21. See, for example, M. Parkinson, H. Russell and R. Evans, *Liverpool City Challenge: First Report of the Independent Evaluation Team* (Liverpool: EIUA, March 1993); A. Harding, *Hulme City Challenge: First Report of the Independent Monitoring Project* (Liverpool: EIUA, January 1993); R. Macfarlane and J. Mabbott, *City Challenge: Involving Local Communities* (NCVO, 1993)

22. Originally called the Urban Regeneration Agency.

23. Manchester, Stockport, Warrington, Chester, Lancaster, Blackburn, Bolton, Bury, Liverpool, Sefton, Hyndburn, St Helens, West Lancashire, Tameside, Wigan. For a similar, more comprehensive

review of Scottish authorities, see R. M. McQuaid, 'Economic Development and Local Authorities: The Scottish Case', *Local Economy*, vol. 8, no. 2 (1993).

24. For example, through promoting community enterprises, providing counselling and resource facilities for the unemployed and direct help for disadvantaged groups within the labour market, especially the long-term unemployed, young unemployed, disabled and ethnic minorities

25. See I. Newman, 'Surviving in a Cold Climate: Local Authority Economic Strategy Today', *Local Economy*, vol. 6, no. 4 (1991).

26. European Regional Development Fund (ERDF) and European Social Fund (ESF). Objective 1 and 2 areas, such as Merseyside and parts of Greater Manchester, are eligible for ERDF. ESF is available in all areas.

27. IDOs have the advantage of requiring collaboration between neighbouring local authorities rather than encouraging inter-authority compeition, as do national government programmes.

28. Current moves toward a unitary system of local government will not improve the 'fit' between local authority boundaries and travel-to-work areas.

29. Authorities in Greater Manchester, for example, have produced an economic development framework for the area in a bid to attract EC funding.

30. Whilst regional government offices will be encouraged to take a regional overview, there are few historical reasons to suggest they will do much more than referee inter-authority conflicts.

31. See A. Harding, J. Dawson, R. Evans and M. Parkinson (eds), *European Cities Towards 2000: Profiles, Policies and Prospects* (Manchester University Press, forthcoming)

32. On the European experience, see M. Parkinson, F. Bianchini, J. Dawson, R. Evans and A. Harding, *Urbanisation and the Functions of Cities in the European Community* (European Commission, 1993)

33. See A. Amin and N. Thrift, 'Globalisation, Institutional Thickness and Local Prospects', paper to the seminar on Challenges in Urban Management, Newcastle University, March 25-7, 1993; J. Peck and A. Tickell, 'Searching for a New Institutional Fix: The After-Fordist Crisis and Global–Local Disorder', in A. Amin (ed.), *Post-Fordism: A Reader* (Blackwell, forthcoming).

III WHAT PAST? WHAT FUTURE?

11 Fifteen Years of Local Government Restructuring 1979–94: An Evaluation

John Stewart and Gerry Stoker

Since coming to power in 1979 the Conservatives have sought to restructure the system of local government. The scale of change attempted has been extraordinary. Huge amounts of legislative time have been devoted to matters concerning local government. This chapter provides an evaluation of the process, progress and impact of central government-inspired change, drawing on the evidence and insights presented in Parts I and II of the book. We do not refer back to individual chapters unless it is not obvious where supporting evidence in the book is to be found.

The first section of the chapter examines the Conservatives' strategy of reform. The process of restructuring has depended on an evolving strategy. The strategy has been driven by broad, strong ideological preferences but has proved capable of pragmatically responding to conditions and circumstances. The nature of the strategy may in part explain some of the success in achieving change. We argue, however, that the process is becoming increasingly incoherent and prone to contradiction. After fifteen years of restructuring there is a need for a reassessment and a restatement of the purposes of local government and democracy.

The second argument of the chapter is concerned with organisational change. The extent to which the Conservatives have shaken the organisational foundations of the system cannot be denied. The organisational map of the system has been transformed but there is an emerging crisis of fragmentation. A third section notes evidence that points to the achievement of a managerial revolution in local authorities inspired by the Conservatives' reform package. The new management orthodoxy, however, has a number of serious weaknesses as well as some strengths.

A fourth section concentrates on the reform of local government finance. The degree of control available to central government is certainly greater than in the past. But the system is unstable and undermines local accountability. A fifth section considers some of the ambiguities and uncertainties that remain about the role and purpose of reform despite fifteen years of Conservative-led initiatives. The existence of contestable and contested areas reflects the influence of other factors on local authorities and the fact that they are political institutions in their own right.

An evolving strategy: the threat of incoherence

As argued in the Introduction to the book it is a mistake to see the Government as having a predetermined strategy which it has consistently put into practice. The Government has been informed by certain ideological stances – a mixture of liberal and conservative New Right positions as described in King's chapter. The agenda of change has also grown out of experience. Themes seen as successful are pursued further as in the case of legislation on competitive tendering which was extended from building work to various manual services and onwards to white collar functions. Policies have been adapted and changed to overcome resistance or implementation failure. The history of legislation in relation to local government finance provides a number of examples of this process of action and reaction.

Part of their success in pushing forward reform may well be that the Conservatives' strategy has been emerging rather than predetermined. Yet there is some unease even within government circles about the consistency and coherence of the Government's approach. Four dilemmas can be identified.

First, there has been some back-tracking which has meant the abandoning of previously cherished policy goals. The most obvious example is the case of the community charge. This reform was promoted as a mechanism for local accountability. On its demise it led to the creation of a system of local finance where accountability at the local level is totally undermined by the weakness of local revenue-raising capacity and the practice of near-universal capping. These arguments will be returned to later in the chapter.

Second, goal-shift in some policy areas has been so radical and rapid that the credibility of the Government's approach is difficult to sustain. Education is one area where the reforms of 1988 appear to have been subject to radical revision contributing to a fundamental shift of policy. The debate about the internal management of local authorities has seen post-Widdicombe legislation requiring that all committees should have a composition in proportion to the balance of parties on the council contradicted by proposals for a local cabinet system and other experimental forms of internal organisation. Urban policy is another area where there has been considerable shifting and changing over the past fifteen years.

Third, the variety of policy initiatives has led to contradictions and conflicts. The introduction of structural reorganisation, because of the complications it brings in its wake, led the Government in December 1993 to announce a substantial delay in implementing the planned extension to white-collar competitive tendering in England. A similar delay has also been announced for Wales and Scotland. In the case of England the first wave of white-collar services will be subject to competition in October 1998 rather that the previous deadline of October 1995.

Fourth, the complexity and scale of what has been attempted has led to a range of unintended or unanticipated consequences. The growth in the number and scale of local quangos is probably more substantial than any government minister or official imagined. The development of voluntary transfer in the housing field appears to have been a policy development which was not foreseen by legislation. The development of a system of community care has been made more difficult by the Government's attempts to control public spending.

The Government's policy style has brought it some success. Its willingness to let its initiatives evolve have given its legislative programme a cutting edge and helped to sustain a momentum of change. Yet the difficulties and dilemmas are mounting. There is a concern that the overall role of local government and democracy is not being considered. It seemed that the review launched by Heseltine on his return to the Department of the Environment in 1990 might spell out the overall implications of the programme but it failed to provide a clear statement or vision. The lack of a clear point or purpose is particularly evident in the case of the

Government's commitment to structural reorganisation. The Government's approach to changing local government has certainly been inconsistent; it is becoming increasingly incoherent.

Changing the organisation map: a crisis of fragmentation

The Conservatives have achieved a considerable amount of organisational change. The institutional map of local government has been transformed. It is possible to refer to the creation of a system of 'local governance' in which local authorities find themselves increasingly working alongside a range of other agencies in their localities. The system has become increasingly differentiated as new agencies and organisations have been given responsibilities which previously belonged to local authorities or as existing institutions have been removed from the control of local authorities and health authorities.

Training and Enterprise Councils took over local authorities' responsibilities in further education for training. Institutions of further education along with sixth form colleges have been constituted as corporate bodies in their own right, following the previous removal of what were then polytechnics and are now universities. In specific areas, Urban Development Corporations and Housing Action Trusts have assumed with the support of central government funds responsibilities for renewal and development. For other functions local authorities have been required to set up companies to take over responsibilities in public transport, airports and waste disposal, sometimes as a means towards privatisation. Provisions for opting out of the control of local authorities and health authorities have led to the creation of grant-maintained schools and hospital trusts as free-standing institutions. As of January 1994 there were 553 grant-maintained secondary and 259 grant-maintained primary schools in England.

The abolition of the metropolitan counties led to the creation of a series of joint boards covering police, fire, public transport and waste disposal. These boards consist of councillors appointed by the constituent authorities but they have their own identity and legal status. The abolition of the Greater London Council led to the creation of a joint board for fire, while London Transport had been removed from the control of the Greater London Council prior to abolition The metropolitan police had always been directly accountable to the Home Secretary. In other fields of London government covering land-use planning and roads, central government has significantly greater powers than elsewhere.

Local authorities themselves have created arms-length agencies, often to involve the private sector. In some cases these have been set up under the direct influence of central government; in other cases they have been a separate response, but influenced by the Government promotion of the involvement of the private sector in environmental improvement and urban regeneration. In other cases changes have reflected local authorities' own interest in economic development and user involvement.

As a result of these changes, the structure of local governance has not merely become increasingly differentiated but more complex with an increasing variety of organisational forms. Stoker[1] has distinguished between:

Central government's arms-length agencies
Local authority implementation agencies
Public private partnerships
User organisations
Inter-governmental forums
Joint boards.

We would now add self-governing institutions in the form of grant-maintained schools, hospital trusts and colleges of further education.

The pattern of organisational restructuring will be further promoted by the process of local government reorganisation launched in the early 1990s. As well as creating a new pattern of authorities this process is also likely to result in the creation of various joint boards and committees.

The emerging structure of local governance marks out a lessening of the role of local authorities within that structure. Even after the 1974 local government reorganisation local authorities remained the key institutional actors in their localities. This supremacy is now under challenge as local authorities share strategic decision-making and service provision in many policy areas with other institutions. In the past the range of responsibilities and legitimacy held by local authorities made them relatively dominant within the overall system, even though there were other agencies involved in providing local services.

The increasing differentiation, along with the weakening of the relative position of local authorities, represents a fragmentation within the overall system. Differentiation has the strength of specialisation and focus. Organisations have a clear if bounded task and bring relevant expertise to that task. But a system of governance has to have a capacity for integration as well as differentiation. The relative weakening of the position of local authorities in the system reduces the capacity for integration through a multi-purpose if not an all-purpose authority.

Many of the new agencies of local governance are subject to direct influence from central government through the appointment of their controlling boards or by way of their funding coming directly or indirectly from the centre. Central government, however, cannot readily provide integrative mechanisms at the local level. The integrative mechanisms of central government, which have themselves often been criticised, focus on the central government departments, the Cabinet and its committees, and processes of consultation. They do not, however, provide integrative mechanisms at the local level.

The need for local integrative mechanisms appears to be accepted by the Conservatives. In November 1993 the Government announced plans to pool the urban and regional budgets of six central departments under the supervision of a new cabinet committee. The administration and management of the budget is to be provided by ten regional offices each headed by a senior regional director. In education, social services and housing similar integrative mechanisms at the regional level are under active consideration.

There are grounds for thinking that these *ad hoc* attempts at integration are inadequate. Moreover, they ignore the potential role that local authorities might play because of their local knowledge, their experience of coordinating and networking in their areas, their capacity for civic leadership and their legitimacy as elected and accountable bodies.[2] In the light of complex social and economic challenges and an increasingly differentiated polity there is a strong argument for bringing local authorities back in to provide a framework in which other agencies and organisations can pursue their specific aims.

A revolution in management: problems and limitations

If the role of local authorities in the system of local governance is changing so is their way of working. A new pattern of working is emerging under the impact of the legislative changes brought about by the Conservative Government and the ideas generated by that legislation. The main dynamic of that change has come from compulsory competitive tendering both in its indirect and direct impacts. It is not that compulsory competitive tendering has led to a high proportion of the work of the authority being contracted out, it is rather that gearing up for competition has led to significant changes in the ways of working within authorities.

Rather than direct control of the service, the role of the client who specifies requirements has been separated from that of the contractor who provides the service to meet those requirements. The relationship between them is governed by the contract which is monitored by the client. Where the contract is made with a direct service organisation of the local authority, that organisation requires and is normally given a degree of freedom from detailed financial and personnel controls to enhance its competitive position. It will develop business plans to ensure its viability. Rather than pay overheads to cover the costs of central services, it will make a service-level agreement covering the services it requires at a specified cost.

The changes in social services again separate the provision of the need for services from an assessment of services. The introduction of local management of schools involves the devolution of budgets, giving boards of governors freedom from detailed financial controls and making many of the support services dependent upon the school as client.

These developments represent a marked departure from past ways of working based on control through hierarchy. What is emerging is management through contracts. The old system of direct overseeing of provision is giving way to a more indirect, arms-length form of management.[3]

The scale and extent of change is confirmed by a Local Government Management Board survey of local authorities undertaken in 1992–3.[4] Competition requirements along with other legislative measures emerge as the strongest motivators for change. The survey found considerable evidence of across-the-board changes with a reduction in the number of departments and subcommittees in many authorities since 1989. The changes detected within service areas were spectacular. In housing, social services and education almost all authorities have reconstructed in the face of new requirements.

> The near-universality of this experience is striking; only four among 292 housing departments responding to the survey had not restructured; this was true of just one social services department and of none of the education departments.[5]

Restructuring has involved establishing client/contractor splits, better provisions for performance review, attempts at customer-orientated provision, mechanisms for user feedback and techniques for managing individual performance. The spread of individual changes reflects a complex pattern. Just 12 per cent of authorities, for example, reported a high use of performance related pay for their white-collar staff.[6] The authors conclude their report with the comment:

> We have mapped the extent of the change that has occurred on a wide range of indicators. It cannot be gainsaid that the magnitude of that change has been huge.[7]

The development of contracting out, the devolution of management and a growing emphasis on the enabling role have necessarily had an impact on the work of committees and of councillors. The work of committees has been divided between the client and contractor roles, with service committees playing the former role focusing upon the requirements from a service and on monitoring whether those requirements are being met, while the contractor roles are controlled through management boards or committees giving greater freedom to management. This has supported a tendency to define the roles of councillors as concerned with strategic management and monitoring performance, although it is not a definition all councillors are ready to accept. Nor does it necessarily take account of the representative role of the councillor.

Other changes as a result of government legislation on policy have had their impact. In the development of policy in community care the inspection role has been separated from the role of provision or

indeed care assessment. The argument for these changes is the need
to ensure the independence of inspectorate, which if associated with
provision can be 'contaminated' by it. A similar argument justified
the removal of local authorities' direct responsibility for waste
disposal, while maintaining their regulatory role. These changes add
to the differentiation within the authority and can secure a new
emphasis on the inspectorate and regulatory roles within local
authorities. Yet while the separation of inspectorate services has a
clear rationale in protecting their independence, there is a danger
that the learning, advice and experience of those services may come
to play less part in the formulation of policy. This is another, if
different, example of the danger that differentiation can lead to
fragmentation.

The changes described above have led, under the impact of
changing management ideas, to an emerging pattern of management
which is becoming the new orthodoxy. The local authority:

- adopts a statement of organisational values
- emphasises closeness to the customer
- develops strategic management to guide the working of the
  authority
- adopts many ways of working, not necessarily assuming an
  authority has to provide a service directly
- devolves management and budgetary responsibility to separate
  cost centres within specified policies
- introduces trading units for the provision of support services
- governs an increasing range of internal relationships by contracts
  or quasi-contractual arrangements
- stresses performance management holding cost centres and
  trading units accountable for predetermined targets
- emphasises total quality management

This emerging pattern of management has powerful arguments in
its favour. The clarification of policy implied by strategic management and the devolution of management responsibility can be seen
as an expression of local government. Too often in the past
committee agendas turned the attention of councillors away from
what is needed from a service, towards how the service should be
run. The specification of requirements makes possible the
devolution of management responsibilities, releasing management

initiative to achieve aims that are set by the political process and within an organisation culture that can give expression to the values of local government. It also makes possible the monitoring of performance and quality. Indeed, it can be argued that separating the purchaser and provider highlights that task which was neglected in the traditional workings of local authorities because the purchaser was also the provider and committees came to identify with the services for which they were responsible rather than with those for whom the service was provided.

The emphasis on the public as customer supports that change of emphasis and opens up the local authority, which in the past was often enclosed within its own procedures. In a different way the recognition that a local authority has an enabling role and need not provide a service directly opens up the local authority to new ways of working.

In these and in other ways the new orthodoxy can be argued to be enhancing the management of local authorities and not merely as local administration but as local government or the expression of local choice. There are however problems in the changes being brought about which derive from three factors.

The first is the danger that the uncritical adoption of the private sector model can lead to a neglect of the distinctive purposes, conditions and tasks of the public domain. To describe, as the Audit Commission has done, developments in management under the title 'The Competitive Council'[8] illustrates the point. A local authority may have to compete in certain spheres, but not as client or when it acts in partnership with other organisations. Nor does the word 'customer' necessarily capture the varying relations between a local authority and its publics. It can conceal the reality that for many services there are more than one customer, whose needs have to be balanced. Who after all is the customer of the school – child, parent, future employer or all three? A local authority imposes as well as services, rations as well as provides. In local government service for the customer has to be balanced against other public purposes.

The second danger is the assumption of universalism or that the same approach to management can govern the whole range of local authority services. In the past the public has been described not as customer, but as client, applicant, user, patient, appellant, suspect, prisoner. It may well be that these words were describing different relationships which are hidden by the use of a single word, customer.

Different activities have to be managed in different ways. One does not manage a home help service in the same way as a fire service. Yet it can easily be assumed that the emerging orthodoxy requires just that. Thus, while contracts have a value in governing certain internal relationships, it can too readily be assumed they should govern all relationships. Experience in the private sector itself suggests that contracts play a role but not a universal role in relationships within or external to organisations.

Developing this theme, the third danger is on over reliance on control through contracts. A local authority will become a series of separate units which conduct their relationships through a series of contractual or semi-contractual arrangements. Each unit will have its own defined task and there will be little or no capacity to look beyond the units or to consider the relationship between them. The result could be a loss of community perspective. Moreover, learning will not easily flow across the boundaries of the fragmented authorities since the responsibilities of the separate units will be limited to their area of concern. The contractors will only inform the clients, if it is in their interest to do so. Learning is necessary if local authorities are to be able to adjust their activities (and their contracts) in relation to the needs and problems of local communities.

Further it is uncertain whether the whole or perhaps even most of the governing process can be reduced to contractual terms. Flexibility and adaptability are conditions of governing in a rapidly changing society. Contracts can be renegotiated but at a cost, which reduces the benefit of contracting. In the final resort a contractor is responsible for fulfilling a contract, but carrying out the contract can be an inadequate response to a crisis in government.

Local finance: central control and the loss of local accountability

The system of control over local government spending is more substantial in 1994 that it has been before. Local taxation in 1993–4 accounted for only about 20 per cent of total local authority income. The remainder of local authority income came from central government and other nationally distributed sources. The break-down was 28 per cent from national non-domestic or business rates,

10 per cent from specific central government grants, 1 per cent from the community care grant and 41 per cent from the general revenue support grant provided by central government. The heavy reliance on non-local revenue creates a substantial opportunity for central government to dictate the level of local spending in aggregate terms. In addition it is able to influence the spending decisions of individual authorities through defining what needs to be spent by way of an annual Standard Spending Assessment (SSA) and by holding capping powers over local budgets to ensure that they do not rise above government-approved levels.

These draconian measures have delivered an increasing degree of control over local spending. Indeed some authorities have had to make drastic cuts. Others protected programmes through various measures and engaged in what is referred to as 'creative accounting'. They have become expert in juggling the books so that the figures for spending match government targets but resources continue to flow to local services. A report for the Joseph Rowntree Foundation found the level of 'overspending' as defined by central government was in 1993–94 virtually identical to that in 1985–86.[9] However over time the scope for creative accountancy has been greatly reduced through new controls and through the costs imposed by the past use of that practice. The threat of capping is giving central government much greater control.

Control has been bought at the price of local accountability. This is the central message of the 'Coventry Declaration' which emerged from a conference organised by the local authority associations in June 1993. With most revenue-raising powers outside local hands and extensive central government capping powers the concept of local choice and therefore local accountability over spending is untenable. Further the system of SSAs has been heavily criticised for being based on difficult-to-defend calculations about local needs. As one speaker at the Coventry conference, a Conservative councillor, put it: 'No-one really knows what the criteria are for SSA decisions. SSAs are like the SAS, shrouded in mystery and secrecy'.[10]

The problems of the SSA system and lack of accountability were also dealt with at length in a critical report by the Audit Commission published in 1993[11] and the Government has responded by setting up a review into its operation. There appears to be some recognition in ministerial circles that the undermining of local accountability is a serious issue.

Contestable and contested areas: uncertainty surrounding the direction of change

It should be remembered that there were other influences upon local authorities, apart from central government legislation. The broad pattern of social and economic changes, shifts in the dominant pattern of management thought and influences from the European Union all have a part to play. Local authorities moreover are political institutions in their own right, developing their response to local needs and problems as well as to central government legislation. We have suggested there is an emerging pattern of local governance and a new orthodoxy of management in local government. However there are also areas which are contested where the meanings to be attached to words or phrases are subject to very different interpretation and where the best way forward is a matter of debate.

The public as customer or citizen

The public can be seen as customer, but the public can also be seen as citizen. The White Paper on the Citizen's Charter, although it uses the word citizen, sees the citizen as a customer. Its emphasis is on the individual user of the services and seeks to give the user as many or as few rights as the customer in the market. The emphasis on the public as customer – whether deriving from the Citizen's Charter or from a local authority's own initiatives – has had a useful impact in opening up the local authority. It has led to a concern for access for the public. Local authorities have sought to learn the public's views on the services they receive through surveys or through other methods. They have set out the standards of service they aim to achieve. In these and other ways local authorities have sought to build services responsive to the customer.

Yet the adequacy of that approach can be challenged by an emphasis on the public as citizen. The citizen has rights that differ from those of the customer. They are not merely the right to vote, but also the right to know, the right to explanation, the right to be heard, the right to be listened to and the right to be involved. To an advocate of this view an emphasis on the individual customer is not enough. Local authorities undertake collective action which rests for its justification and legitimacy on the support of the citizenry.

The customer and citizen perspectives are not necessarily always opposed. They are both oriented towards opening up the authority to the public. Collective action can leave space for responsive service and to that extent the public is both customer and citizen. Yet while a balance can be sought the Conservatives' agenda as it stands neglects the role of the citizen.

The enabling authority

The enabling authority can be given a wide variety of meanings. At one extreme is the position taken by Nicholas Ridley in the title to his pamphlet *The Local Right: Enabling not Providing.*[12] The task of the enabling authority was to get other organisations to provide services and carry out its responsibilities. Another model is based on enabling communities to resolve their problems and meet their needs in the most effective way.[13] The second approach differs from the first in not ruling out the possibility that the authority will provide services directly. The test is which is the most effective way. Both however share a rejection of the assumption of self-sufficiency that given a responsibility the local authority should necessarily discharge that responsibility directly, itself employing all the staff required.

There is another critical difference of greater relevance as the fragmentation of the system of local governance grows. Whereas the Ridley model is basically focused on the services provided by the authority and is concerned with the way they are delivered the alternative model focuses on communities and the way their needs are met. It is therefore concerned with the wide range of agencies through which those needs are met. The broader concept of enabling rests on an assertion of the role of the local authority to act as a representative of its local community. In undertaking this role it has the right to call other agencies to account in terms of how far they are meeting the needs and concerns of the area.

The principle of subsidiarity

European influence shows itself in interest in the principle of subsidiarity. The principle can be seen as government ministers use it to define the relationship between the European Union and national governments. However that is to restrict the relevance and the meaning of the principle. As Norton has argued:

It is a universal principle: applicable to levels of organisation from the United Nations through all intervening bodies down to the individual person. It puts first the placing of responsibilities for action as close as can be reasonably justified to the individual citizen. It therefore favours the smaller organisation rather than the larger: the level at which the individual counts most. It has the implication for government structures that institutions that serve the community should lie as close to the individual as is compatible with other priorities. It is not confined to public bodies but extends and gives priority to voluntary and other private bodies where it is to the general good that a function should be outside the public sector.[14]

The principle does challenge the growth of central control. However, in applying the principle local authorities have also to consider its meaning for their own working and its implications for their relations with communities and individuals. What is at stake is the devolution of power as opposed to organisational decentralisation to enhance management responsibilities and effectiveness. Subsidiarity is ultimately about a new relationship between governors and the governed.

Public accountability

There is an emerging crisis of accountability in the system of local governance. The overall effect of the changes is to reduce local accountability. There is a combination of two factors. The first is the reduction of local choice given the assumption of responsibility by central government for local expenditure decisions taken by local authorities and also the decisions taken by many of the new institutions of local governance. The second is the growth of a new magistracy, or lay elite appointed to the rising number of local quangos or appointed boards. They constitute the new unknown local governors overseeing in total public spending equivalent to that of elected local government.[15]

The Conservatives reject the charge that increased central control and the rise of appointed bodies represents a decline in accountability. William Waldegrave, a government minister,[16] argues that the emerging system is more accountable because:

1. Central government has taken the responsibility for laying down the framework and ground rules for what should be provided. In the case of the National Curriculum, for example, parents are able to clearly see what is expected. The Government is accountable for the broad framework, individual schools for the standards of teaching within that framework.
2. More information is provided to the citizen. Again in the case of education parents are entitled to a full written report once a year on their child, comparative examination results and truancy tables. Knowledge of this sort gives parents the opportunity to hold service providers to account.
3. The creation of a new magistracy of appointed members broadens the base and creates identifiable local figures in terms of those drawn in to oversee services. It brings in local people with different expertise, skills and interests. Members of school governing bodies are, for example, likely to run a school more efficiently, effectively and with a greater sense of responsibility to pupils and parents than officials within the local council structure.

Critics, however, can suggest counter-arguments to each of the above claims. The more prominent role for central government overburdens a relatively small group of ministers and civil servants with responsibilities and authority which they may be unwilling to accept. Reserving the right to make policy to the centre and placing all other agencies, including local authorities, into the role of implementation creates a long and unsustainable line of accountability. Ministers lack the time, capacity and legitimacy to rule when local disputes arise as they always will. Moreover they lack local knowledge and flexibility to match policies to local circumstances.

Providing more information can help aid accountability as long as the information is of adequate quality. Yet the rise of appointed boards is not always accompanied by the kind of information provision and open access associated with the best practice of local authorities. Meetings of some appointed bodies are not subject to the same level of external scrutiny – by the media and by the public – as is commonplace in local authorities

Waldegrave's position can be seen as confusing the prospect of customer satisfaction with the requirements of public accountability. It may be that appointed bodies (especially if provided additional funding by central government) will in some cases offer better service. If they fail to satisfy, however, local citizens have few options to bring them to account. Many of the key decision-makers, whether appointed lay-persons or managers, will be unknown to the public. Nor is there in most cases a strong local mechanism to remove them from office.

The emerging of a system of local governance is creating a confusing pattern of accountability. Appointed bodies are both accountable to central government and at the same time claim local accountability. The variety and mix of organisations leads to uncertainty in the public's mind about who is responsible for what. Local government reorganisation is not going to resolve this problem. The impending crisis in accountability derives from confusion as to where accountability lies, the growing weakening of local accountability and the increasing burden of accountability on ministers which stretches the doctrine of ministerial responsibility to breaking point. The contestable and contested area is how to give new meaning to public accountability.

Conclusions

The Conservatives have changed the face of local government. The key driving forces for change have been central government legislation and shifts in managerial thought. The key changes have been in institutional arrangements, management systems and an attempted assertion of control by central government.

Throughout 'ordinary' citizens have largely been on the sidelines with occasional demonstrations of support as in the case of council house sales or forthright opposition as in the case of the poll tax. The new system that is emerging is not the haven of consumer sovereignty and active citizenship dreamt of by the liberal wing of New Right think-tanks. Equally supporters of local government must be chastened by the relative lack of interest of the public as measure after measure undermined *their* local council. Even the reorganisation debate has attracted only modest and locally specific public interest.

Ordinary service providers in local government might also regard themselves as victims rather than instigators of change. They have found themselves criticised for their self-interest and inefficiency. A MORI survey for the Local Government Management Board in 1993[17] revealed considerable disquiet about the future of local government: 65 per cent were pessimistic about future morale and 52 per cent described themselves as pessimistic about the future of local authorities (only 12 and 18 per cent respectively identified themselves as being optimistic). A considerable amount of change has been coped with and undoubtedly some employees have relished the challenge of competition or customer-orientation. But there are signs that change fatigue may be setting in. There are also deeper issues about the nature of public service in light of the encouragement of a more commercial ethos. There is a danger that the commitment to the public and ethical standards of the old system may be lost.

The rebuilding of a case for local government and democracy needs to start from a realistic assessment of the position of these groups – the public and the providers – who have thus far stayed on the sidelines. Their interests are not wholly incompatible. A more responsive and effective system of local government and democracy would emerge if their interests were given more prominent and soundly based expression.

Notes and references

1. See G. Stoker, *The Politics of Local Government*, 2nd edn (Macmillan, 1991) ch. 3.
2. For a development of this argument see G. Stoker and S. Young, *Cities in the 1990s* (Longman, 1993) ch. 1.
3. For an early discussion of management by contract see G. Mather, 'Thatcherism and Local Government: An Evaluation', in J. Stewart and G. Stoker (eds), *The Future of Local Government* (Macmillan, 1989) pp. 232–4.
4. See K. Young and L. Mills, *A Portrait of Change* (Local Government Management Board, 1993).
5. Ibid., p. 19.
6. Ibid., p. 36.
7. Ibid., p. 65.

8. The Audit Commission, *The Competitive Council* (HMSO, 1988).
9. R. Hale and Associates *The Effect of Standard Spending Assessments* (Joseph Rowntree Foundation, 1993).
10. See *Association of Metropolitan Authorities News*, No. 739, (July 1993) p. 80.
11. The Audit Commission, *Passing the Bucks* (HMSO, 1993).
12. See N. Ridley, *The Local Right: Enabling not Providing* (Centre for Policy Studies, 1988).
13. See J. Stewart and G. Stoker, *From Local Administration to Community Government*, Fabian Research Series 351 (Fabian Society, 1988) and M. Clarke and J. Stewart, *The Enabling Council* (Local Government Training Board, 1988).
14. A. Norton, *The Principle of Subsidiarity and its Implications for Local Government* (Local Government Management Board, 1992).
15. For a development of these arguments see J. Stewart, *The Rebuilding of Public Accountability* (European Policy Forum, 1992); J. Stewart, 'Defending Public Accountability', *DEMOS Quarterly* (Winter, 1993); H. Davis and J. Stewart, *The Growth of Government By Appointment Implications for Local Democracy* (Local Government Management Board, 1993); K. Morgan and E. Roberts, *The Democratic Deficit: A Guide to Quangoland* (Department of City and Regional Planning, University of Wales College of Cardiff, 1993). The phrase 'the new magistracy' was first used by Bob Morris. See B. Morris, *Central and Local Control of Education after the Education Reform Act* (Longman, 1990).
16. W. Waldegrave, *The Reality of Reform and Accountability in Today's Public Service* (Public Finance Foundation, 1993).
17. MORI, *Employee Attitudes in Local Government* (Local Government Management Board, 1994).

12 The Post-Fordist Local State: The Dynamics of its Development

Gerry Stoker and Karen Mossberger*

The starting point of this chapter is that the post-Fordist literature has a reasonable claim to have most effectively captured the broad complexity of the changes that are occurring in the system of local governance. The first two sections of the chapter re-state the main contributions of regulation theory in this area and provide a brief specification of the Conservative-inspired post-Fordist local state that appears to be emerging. The remainder of the chapter is devoted to examining just how messy, problematic and uneven the process of change has been and is likely to continue to be. The brave proclamation of a 'Post-Fordist Local State' in the title of the chapter is heavily qualified by a concern to understand the complex and uncertain processes involved in its development.

The dynamics of development are influenced by the attempt at a 'vertical' imposition of change by central government and complex 'horizontal' processes reflecting different conditions in different localities. The second half of the chapter presents and explores a typology of local response and characterises differences in local authorities according to whether they are early adherents, pragmatic or critical compliers or late adopters. The aim is to explore the differential diffusion of post-Fordist local government in Britain.

---

*An earlier version of this chapter was presented at the 'Towards a Post-Fordist Welfare State' conference, University of Teesside, Middlesbrough, 17/18 September 1992. Presentations were also made at Manchester University and Glasgow Caledonian University. The authors are grateful for helpful comments and criticisms made at these presentations. They are also grateful for the funding provided by Strathclyde University which enabled Karen Mossberger to be Gerry Stoker's research assistant during the academic year 1992–93.

The contribution of regulation theory

Regulation theory has proved itself useful in clarifying changes in the form of local governance and the changing place of local governance in the overall national and international political system. Such a presentation eschews a narrow focus on changes in labour processes and systems of industrial production and opts for a broad concern with changes in the 'general pattern of social organisation'. The regulationist account takes as a starting point changes in the organisation of the economy but moves on to consider developments and trends in social and political structures. Together these structures interact and influence one another in a complex way. The changing system of local governance is affected by these developments and at the same time its institutions have the ability to intervene in the process. Moreover a system of local governance may have a central role in establishing the stability of a particular system of regulation.

Starting with the work of Aglietta regulationist theory has developed in many different directions but especially relevant to those with an interest in the state is the work of Lipietz and Jessop.[1] A number of writers have sought to apply insights from regulation theory to the position of local government and the changing nature of intergovernmental relations.[2] The regulationist approach views the role of the state and local government as the product of social struggle in an unstable society. The role of the state and other economic and social institutions may reflect the strategic ambitions of key political forces but roles are also defined by the unintended and unanticipated outcomes of political conflict. The coming together of a set of mutually supporting institutional arrangements and social structures 'are chance discoveries made in the course of human struggles and if they are for a while successful, it is only because they are able to ensure a certain regularity and a certain permanence in social reproduction'.[3] The theory combines a dynamic of human struggle and conflict with a recognition that certain social and political arrangements are conducive to societal functioning. The tensions and conflicts of developing capitalism are such that the emergence of a relatively stable system of institutions and social relations (a mode of social regulation) to manage and sustain the conditions for sustained economic growth is problematic. Any mode of social regulation is prone to break down and collapse.

The changing pattern of local governance can be examined in the context of this complex historical process.

Regulation theory argues that from a period stretching roughly from the 1930s to the early 1970s a relatively stable model of social regulation was established in capitalist societies although the timing and pattern of development varied between nation states. The label 'Fordist' is given to this period of mass production and consumption. Regulationists see a distinctive role for the state in the Fordist period. State intervention in the economy to manage and sustain demand for, and provide the infrastructure necessary to, mass production is seen as essential. The state also takes an increased role through the collective provision of education, health, housing and Income Support. This increased role is seen as the product of several forces. In part it reflects working-class demands for better social conditions. Yet the welfare state is also essential to the Fordist regime of mass production and consumption. It enables the workforce to support and reproduce themselves and their dependants while at the same time operating the long working hours demanded by the economic system. It also helps to sustain the norm of consumption, providing the social stability and security in which mass consumption could flourish. Local government because of its key role in Britain in organising and operating the welfare state has a core part in the Fordist mode of social regulation. It has also been influenced by the dominant organisational ethos of the era to develop a commitment to large-scale, hierarchically controlled, standardised service provision.

The changed context for local governance in the 1980s is explained by the gradual collapse of Fordism. The implications for local government are at base a challenge to its established role. The old mode of regulation is breaking down and new institutions are emerging. 'Cautious' versions of the argument stress that the emerging developments do not necessarily lead to a major role for a new post-Fordist local government and indeed the particular thrust of changes and Conservative government policies may be antipathetic to the attempt to establish a new regime to support sustained economic growth.[4] More 'heroic' versions of the argument identify a new role for local government in an emerging post-Fordist system. This new role is a product of a Thatcher-initiated attempt 'to change the role and functions of local government to make its activities, organisation and orientation compatible with the flexible economic structures, two-tier welfare system and enterprise culture which in the Thatcher vision constitute the key to a successful future for the UK'.[5] Local government also finds itself influenced by new management thinking, stimulated by the breakdown of Fordism, and so seeks to change its management systems to meet the new demands of customer-orientation and flexibility.

Criticism of this regulationist interpretation has been made on two main grounds. First it is argued that the Fordist/post-Fordist distinction is misleading and inadequate as a historical interpretation.[6] The depiction of the Fordist period ignores counter-evidence and features that do not fit. The speculation about post-Fordism seizes on selected examples and is long on hype and short on substance. Above all it is misleading to think of history in such binary terms. The second main criticism is that the mechanisms driving change in the model are not clear. Cochrane argues:

> It sometimes looks as if the theorists of post-Fordist local government . . . want to have it both ways: on the one hand the theoretical approach implies a structural shift, whose key features can be identified from first principles; but as soon as its proponents are accused of determinism, or it is suggested that some of the changes it appears to predict are not taking place, then the notion of post-Fordism becomes increasingly slippery.[7]

Defenders of the regulationist approach have been able to reply to these two criticisms but have conceded some ground. First the Fordist/post-Fordist paradigm can be defended as a simplified depiction which nevertheless captures significant elements in the history of modern capitalist societies.[8] Painter and Goodwin[9] offer an empirical defence in support of the existence of an era of Fordism in Britain stretching from the 1950s to the early 1970s. They concede that the notion of post-Fordism (as indeed many recognise) is problematic but argue that regulation theory does not necessarily require a new mode of social regulation to emerge. The point about lack of clarity with respect to the driving forces of change finds more purchase. The open-ended process and unintended outcomes which underlie the regulationist depiction of change provide hints as to the relevant factors but not a coherent statement. Reference to 'chance discoveries' avoids the charge of determinism but leaves a considerable vacuum in the attempt to explain change. Even critics, however, are moved to comment – 'It is nevertheless important to acknowledge that these debates [about post-Fordist local government] have drawn attention to significant changes which are taking place, and have taken the important first steps of relating local government to those changes.[10]

The centralised Conservative road to the post-Fordist local state

A distinctive feature of the British response to the decline of Fordism is the prominent role taken by the nation state in leading the way in the search for new ways forward. This observation is particularly apt when considering the changing form of local governance. A series of reforms, initiated by central government since 1979, can be seen as a Conservative attempt to impose a new role on local government to meet the demands of a changing political economy.

The process is complicated by at least two factors. First, the strategic vision of the Conservatives has not always been clear and the jumble of initiatives and experiments reflect a variety of motivations that include short-term political concerns. Nevertheless it is possible to discern some vision behind the reform programme. Second, local authorities and other interests have not simply been passive recipients of change but have sought themselves to respond to the new environment in which they find themselves. In many instances the Conservatives have either taken forward and extended local developments of which they approve or in other cases they have moved to close down options of which they disapprove.

Bearing in mind these qualifications and recognising that what is being described is a model which has only partially been established in practice it is possible to identify a Conservative-inspired post-Fordist local state. Details of the various changes have been discussed in the first half of the book. Set out below is the emerging overall pattern, organised under four dimensions: economic, social, political and managerial. This multi-dimensional analysis is a useful corrective to some approaches that refer to a shift from a 'managerialism to entrepreneuralism in urban governance'[11] or a transfer from 'welfare state to an enterprise state at the local level'.[12] Such analyses over-concentrate attention on the growing prioritisation of economic development measures and policies within the system of local governance. The insights of regulation theory encourage a recognition of an interconnected pattern of economic, social and political change.

- *economic*: supply-side intervention, promoting competition and labour flexibility; local economic strategies; attraction of capital and high-income residents
- *social*: two-tier service provision; constraints on public spending
- *political*: 'networking' and external focus; European Community and transnational influence; private sector involvement in policy-making
- *managerial*: 'new management' thinking; dominance of private sector methods

Regulation studies of the changing nature of economic policy suggest a trend towards increasing intervention in the supply side of the economy in order to promote international competitiveness and labour market flexibility. The local or regional level is seen as particularly appropriate for such activity by the state and indeed there is increased evidence of investment in local economic strategies at a subnational level. Local authorities have in many instances given a higher priority to economic development – Birmingham City Council, for example, has increased its spending in the economic development field from 2.1 per cent of its budget in 1980–81 to 4.1 per cent of its budget in 1989–1990. Since the mid-1980s local politicians and officials have increasingly presented their localities as involved in a fierce global competition with the need to make them as attractive to mobile capital and high-income social groups as possible. This approach has been actively encouraged by central government in its own rhetoric and in its willingness to lend financial support to 'flagship' projects such as the Manchester Olympic bid. Beyond local authorities a range of other institutions have established a stake in local economic development: Training and Enterprise Councils (TECs) in England and Wales, Local Enterprise Companies (LECs) in Scotland and Urban Development Corporations (UDCs) which operate in various locations are expressions of this increased interest. As well as these central government-sponsored bodies the private sector too has set up various agencies and generally sought to give local chambers of commerce a more effective role.[13]

Changes in the welfare role of the local state suggest a move away from universal traditions towards a more differentiated pattern of social consumption. One of the authors of this chapter has earlier argued:

> Among the consumers of welfare the divisions will increase between: those who can afford to take on 'private' solutions to housing, health care, transport or pension provision; those who have the skills (or good fortune) to get access to a high-quality public sector 'trading' provision such as CTCs (City Technology Colleges), opted-out schools, housing associations and some local authority services; and those who have access to basic no-frills local authority provision.[14]

Conservative-sponsored changes in education, housing and community care, analysed earlier in this book, would only seem to confirm this analysis. The local state's role in underwriting a system of large-scale industrial production by providing a numerous and satisfied workforce has been undermined through constraints on public spending, the creation of a substantial pool of long-term unemployed and the demands that state provision match the expectations of the more affluent and discerning of its consumers. Under the post-Fordist local state those with the appropriate capabilities (either resources of their own or designation as respectable consumers) acquire good-quality services and those that lack such resources are left with a basic, minimalist service.

Developments on the political front are reflected in an increasing concern with external relations and networking and the breaking down (but not the removal) of barriers of access to the internal decision-making structures of local authorities. In short there is a growing awareness of the need to 'manage' the environment and beyond. The concern with networking in part corresponds with the fragmentation of the system of local governance. In the 1960s and 1970s local authorities were the prime if not the sole local political institutions. During the 1980s and 1990s they have had to increasingly share this political space with a range of non-elected governmental institutions, the private sector and third force or voluntary sector agencies. The prominence of the European Union on the scene has led to increased local–EU exchanges as well as transnational networking by localities. Central government has initiated a number of these developments and kept a watchful eye on local experiments. The involvement of local 'new magistracy' figures other than councillors appears to be a key element in Conservative thinking. Business interests and others are to be encouraged to have a more direct involvement in local policy-making.

In the changing management of the local state it is the nature of post-Fordism as a hegemonic project that comes to the fore. The 1980s and 1990s have seen a wave of new management thinking. New management is associated with the transition from Fordism in two senses. In part it is a reflection of changed private sector practices and organisation in the search for economic regeneration. Although private sector practice is more varied than some advocates of new management realise, new wave management is a particular distillation of private sector practice and promotes itself as a model to follow. It combines selective description with prescription. It is precisely this characteristic which has attracted the criticism of social scientists that, at the same time, makes the new management wave a powerful tool of its consultant advocates.[15] Leading lights in the new management wave, Peters and Waterman, have in joint and separate publications[16] sold books in their millions to private and public sector managers. The core themes of the new management wave are summarised in Table 12.1. What is crucial is to recognise that new wave management has a momentum of its own and although it has its origins in private sector management approaches many of its themes and ideas have been taken on board by the public sector. This reflects the cultural dominance of the private sector and matches earlier transfers of the 1970s, notably ideas surrounding corporate management and planning.[17] Another factor is the active support of central government for some versions of new management thinking. The most obvious and powerful expression of this phenomenon is the use of compulsory competitive tendering measures in an increasing range of local authority activities.

Explaining change: the dynamics of diffusion

The broad trends identified by regulation theory and the model of a post-Fordist local state inspired by the Conservatives' reform programme provide a valuable starting point to understanding the changing nature of local governance. Yet as noted earlier the specific

Table 12.1 New wave management: the '4' S model

	'Traditional' management	'New wave' management
Structures	Bureacratic Hierarchical Centralised	Tight centre Broad, flat periphery Decentralised
Systems	Central 'hands-on' control Detailed oversight exercised through multiple tiers	Performance targets Cost centres, tasks and teams Internal markets/trading 'Hands-off' control
Staffing	Large staff corps Fixed, permanent Centralised bargaining	Small core Flexible, large periphery Localised bargaining
Superordinate culture	Sound administration Legal and financial probity Professional Quantity in service delivery	Flexible management Measuring output Managerial Customer-orientated Quality in service delivery

dynamics of change require investigation and analysis beyond the boundaries of contemporary regulation theory. Writers sympathetic to a regulation approach have sought to explain patterns of economic change and organisation through introducing concepts such as transaction costs, networking and co-evolution.[18] This fine-grain analysis suggests that change occurs through a process of experimentation. Through trial-and-error individuals and organisations learn and make discoveries. Emulation is an important part of the process. Successful initiatives are seized upon and generalised. In some cases the changes may have a hegemonic quality which carries them forward in a broad and strong wave and gives them a force beyond the impetus provided by the original propagators.[19]

There is no doubt that such fine-grain analysis is needed to make sense of changes in political as well as economic systems. Yet in the political world policy diffusion is a result of both pull and push factors. Some learning is 'voluntary' as local authorities borrow, adapt and emulate changes of which their leaders approve, pulling out the experience and best practice of other organisations. Equally ѕome diffusion is 'forced' by central government when local authorities are pushed into changes by legislation. Over the past decade or more centrally decreed changes in local government conform more to a type of diffusion that has been called 'authority-innovation decisions'. Forced upon subordinates by a higher authority this type of policy diffusion is often more complex and ineffective than others because it may breed 'dissonance' among those charged with implementation.[20]

The prominent role of the central government in the British case is remarkable not only because of the intensity of its involvement but also the manner in which it has sought to develop and implement its programme. Consultation has been kept to a minimum and the Conservative governments since 1979 have deliberately adopted a top-down approach to putting policy into effect. This process requires the following conditions:

1. knowing what you want to do;
2. the availability of the required resources;
3. the ability to marshal and control these resources to achieve the desired end;
4. if others are to carry out the tasks, communicating what is wanted and controlling their performance.[21]

The difficulty confronting any government adopting such a top-down approach is that the above conditions are likely to be extremely difficult to meet. In short an implementation gap is to be expected because the centre's objectives may become ambiguous and inconsistent, instruments to achieve compliance are absent or limited and other interests may actively oppose or at least be reluctant participants in the process of change. Rhodes and Marsh go as far as to argue:

The Conservative Government of the 1980s deliberately adopted a top-down model and either failed to recognise, or chose to ignore, the known conditions for effective implementation in its determination to impose its preferred policies ... Implementation problems may be common to all governments but they were uniquely severe for the Conservative Government because it insisted on an inappropriate (and ill-considered) model of implementation.[22]

The lesson to be drawn is that change imposed from above is likely to have a patchy and complex impact at the implementation stage.

When looking at the process of change towards the post-Fordist local state the environment of centrally driven initiatives creates the conditions for disinformation. The rhetoric of change may be exaggerated to appease the centre and the substance of change may be less firmly established. The centre may over-promote a few exemplary cases in order to provide a lesson for others and justify its claims of success. In short the extent and nature of change should always be questioned.

A process of uneven development towards the post-Fordist local state should also be expected. The ESRC Locality Studies provide clear evidence of patterns of change taking different forms in different localities and the specific dynamics of local institutions and actors playing a part in explaining the process of change.[23]

It is clear that post-Fordist changes have transformed some localities while leaving barely an imprint upon others. How can this variation be characterised? In the economic sphere, the uneven development of capitalism has created a varied landscape, and despite a general trend toward post-Fordism, different forms of production coexist. Capitalist restructuring proceeds in different ways, creating new industries in the South, destroying the old economic order in the North, and little affecting some rural areas. Social institutions, including the local state, reflect the process of uneven development as well. Further social change is an active process rather than a passive one, and individuals and institutions mediate the process of transformation. Locality is important for two reasons: (1) global or national forces play out differently in different settings and (2) there is an undeniable local logic at work as individuals and institutions seek to respond to and shape change within their home territory.

The process of change to a post-Fordist local state has both vertical and horizontal dimensions. Change and particular models of operation and organisation are imposed by central government. Local authorities react in different ways to this imposition. Equally there is a horizontal dimension as circumstances and actors create the conditions for specific alliances and particular ways forward in different localities.

Towards a typology of local response

A typology is needed to characterise differences in local authority response to post-Fordist restructuring of the local state. Drawing upon the literature on policy diffusion and policy implementation, several categories can be formed which describe willingness to adopt change.[24] One criterion is timing, or relative speed of policy adoption compared to other local authorities. A further criterion driving the typology is the extent or depth of change. Is the organisation committed or just going through the motions? Are the organisations enthusiastic adopters or compliers?

The use of the terms 'adopter' or 'complier' is not meant in the narrow sense that local authorities are merely responding to directives from central government. Adoption is a synthesis of response to both external and internal pressures. In the case of the early adherents, many would have undertaken post-Fordist restructuring at some level even without the external stimulus of central government. And among others, restructuring is being shaped to fit local needs rather than adopted unquestioningly. With this cautionary note, then, below is a typology of local authorities and their response to post-Fordist restructuring:

- *Early adherents*: the earliest adopters, who display leadership and enthusiasm for implementing changes.
- *Pragmatic compliers*: the second wave of adopters, who emulate the innovators. They may adopt programmes only nominally, but wish to be viewed as 'up to date' or 'in compliance'. They avoid risk, and even if they equal the efforts of the early adherents, seldom expand upon or improve upon them.
- *Critical compliers*: later adopters who reshape policies and programmes to fit local need and preferences. Level of innovation could equal or surpass the efforts of early adherents if conditions warrant. Delay is 'strategic'
- *Late adopters*: they act with little enthusiasm, and most importantly, little need, for the policy innovation. Compliance is usually limited to minimal requirements as well as delayed

The policy diffusion literature[25] suggests a number of variables that may affect policy adoption, some of which are outlined below.

Local characteristics affecting subnational policy diffusion

Salience – or policy 'fit' with local problems
Problem severity
Continued public attention to problem
Policy 'fixers' (to adapt) or 'entrepreneurs' (to sell)
Change agents
Advocacy coalitions
Support or opposition from organised interests
Support or opposition from elected officials and administrators
Political leadership
Organisational structure
Number of agencies involved on local level
Organisational goals (bureaucracy and council)
Organisational capacity (including personnel and fiscal resources)
Personnel – goals, skills, commitment
Bureaucratic consolidation
Professionalism of administrators and elected officials
Partisan politics/inter-party competition
Wealth (personal income, per capita spending, median family
    income, and percentage poor)
Industrialisation
Urbanisation
Educational level of populace
Population size
Socioeconomic change
Public opinion
Openness to public participation in decision-making
Openness to innovation
Political culture

   Most of these variables, ranging from macroeconomic factors to
micro-level motivations, offer useful explanations for the differential
diffusion of post-Fordist local government in Britain. Still, a few
alterations must be made. Along with problem severity, 'opportunities' should be added, for post-Fordism presents opportunities for
some localities, like Swindon and Cambridge, as well as problems
for conurbations like Glasgow or Merseyside. The US policy
diffusion literature makes no explicit mention of class relations or

social structure, although that could be subsumed under 'socio-economic' conditions.

It is useful to cluster together various influences in order to make analysis more manageable. Five clusters are identified below:

1. *Socio-economic conditions*: pressure for change, which can be either negative (problem-driven), positive (opportunity-driven) or largely absent. Economic variables such as high unemployment or rapid growth are clearly relevant, as well as types of economic activity (industrial, coal-mining, high-tech, etc.).
2. *Social structure*: population shifts that cause a change in class and social structure.
3. *Political conditions*: the influence of partisan politics, political culture, public opinion and interest group politics
4. *Values and ideology of the local officialdom*: how dissatisfied with existing circumstances, degree of concern with personal and career advantage, sense of local identity and appropriate behaviour, fear of change
5. *Integration into 'national' networks*: extent and nature of non-local orientation, local visibility in national political arena

The variable grouping of these clusters in different localities is translated into discernible patterns of response to post-Fordism. While the typology of response and links with these explanatory variables are subjects for further research, it is possible to present a number of suggestive connections.

Local authorities who are early adherents are in a political and economic position to employ a post-Fordist outlook in the first place. The actions of central government, promoting privatisation and local government restructuring, act as an impetus rather than a primary cause for change. High-tech industries, financial institutions or universities dominate the local economy, and population shifts caused by gentrification create a supportive middle-class and upper-working-class social base for post-Fordist policies. Rapid changes in the locality have created new opportunities and new demands, to which councillors are sensitive. Politically, local authorities are New-Right Conservative, ideological brethren of central government. They have senior council officers who highly value managerial expertise. Local politicians have the ability to capture the national limelight, thereby promoting the political or professional careers of innovators. The London borough of Wandsworth is one example of an early adherent, as is Kent County Council.

Pragmatic compliers have the professional desire to employ the latest techniques, and the political desire to conform with central government requirements or at least avoid a confrontation over them. No overwhelming pressure for change exists. Economic conditions remain stable, or an autonomous local economy is virtually non-existent, as in suburban 'bedroom' communities. The fairly stable population, predominantly middle-class, voices few demands upon government, presumably out of satisfaction with the status quo. In the political vacuum, individual councillors and staff respond to individual political and professional incentives to enhance their work environments and reputations, avoiding unnecessary risk (blame-avoidance is a more powerful political motivation than credit-claiming). Southern coastal towns or comfortable south-east suburbs in England exemplify this type of locality.

Critical compliers feel the sting of negative pressure for change, as their localities have been sorely impacted by post-Fordism. The once flourishing mining and industrial regions, now faced with high unemployment and a dwindling population, must respond to demands for jobs and services among an increasingly elderly and welfare-dependent population. The working-class and trade union politics of these localities rejects the ideology of Thatcherism, but may be responsive to other facets of 'post-Fordism' including community empowerment and decentralisation of services. Economic development activities become a necessity, but are undertaken in ways that are maintaining public sector initiative and involvement (rather than attempting to promote private sector solutions as necessarily superior). Such authorities usually have Left Labour councils, and local politicians with a national audience. The conurbations of Glasgow and Merseyside, and cities such as Manchester or Sheffield illustrate this type of local authority.

Late adopters exist outside the mainstream of economic change and national politics, feeling little pressure to change or to conform to any national or professional standards. Usually rural, their social base is unchanging and homogenous, and politics is parochial. Neither Fordism nor post-Fordism have provoked many changes in these localities, in the remoter reaches of Wales or the Scottish islands, for example.

Conclusions

This chapter has explored the dynamics of differential diffusion in the development of the post-Fordist local state. The response of local authorities has been characterised according to a fourfold typology: early adherents, pragmatic compliers, critical compliers and late adopters. Further conceptual refinement and empirical research will be necessary before a more complete picture of the uneven and uncertain development of the post-Fordist local state can be provided. This chapter seeks to provide a starting point for such an analysis.

Unlike changes in economic organisation it is argued that change in the political field in Britain involves an attempted imposition of new structures and practices by a higher authority aided by a whole raft of new quasi-government agencies and consultants preaching the virtues of new management doctrines.

Compared to the non-local sources of policy change identified by Dunleavy[26] in the heyday of the Fordist welfare state the key exporters in the contemporary period are: (1) central government rather than the national local government system of local authority associations, conferences and networks; and (2) managers and management consultants rather than professionals. Further, quasi-governmental agencies have moved from the periphery of policy change to become major agents of new policies and approaches. This changed pattern in the leading exporters or promoters of policy change provides the framework for the development of a post-Fordist local state. The process is further complicated by the influence of local circumstances and actors.

Notes and references

1. See A. Lipietz, *Mirages and Miracles* (Verso, 1987); B. Jessop, 'Regulation Theory, Post Fordism and the State', *Capital & Class* no. 34 (1988) pp. 147–68 and 'Regulation Theories in Retrospect and Prospect', *Economy and Society*, vol. 19, no. 2 (1990) pp. 153–216. The discussion in the section below draws heavily on G. Stoker 'Intergovernmental Relations', *Public Administration*, forthcoming 1994.
2. P. Hoggett, 'A Farewell to Mass Production' in P. Hoggett and R. Hambleton (eds), *Decentralisation and Democracy*, Occasional Paper

No. 28, School for Advanced Urban Studies; M. Goodwin, S. Duncan and S. Halford, 'Regulation Theory, the Local State and the Transition of Urban Politics', *Environment and Planning D: Society and Space*, vol. 11 (1993) pp. 67–88; J. Painter, 'Regulation Theory and Local Government', *Local Government Studies*, vol. 17, no. 6 (1991) pp. 23–43; G. Stoker, 'Creating a Local Government for a Post-Fordist Society: the Thatcherite Project?', in J. Stewart and G. Stoker (eds), *The Future of Local Government* (Macmillan, 1989) and 'Regulation Theory, Local Government and the Transition from Fordism', in D. King and J. Pierre (eds), *Challenges to Local Government* (ECPR/Sage, 1990); A. Tickell, and J. Peck, 'Accumulation, Regulation and the Geographies of Post-Fordism', *Progress in Human Geography* vol. 16, no. 2 (1992), pp. 190–218.

3. A. Lipietz, *Mirages and Miracles*, p. 15.
4. M. Goodwin and J. Painter, 'Local Governance, the Crisis of Fordism and Uneven Development', paper presented to Ninth Urban Change and Conflict Conference, 14–16 September 1993, University of Sheffield.
5. G. Stoker, 'Creating a Local Government for a Post-Fordist Society', p. 141.
6. A. Sayer, 'Post Fordism in Question', *International Journal of Urban and Regional Research* vol. 13, no. 4 (1990) pp. 666–95.
7. A. Cochrane, *Whatever Happened to Local Government?* (Open University Press, 1993) p. 92.
8. G. Stoker, 'Regulation Theory, Local Government and the Transition from Fordism'.
9. M. Goodwin and J. Painter, 'Local Governance, the Crisis of Fordism and Uneven Development'.
10. A. Cochrane, *Whatever Happened to Local Government?*
11. D. Harvey, 'From Managerialism to Enterpreneurialism: The Transformation of Urban Governance in Late Capitalism', *Geografiska Annaler*, vol. 1 (1989) pp. 3–17.
12. A. Cochrane, 'The Changing State of Local Government' *Public Administration*, vol. 69, no. 3 (1991) pp. 231–303.
13. A. Harding, 'Central Control in British Urban Economic Development Programmes', in C. Crouch and D. Marquand (eds), *The New Centralism: Britain Out of Step in Europe?* (Blackwell, 1989).
14. G. Stoker, 'Creating a Local Government for a Post-Fordist Society', p. 162.
15. S. Wood, 'New Wave Management?', *Work, Employment and Society*, vol. 3, no. 3 (1989), pp. 379–402.
16. See, for example, T. Peters, *Thriving on Chaos* (Macmillan, 1987) and T. Peters and R. Waterman, *In Search of Excellence* (Harper & Row, 1982).
17. Cf. C. Cockburn, *The Local State* (Pluto, 1977).
18. See A. Scott, 'Flexible production systems and regional development', *International Journal of Urban and Regional Research*, vol. 12, no. 2 (1988) pp. 171–85 and J. Murdoch, 'Regulation Theory, Flexible

Specialisation and Network Analysis: Towards a Co-evolutionary Account of Economic Change', unpublished paper, 1993.

19. This argument is inspired by H. Ward's 'State Exploitation, Capital Accumulation and the Evolution of Modes of Regulation: A Defence of Bottom-Line Economism', Political Studies Annual Conference, University of Leicester, April 1993.

20. Cf. E. Rogers, *Communication of Innovations: A Cross Cultural Approach* (Free Press, 1971).

21. R. Rhodes and D. Marsh, 'Thatcherism: An Implementation Perspective' in Marsh and Rhodes (eds), *Implementing Thatcherite Policies: Audit or an Era* (Open University Press, 1992).

22. Ibid., p. 9.

23. See, for example, P. Cooke (ed.), *Localities* (Unwin Hyman, 1989) and M. Harloe, C. Pickvance and J. Urry (eds), *Place, Policy and Politics: Do Localities Matter?* (Unwin Hyman, 1990).

24. H. Wolman, 'Innovation in Local Government and Fiscal Austerity', *Journal of Public Policy*, vol. 6, no. 2 (1987) pp. 159–80; E. Rogers, *Diffusion of Innovations* (3rd edn, Free Press, 1983); Rogers, *Communication of Innovations: A Cross Cultural Approach*; J. Walker, 'The Diffusion of Innovation Among American States', *American Political Science Review*, vol. 53, no. 3 (1969) pp. 880–99; J. Clark, 'Policy Diffusion and Program Scope: Research Directions', *Publius* vol. 15, no. 4 (1985) pp. 61–70; M. Goggin, A. Bowman, A Lester and L. O'Toole *Implementation Theory and Practice: Towards a Third Generation* (HarperCollins, 1990); R. Savage 'Diffusion, Research Traditions and the Spread of Policy Innovations', *Publius*, vol. 15, no. 4 (1985), pp. 1–27.

25. See Goggin *et al.*, *Implementation Theory and Practice*; and Savage, 'Diffusion of Research Traditions'.

26. P. Dunleavy, *Urban Political Analysis* (Macmillan, 1980) pp. 102–20.

13 From the Urban Left to the New Right: Normative Theory and Local Government

Desmond King

British local government has undergone major changes since 1989.[1] These changes reject conventional conceptions about the purposes of local government and the political values which should be embodied in the political institutions of local authorities. This chapter reviews the political values commonly imputed by the Left and the Right to local government institutions and assesses how these values have fared in national and local policy during the 1980s. The chapter is therefore concerned with normative arguments and not simply with describing government policy. It is not assumed that there is any direct relationship between political values and public policy but it is assumed that political principles constitute relevant criteria with which to discuss public policy.[2]

The chapter is divided into two parts, the first reviewing the political values for local government inherited from the liberal and social democratic traditions. The second part develops a typology of Left and Right theories of local government, relates them to the earlier values, and discusses them critically in the light of illustrative policies. The concluding section critically examine the epistemology of both Left and Right theories.

Political values for local government

The core liberal values: liberty, participation and efficiency

In the liberal tradition of writing about local government the dominant intellectual influence is John Stuart Mill, who valued politics as a means of achieving freedom, nourishing the self-development of the individual and satisfying the imperatives of allocative efficiency.[31] Local government supposedly enhances *liberty* by forming a bulwark against the power of the state. More recently, scholars argue that local government diffuses power in the political system.[4] Instead of concentrating all political power centrally, local government and the division of power it sustains makes the polity pluralist. In Britain the diffusion argument is important as a political objective in a highly unitary state. Its realisation is constrained by the constitutional supremacy of Parliament. Local government allows some diffusion of power but since local institutions are constituted and reconstituted at central discretion this attribute is relative.[5] Without constitutional changes it is difficult to see how the argument could be sustained.

For the 'New Right', freedom is defined by the 'power to choose'. Exercising individual choice through local government is a further dimension of the political value of freedom. This objective has its most rigorous formulation in public choice theory of which the 'Tiebout hypothesis' is representative.[6] Tiebout argues that for each unit of local government there is a natural 'optimum community size' based on the mixture of taxes levied and services provided towards which all local governments should strive. This 'optimum community size' will be achieved as a consequence of individual consumers 'searching around' to find that community which suits their needs best. Individual choices determine local authority behaviour. If taxes rise intolerably or desired services are not provided, then consumers/voters will respond through either 'voice', articulating their discontent, or 'exit', departing from the jurisdiction. A local authority concerned about its fiscal buoyancy must respond to such consumer dissatisfaction. Those consumers unable to exercise these options or convinced of the rightness of the changes will maintain 'loyalty'.[7]

Political participation is a value also imputed to local government. The central claim is that citizens can participate in the running of those affairs which affect them directly and can hold accountable their elected representatives. Participation is at the core of Western ideas about political democracy and a number of claims about its utility can be distinguished. First, participation can be advocated as the basis for self-development, a key part of Mill's theory. However, while self-growth is now universally praised it is seldom invoked for its own sake. Second, participation is the necessary basis for the exercise of individual choice by voters. This argument links with the third claim of realising policy objectives and ensuring that certain principles and criteria (for example, non-discrimination and allocative efficiency) are met in local policy.

Fourth, participation can be joined to ideas about community-maintenance and respect for historical traditions. One of the reasons for local government is to allow those citizens who feel part of a particular community to govern themselves and to make decisions about those issues affecting them directly. Political participation is the necessary basis for such local self-government since it enables citizens to express themselves and their concerns about their community. The great difficulty with this argument is how to define community. Is it a sociological phenomenon, a geographical area or a psychological feeling, or all three? Furthermore, the changes in local government boundaries and rapid growth of cities in the twentieth century have eroded the direct link between sociological communities and administrative units. Fifth, Jones and Stewart stress 'localism' in local government, which again requires participation.[8] The claim here is that 'local government is local' and therefore best able to address the needs of local voters, who reside in a particular area and hold opinions about its governance. People require a local political institution through which to address their local needs and to express their desires for that community. Local government can undertake this role more effectively than central government because it is closer to people, has greater contact with them and can respond to changing needs. It is a position opposed directly, therefore, to one based upon national minimum standards. Finally, participation might be pursued for socialist reasons. Participation and control of local government could provide the means for pursuing policies which, for example, aim to transform the local economy and its relationship to the community.

The third core liberal political value for local government is allocative *efficiency*. Local government can allocate public goods and services in the most economically efficient way, a point noted by Mill. Local authorities can address the requirements of their jurisdiction and can equalise service provision across the system of local government – though the liberal theory of local government presumes diversity and differences in the system. Within national parameters local authorities should have the discretion to allocate services according to local needs. However, if the premises of the Tiebout hypothesis are operating – the maximisation of individual choice – and local governments have discretionary powers, then interregional inequalities are more likely to result than equalities because authorities have quite different fiscal bases with which to fund local services.[9]

Some observations about the core liberal values

The three core liberal values each reflect the liberal principle that people should be able to engage in any activity which does not have consequences for others, a claim about which some remarks can be advanced. First, the apparently uncontroversial idea that local authorities know best the needs of their locality and should therefore exercise control over service allocation masks a deeper question: how are local powers of policy-making to be reconciled with national standards? This question is an important one if some political principles and objectives are valued more than others by the national political community – for example, that discrimination by gender or race should not be tolerated or that certain rights should be available to all members of the community irrespective of in which local authority's jurisdiction they reside. There are several answers to this quandary. One empirical response holds that discussion of national standards neglects how these are established through local practice:

> national minimum standards, in statutes or statutory instruments, are in fact rare. Most mandatory obligations laid on local authorities are general, empowering local authorities to perform certain functions, giving them duties and laying down procedures, while leaving local authorities discretion about the level and extent of the service provided, its frequency and intensity. The standards which have emerged are not nationally determined. Such standards are in effect standards achieved through local choice.[10]

This judicious response derives from the pivotal role of local authorities, through implementation, in shaping policy. Elsewhere, Jones has elaborated upon the practical difficulties of determining national minimum standards and the difficulties of enforcing them through various performance indicators. He concludes that 'the consequence of the standards approach will be an increase in central civil servants, situated in regional offices so that they can inspect local authorities, to ensure that they conform to the minimum, and can check their claims about the costs of standards . . . Thus the minimum standards solution is highly centralist'.[11] This argument can be criticised for exaggerating the problems of a minimum standards approach and for neglecting the potentially undesirable results of expanding local powers: the difficulty of devising input measures is hardly insurmountable for ensuring that political objectives agreed upon nationally are being enforced in a non-discriminatory fashion.

A second response is to ensure that national and universal parameters are drawn for policy within which local authorities must modify their policies as they see best for their local needs. It is this second response which seems the more cogent but here the difficulty is ensuring that the powers accruing to local authorities are significant.

The difficulty with these responses is determining how local choice can be both faithful to national priorities and guarantee consequential local power. Can either be achieved without compromising the other? Furthermore, achieving the appropriate balance is difficult enough when there is national agreement about specific priorities, but when that agreement itself is eroded – as it has been during the 1980s – then reconciling local choice and national standards is even more complex. If local choice is granted under these circumstances there are dangers of local abuses of power, the pursuit of discriminatory policies – think of the American South before 1965 – and the growth of significant inequalities between different regions of the country. Central government cannot be viewed as a panacea to all problems of inequality, discrimination and interregional variations – a point repeatedly made by local government advocates. But national government can set standards, derived from national consensus, with which to guide policy. These standards may compromise the capacity of local authorities to enjoy considerable powers of local choice. If local government is given substantial local powers they may wish, for instance, to expand the role of the market in meeting their statutory obligations. Historical experience suggests that market processes generate inequalities and discrimination, which is why the welfare state was instituted.[12]

Having reduced the role of the market at the national level it seems strange to allow its reintroduction at the local level, yet such a development must be tolerated if local powers are to be real. If left wing politicians want to devolve power they should acknowledge the likely consequences of such actions: while one authority pursues policies they approve of, another will behave quite differently.

This conclusion leads to a related issue: the tension often ascribed to the relationship between allocative efficiency and political participation. Both are important political values but facilitating wide participation may produce policy mixes which do not maximise the efficient allocation of local services. This tension has been recognised in a series of government commissions on local government. For instance, it is commonly argued that economies of scale can be realised in particular local government boundaries and not in others, an argument which may be used to oppose the construction of small authorities based on particular communities.

Social democratic values: redistribution and autonomy

Social democrats do not dispute the importance of liberty, participation and efficiency as foundational values of political institutions. They add a fourth value, that of redistribution. The pursuit of allocative efficiency should be tempered by a concern for economic redistribution. Such redistribution may be a necessary basis for attaining liberty and participation. In practice, redistribution has meant introducing a progressive tax system which levies tax proportionate to income and uses these revenues to fund public institutions such as schools, hospitals, housing and universities, which establish equality of opportunity and advance equality of outcome. But these social democratic objectives have been considered the appropriate business of national, not local, government. Local authorities have lacked the requisite resources and interventionist powers to make binding policy and, for the same principles valued by Tiebout, they cannot coerce citizens into remaining within their tax regime. Accordingly, the national arena is designated as the one through which redistributive social aims are best pursued.[13]

A fifth value imputed to local government by some socialists – at least by implication – and other theorists is that of autonomy. The idea here is that local governments require a minimum of independence if they are to be able to pursue their own policies.

Autonomy has both fiscal and political aspects. In the British political system both attributes of autonomy are weak: the doctrine of *ultra vires* undercuts local political power while the reluctance of the central government to grant fiscal control to local authorities reduces the scope for financial independence. The issue of local finances runs through numerous government commissions, with the principal conclusion that the absence of significant revenue powers – a revenue base independent of central government interference and influence – makes local autonomy precarious.[14] Advocates of local government recognise this problem and promote a local income or other tax which local authorities can control and direct as they wish. The main practical constraint with this proposal is the link between local and national tax systems and the consistent unwillingness of governments to leave local finance to local authorities. For instance, the poll tax intended allegedly to increase local financial accountability but its rate was subject to national controls.

Theories of local government: a Left–Right typology

The distinction drawn between the New Right and the Left can be further subdivided into two and three perspectives respectively. The New Right embraces both liberal and conservative variants, each implying a different role for local government. The Left covers three distinct groupings. first, the old statist Labour Party tradition, much criticised now, which was responsible for removing functions from the local to the national level in the post-1945 period; second, the Labour groups commonly referred to as the 'New Urban Left', in many ways a reaction to the statist tradition, active in the 1980s; and third, the movement towards community control or 'enabling', not necessarily linked to the Labour Party though enjoying support within certain parts of it.

The Right and local government

The liberal New Right

The Conservatives have traditionally supported local government and, in theory, decentralised local government has a significant position within right-wing arguments. The liberal Right is committed to maximising individual freedom and to limiting government. Both aims imply decentralisation and considerable powers of local government. The post-1979 Conservative administration has, however, drawn not only upon a liberal political and economic tradition but also upon a conservative, authoritarian one which contradicts, many commentators suggest, the liberal precepts.[15]

Representative of the liberal theory is the 'Tiebout hypothesis'. Tiebout argued that there was an 'optimum community size, toward which local governments could strive'. Optimality pertains to the efficient allocation of municipal services, defined 'in terms of the number of residents for which this bundle of services can be produced at the lowest average cost'.[16] Such efficiency will increase individual freedom and choice since citizens will calculate the cost–benefit ratio of service provision (that is, costs in taxes paid and benefits in standard and appropriateness of the services provided) in other jurisdictions before deciding upon a particular residence. Such rational behaviour forces local government to be cost-efficient in its provision of services and to maintain a prosperous economy.

The 'Tiebout hypothesis' prompted the poll tax and the introduction of compulsory competitive tendering by local authorities, a strategy which reflects other New Right criticisms of the inefficiency of the public sector. The poll tax was supposed to link directly the consumption of local services with their cost.[17] Accountability was defined in fiscal terms. This interpretation is supported in the arguments marshalled by the minister introducing the changes when he emphasises how the poll tax would permit voters to compare the policies of different local authorities: 'there will therefore be a direct relationship between each authority's spending level and the Community Charge which it has to levy. And the electorate will be able to make direct comparisons between different authorities on the standards of service they provide and the level of charge they levy.'[18] If the Tieboutian principles were employed fully, local authorities would have retained complete control over the level of the new charge.

The inconsistencies of the poll tax can be joined with flaws inherent in the Tieboutian logic. For example, there is little evidence that local residents are able either to calculate their cost–benefit function or to choose to live where they can afford to. Most people live where they do because there is employment there. While some citizens may be able to pick and choose jobs in different areas many people cannot. Feelings of community and belonging may discourage residents from 'exiting' an unfavourable tax zone; 'voice' or sullen quietism may be a more likely response.

Politically, the Tiebout hypothesis is appealing to the New Right for another reason. One empirical consequence of this theory is the promotion of interregional inequality and the diminution of local government's redistributive role. Local authority power to set their local taxes and to allocate their local public goods will generate inequalities because some communities have a wealthier fiscal base than others with which to finance services. This outcome is problematic only if policy-makers are committed to certain national standards and the New Right is intent upon the erosion of such standards. The Tieboutian logic imposes costs on local authorities which do pursue redistributive policies, a point noted by Peterson:

> efficiency in local government promotes city interests. [T]he closer any locality moves toward this ideal match between taxes and services, the more attractive its land becomes. It is thus in the interest of local governments to operate as efficiently as possible. Operating efficiently hardly means operating so as to enhance equality.[19]

For the liberal New Right, welfare consists in the maximisation of collective good regardless of how this aggregation is distributed across individuals or, in the case of local government, spatially, an approach which ultimately equates social justice and efficiency. The liberal political value of allocative efficiency trumps any concern with redistribution for social justice.

The Conservative new right

When he was responsible for local government, the late Nicholas Ridley provided a major statement of Conservative policy towards local authorities.[20] The author proclaims Conservative commitment to local government and to encouraging local diversity and innovation. Yet throughout his pamphlet it is the New Right values associated with conservatism, not liberalism, which predominate. The value of allocative efficiency preempts those of liberty and participation.

Parliamentary sovereignty is paramount: 'Parliament must continue to play a role in determining the essential framework in which local authorities operate.'[21] The central government should specify local functions, the constitutional position of local authorities, their taxation levels, 'standards of provision for services of a national character',[22] and ensure allocative efficiency in local service provision. The author is clear about public expectations too: 'what the general public wants of local government is that it should provide good services as efficiently as possible',[23] an objective which requires a commitment to competition, personal responsibility, and increased use of the private sector.

Ridley's view of local authority service provision is not unambivalent. The Conservatives allegedly want to grant considerable powers to local authorities. However, they fear the fiscal consequences of so doing. The Conservatives are enthusiastic about local government as long as these local authorities satisfy central criteria and aims, as the following passage indicates:

> what is clear . . . is that the more effectively and efficiently local authorities operate in providing services in an accountable way, responsive to needs of their local communities and competing effectively with other providers where that is relevant, the less need there is likely to be for central government and detailed control . . . Conversely, where local responsibility breaks down there is inevitably stronger pressure for central intervention.[24]

Absent from this position is a willingness to grant greater local freedom *per se*; rather there is a reliance upon the conservative, 'strong state' strand of New Right theory. This centralist position is buttressed by the constitutional position of Parliament. It is revealing that the Conservatives are unwilling to query this status.

The Conservatives emphasise accountability defined fiscally as a 'more direct relationship between payment for local services through local taxation and the services being provided'.[25] The community charge would force financial prudence upon authorities and stimulate greater participation by voters acting as consumers with precise fiscal objectives and worries: 'the level of the Community Charge and the costs of services provided by different councils will be compared and questioned'.[26] But there are major areas of Conservative local policy which are not subject to the imperatives of accountability and participation. For instance, the financially large Urban Development Corporations have been established without significant local representation. These corporations are administering large budgets and implementing policies with fundamental implications for the development of the local communities, yet these latter are denied effective representation and cannot therefore hold the corporations accountable, however this value is defined.[27]

In sum, the New Right liberal strand has a philosophy of local government based on the principle that local communities should control taxing and spending policies which best satisfies their voters. The key political values are those of liberty and accountability, defined fiscally, and allocative efficiency with a constant attention to reducing government and expanding private sector responsibilities. These are the values and aims which have been promoted by the New Right think-tanks such as the Institute of Economic Affairs, the Adam Smith Institute and the Centre for Policy Studies.

The Left and local government

The postwar statist tradition

Like the Conservatives, the Labour Party have long paid lipservice to the importance of local government. In practice they have concentrated upon national policy. The postwar welfare state initiative was a national policy, though many of the policies were administered locally within national parameters – for example, the introduction of comprehensive education at the secondary level. Between 1945 and the mid-1970s, the Labour Party's dominant policy focus was upon nationalisation policies and the pursuit of equality of opportunity through national redistributive policies.[28]

This statist tradition, the reliance upon national planning, signalled, to some extent, the decline of local government as a policy-making and independent entity. Labour's political priorities, such as those associated with the welfare state, were judged national responsibilities to be pursued in universal public policies. Local government was, as a consequence, reduced increasingly to an administrative role, a conception strengthened by the new professionals increasingly dominating local authorities in the post-1945 decades. Regional and urban policies were nationally formulated with the objective of eliminating interregional and inter-urban inequalities. Such egalitarian aims were considered national, not local, responsibilities. The commitment to national standards of equality of opportunity implied that the freedom of local authorities to pursue their own policies should be limited, except in those areas where local initiatives did not contravene national objectives.

The neglect of local government by the Labour Party informs David Blunkett and Keith Jackson's book. They criticise the postwar Labour administration's welfare state policies for neglecting the potential of local authorities. They characterise this strategy as 'Labour's great mistake'.[29] The statist tradition is now repudiated by Labour Party members nationally and locally. In common with the Conservatives, Labour stress now the rights and needs of the consumers of state services. Gone is the automatic commitment to the nationalisation of large industries and the public ownership of the means of production. Statist Labour activists remain committed to a national policy for pursuing citizenship and reducing inequalities, however, and this commitment implies a more modest evaluation of local government's potential. At the local level, the themes of decentralisation, greater participation and consumer control were developed by the 'New Urban Left'.

Local government for redistribution: the Urban Left

By the mid-1970s the statist tradition was questioned not only over national policy but for local government too. This questioning attained its fullest local expression in a phenomenon dubbed the 'New Urban Left'. This loose political grouping was concentrated in the larger metropolitan authorities and London for a decade after the mid-1970s. Even as a loose category the term is problematic. Scholars now draw two clear divisions – between Liverpool and other cities, querying the inclusion of the policies of the former within the Urban Left; and between the remaining metropolitan counties and London, the latter holding the most 'radical' conception of the transformative potential of local government.

The New Urban Left encouraged the establishment of new committees dealing with race relations, women's issues and police accountability among other topics. New Urban Left activists were committed to local government as an arena for change and radicalism and not simply as a forum from which to stage a career in Parliament. The most ambitious initiative for producing significant change was economic. The New Urban Left were responsible for the founding of local enterprise boards which attempted to give local authorities the capacity to intervene in their local economies, but to intervene in a socially positive sense.[30] An important division lies here between the Greater London Enterprise Board (GLEB) and the boards of the other authorities, since the former's investment and employment strategies are generally interpreted as the most socialist.[31]

The development of local economic strategies broke with the postwar statist tradition's national focus.[32] For various reasons, principally the dominance of the Conservatives nationally, the Urban Left pursued the possibilities for redistributive socialist policies at the local level.

The Urban Left's political values were social democratic; the reduction of inequality, combined with a commitment to greater participation in local government and an attentiveness to allocative efficiency. Change was to be brought about at the local level with the active participation of those citizens affected directly. In this sense it was a localist strategy and one which could have different results in different areas, intensifying interregional inequalities – a paradoxical outcome for socialists. The Urban Left assumed the maintenance of national welfare state standards but wanted to advance socialist economic and political objectives by direct, local investment policies.

The New Urban Left illustrates the potential for local government. Local politics can be the location of new political developments in ideas and movements, as has been illustrated historically by municipal socialism and the rate-payers' movement among others. The commitment to redefining socialism, to establishing local institutions of democracy and to undertaking local initiatives suggest the resilience of local politics. Undoubtedly, the unfavourable national arena influenced this development significantly as did policy debates within the Labour Party. But the New Urban Left indicates also the sharp limitation to local politics in Britain. Ultimate power rests with Westminster and its exercise is relatively easy, as demonstrated by the abolition of the GLC and MCCs in 1986 – all loci of political opposition to the national administration. If the political party roles were reversed and it was a 'New Local

Right' opposing a Labour Government there is little grounds for thinking that it would not exercise the same constitutional powers to impose its will which the Tories have used in the 1980s. At the core of the dilemma is the lack of a normative theory of local government which specifies clearly what powers are available to local authorities and what initiatives they can pursue within this framework. Such a theory might be less agreeable to the New Urban Left than to the local Right, since real powers of local initiative could be expected to compromise national standards to which the Labour Party has been committed historically.

Communitarian local government: enabling local government

There is a third strand to current Left, or quasi-Left, theories of local government whose practitioners want to grant local government 'enabling' powers to bring the community into decision-making as fully as possible. For Blunkett and Jackson local politics is defined as a means by which 'people can run their own affairs, adopting an increasingly broad perspective as confidence in democracy grows'.[33] In contrast to the New Right, Blunkett and Jackson have a richer notion of how communities underpin local political institutions and provide the basis for self-government. Their concern is the erosion of local government powers in the 1980s. They conclude rightly that the 'conflict between central and local government has been fought not over economic or technical issues but over different views of the world'.[34]

Unlike the New Right, Blunkett and Jackson recognise that reform requires a change in the position of Parliament, though they do not advocate ending *ultra vires,* but rather legislating specific local powers.[35] First, local authorities must have the power to initiate policy in areas which affect their jurisdiction, a classic liberal objective; second, the power to set their own taxation levels and thus to have local revenue autonomy, a prerequisite for effective local participation and policy-making; third, the ending of capital borrowing restrictions; and, fourth, the removal of legal restraints on trading. These are reasonable proposals and build on political values such as participation, representation, allocative efficiency and redistribution. However, Blunkett and Jackson do not consider accountability and efficiency in the exclusively fiscal sense attributed to the New Right above. These values arise from the shared sense of community – though this term is not well defined – and the desire for self-government to formulate collective responses to specific needs which this community sense induces.

Absent from this analysis is any discussion of the consequence of greater local autonomy for equality and inequality. Local government is not idealised: there are many criticisms of existing practices and attitudes in local government. But there is no evaluation of the problems resulting from interregional inequality. They are very keen on the progressive initiatives undertaken by Sheffield City Council but have nothing to say about 'unprogressive' local initiatives – a likely consequence of granting greater initiatory powers to all local authorities. Blunkett and Jackson continue to subscribe to the social democratic welfare state model with some decentralisation thrown in. There is insufficient acknowledgement of the divisions about the purposes of local government and how these are to be resolved.

There will always be variation between policy delivery in different local authorities and such variation need not correspond with inequality of service delivery either between persons or areas. In this chapter the term 'variation' is used to refer to those outcomes which do promote inequality between persons or jurisdictions. However, a commitment to equality of opportunity, imputed here to the postwar statist tradition in local government, will normally imply a commitment to diminishing variations in service outcomes within and between local authorities.

Table 13.1 summarises the five theories of local government. It indicates their respective implications for the role of local government and likely policy outcomes. The table includes a policy to illustrate each theory. The poll tax with its liberal pretension of devolving power and maximising individual choice seems to represent that strand of New Right theory. The Urban Development Corporations with their accountability to the centre reflect the centralist thrust of New Right conservatism. The National Curriculum is a more recent example. The centrally determined introduction of comprehensive schools is an example of the old statist Labour Party tradition: the centre decides upon the appropriate policy and standards and leaves implementation to subnational authorities. The New Urban Left's keenness upon local redistributive experiments is well-represented by the policies of local enterprise boards, while the enabling aims of community theorists

Table 13.1 Five theories of local government

	Ideological level				
	New Right		Urban Left	Left	
Variants	Liberal New Right	Conservative New Right	Urban Left	Communitarian	Statist
Values	Liberty Participation Efficiency	Central authority/ efficiency	Redistribution/ participation	Liberty Participation Redistribution	Social citizenship
The role of local government	Serves community	Central agent	Serves community	Serves community	Central agent
Illustrative policy	Poll tax	National Curriculum	Enterprise boards	Local income tax	Comprehensive education
Policy outcome	Promotes variation and inequality	Central pattern of services within efficiency criteria	Inter-personal and -regional variation in services	Inter-personal and -regional variation in service delivery	Central pattern to reduce inequality

suggests the introduction of a local income tax with which fiscal base local authorities can pursue whatever policies the community supports. The statist Left tradition minimises variation (to minimise interpersonal and interregional inequality) between authorities, a power which the authoritarian New Right theory potentially holds too. The liberal New Right and the community theories both imply significant differences between local authorities as determined by their respective constituents. The New Urban Left also implies interpersonal and interregional inequality across localities, though this outcome is less favourably embraced by them than by the liberal Right or community Left. These differences reflect the different conceptions of the appropriate role of local government: either as central agent or local representative body.

Conclusion: the ubiquity of liberalism

This chapter has reviewed the approaches of the Left and Right to the central theoretical problem of local government: in a unitary state, how are powers and responsibilities to be divided between the national and local tiers of government? If a political community is committed to national objectives and standards then the scope for local government autonomy will be necessarily constrained. Certainly, some local discretionary powers can be retained to address local circumstances but the criteria by which this discretion is exercised will be national ones. Broadly, this was the practice of the three postwar decades in Britain when both the Left and Right shared a commitment to the expansion of welfare state institutions, thereby according local authorities an increasingly administrative role. This practice was coupled with a continued rhetorical commitment to the importance of local government and of local political participation but an actual weakening of these local institutions.

Of the five normative approaches to local government sketched above, the two most coherent positions are the liberal right and statist left. The former declares: devolve power and accept the consequent inequality and variation across districts. The statist Left pursues the elimination of inequality and, on that basis, constructs national priorities and criteria to be satisfied in local policies. While this latter stance looks rather dated in relation to the Morrisonian nationalisation tradition it retains value in the promotion of the social rights of citizenship.[36]

Although these two theories are the most robust, they are also vulnerable to recent theoretical criticism. Both approaches share a similar liberal epistemology, methodological individualism, with a common construction of the individual. This criticism has been advanced by communitarians and feminists.[37] Many feminists, for instance, have argued that traditional liberal arguments about justice are male-biased; other feminists have dismissed the very subject of justice as unduly male-constructed, and argued for its replacement with the subject of caring. Communitarians reject the epistemological core of liberal and rational choice theory. They argue that these approaches misunderstand individuals' capacity for self-determination and self-articulation of interests, and neglect unduly the social context in which aims and understandings are formulated. Liberals, influenced by Kant, believe the self is unproblematic – in Rawls's words the 'self is prior to the ends which are affirmed by it'.[38] This position is rejected by communitarians because it 'ignores the fact that the self is embedded or situated in existing social practices, that we cannot always stand back and opt out of them. Our social roles and relationships, or at least some of them, must be taken as givens for the purposes of personal deliberation'.[39] For such communitarians the liberal conception of the self 'is empty, violates our self-perceptions and ignores our embeddedness in communal practices'.[40]

These are serious criticisms. That the communitarian critique can be harnessed by both the political Left and Right in defence of local government suggests the complexity of the issues and the ambiguities of key terms. If theorists of local government are to produce defensible and plausible arguments about its organisation, and the values upon which it should be based, then they will need to engage with these important issues.

Notes and references

1. For details see Desmond King, 'Government Beyond Whitehall: Local Government and Urban Politics' in P. Dunleavy *et al.* (eds), *Developments in British Politics 4* (Macmillan, 1993).
2. On the importance of political principles and values see Brian Barry, *Political Argument* (Harvester, 1965) and Jeremy Waldron, *Liberal Rights* (Cambridge University Press, 1993). For their application to local government see amongst others David Harvey, *Social Justice and the City* (Edward Arnold, 1973); Paul Peterson, *City Limits* (University of Chicago Press, 1981); A. Seyd, *The Political Theory of American Local Government* (Random House, 1966); S. Elkin, *City and Regime in the American Republic* (University of Chicago Press, 1987).
3. J. S. Mill, *Considerations on Representative Government* (Dent, 1972); L. J. Sharpe, 'Theories and Values of Local Government', *Political Studies*, vol. 18 (1970) pp. 153–74, and Dilys Hill, *Democratic Theory and Local Government* (Allen & Unwin, 1976). See also R. Bellamy, *Liberalism and Modern Society* (Polity, 1992). See also C. Tiebout, 'A Pure Theory of Local Expenditures', *Journal of Political Economy*, vol. 64 (1956) pp. 416-24.
4. George Jones and John Stewart, *The Case for Local Government*, 2nd edn (Allen & Unwin, 1985); and David Widdicombe (Chairman), *Report of the Committee of Inquiry into the Conduct of Local Authority Business*, Cmnd 9797 (HMSO, 1986).
5. See D. S. King, 'Political Centralization and State Interests in Britain: The Abolition of the GLC and the MCCs', *Comparative Political Studies*, vol. 21 (1989) pp. 467-94; and T. R. Gurr and D. S. King, *The State and the City* (University of Chicago Press, 1987) ch. 4.
6. Tiebout, 'Pure Theory of Local Expenditures'. For criticisms see J. R. Logan and T. Swanstrom (eds), *Beyond the City Limits* (Temple University Press, 1990).
7. Albert Hirschman, *Exit, Voice and Loyalty* (Princeton University Press, 1970).
8. Jones and Stewart, *Case for Local Government*.
9. This outcome is apparent in the USA: see Desmond King, 'The Politics of Urban Policy', in G. Peele *et al.* (eds), *Developments in American Politics 2* (Macmillan, 1994); and E. S. Mills, 'Non-Urban Policies as Urban Policies', *Urban Studies*, vol. 24 (1987).
10. Jones and Stewart, *Case for Local Government*, pp. 81–2.
11. George Jones, *Responsibility and Government*, Inaugural Lecture, London School of Economics and Political Science, 1977.
12. See R. E. Goodin, *Reasons for Welfare* (Princeton University Press, 1988); and Raymond Plant, *Equality, Markets and the New Right* (Fabian Society, 1984).
13. Harvey, *Social Justice and the City*; and Paterson, *City Limits*.
14. F. Layfield (Chairman), *Local Government Finance; Report of the Committee of Inquiry*, Cmnd 6453 (HMSO, 1976).

15. See D. S. King, *The New Right* (Macmillan, 1987); K. Hoover and R. Plant, *Conservative Capitalism* (Routledge, 1988); and A. Gamble, *The Strong State and the Free Economy* (Macmillan, 1988).
16. Tiebout, 'Pure Theory of Local Expenditures', p. 419.
17. See D. Mason, *Revising the Rating System* (Adam Smith Institute, 1985). In the Green Paper preceding the poll tax the Government explained the scheme's role in increasing local authority accountability to voters: 'the main role of local government is to provide service in a way which properly reflects differences in local circumstances and local choice. A council's powers to raise taxes locally, and the grant it gets from the national Government, should be designed to ensure that the council can provide adequate services. They should also be designed to ensure that the local electors know what the costs of their services are, so that armed with this knowledge they can influence the spending decisions of their council through the ballot box. Effective local accountability must be the corner-stone of successful local government' (Department of the Environment, *Paying for Local Government*, Cmnd 9714 (HMSO, 1986 p. vii)).
18. Nicholas Ridley, *Local Right* (Centre for Policy Studies, 1988) and see parliamentary debates during the third reading of the Local Government Finances Act 1988, Hansard, especially 18 April 1988, vol. 131, cols 569–642.
19. Peterson, *City Limits*, p. 37.
20. Ridley, *Local Right*.
21. Ibid., p. 10.
22. Ibid., p. 11.
23. Ibid., p. 28.
24. Ibid., p. 13.
25. Ibid., p. 8.
26. Ibid., p. 33.
27. See King, 'Government Beyond Whitehall'.
28. C. A. R. Crosland, *The Future of Socialism* (Cape, 1956).
29. David Blunkett and Keith Jackson, *Democracy in Crisis* (Hogarth, 1987) p. 64.
30. See D. S. King, 'The New Urban Left and Local Economic Initiatives: The Greater London Enterprise Board', in D. S. King and J. Pierre (eds), *Challenges to Local Government* (Sage, 1990).
31. John Gyford, *The Politics of Local Socialism* (Allen & Unwin, 1986); Hugh Morison, *The Regeneration of Local Economies* (Oxford University Press, 1987).
32. There are historical precedents on the Left, however: see Andrew Sancton, 'British Socialist Theories in the Division of Power by Area', *Political Studies*, vol. 24 (1976) pp. 158–70.
33. Blunkett and Jackson, *Democracy in Crisis*, p. 5; see also Jones and Stewart, *Case for Local Government*.
34. Blunkett and Jackson, *Democracy in Crisis*, p. 189.
35. Ibid., pp. 204–6.
36. Goodin, *Reasons for Welfare*.

37. See I. Young, 'Polity and Group Difference: A Critique of the Ideal of Universal Citizenship', *Ethics*, vol. 99 (1989) pp. 250–74; S. Okin, *Justice, Gender and the Family* (Basic Books, 1989); and C. MacKinnon, *Feminism Unmodified: Discourses on Life and Law* (Harvard University Press, 1987).
38. J. Rawls, *A Theory of Justice* (Oxford University Press, 1971) p. 560.
39. W. Kymlicka, *Contemporary Political Philosophy* (Oxford University Press, 1990) p. 207.
40. Ibid., p. 208.

14 A Future for Local Authorities as Community Government

John Stewart

This book has recorded a series of changes in the nature of local government brought about by legislation introduced by the Conservative Government. Chapter 11 argued that there are problems associated with the direction of change that the restructuring of local government has been taking. This chapter sets out an alternative scenario based on alternative policies.

The limitations of structural change

Much consideration of the future for local government is concentrated on issues of structure highlighted by the Local Government Commission. The Commission focuses its attention on whether and how unitary authorities should be created outside the metropolitan areas. In the past, discussion has raised and doubtless will again, the issue of whether a regional tier of government should be created. Yet if an alternative to the Government's programme for the future of local government is to be developed, it must escape from regarding discussion of structural change as primary.

To discuss structural change is to evade the real challenge of the Government's legislation, which is to the nature of local government: its role and way of working. To focus on structure is to assume either that these issues have all been resolved by the Government's programme or that all that is required is to restore local authorities to their previous position. Neither is an adequate response. The Government's programme is incomplete – further change is inevitable and is already taking place. It would be an equal mistake to assume that a return to the past was possible. The slogans 'Defend Jobs and Services' and 'Defend Local Democracy' aroused but little response because they assumed too readily that all was well in local government.

The consideration of structure is a distraction from – as it has so often been in the past – the real issue of the role and way of working of local authorities. It is only when we know the nature of local government sought that it is meaningful to discuss such issues as structures, tiers and boundaries. That is a weakness in the work of the Local Government Commission. It would be an equal weakness if an alternative policy for local government took structural change as its starting point. The challenge of the Government's programme is not met by proposals for a new structure. If a development of that programme is not to be the only future discussed, an alternative programme has to be developed for local government, which takes as its starting point the role of local government, its functions and its method of working.

The lessons of the experience of Western Europe

To develop an alternative future it is necessary to break out of the constraints on thinking imposed by past experience. We assume too readily that local government has to be the local government that we have known. The value of European experience – or indeed of comparative experience generally – is that it challenges our past concepts of the nature of local government.

The experience of increasing control over local authorities in the UK differs from the recent trend in Europe and in other countries. While in this country the effect of the Government's actions over a period of ten years has been to weaken local government and to extend the powers of central government, the trend elsewhere has been the reverse. Writing about North-Western continental Europe, Norton concluded 'there has been almost everywhere a serious attempt to decentralise power from state government to local government, with major reforms in practice in Scandinavia and in France and some modest achievement in Germany'.[1] There is a realisation in those European countries that there is only a limited capacity in central government to meet the challenges of a changing society and that there is a need for central government to focus on the issues which it alone can deal with, strengthening local government to increase the overall capacity of the governmental system.

The European pattern reflects a different concept of the role of local government from that dominant in the UK. It has been customary to regard the UK as having a strong system of local government, since local authorities have a wide range of responsibilities. Those responsibilities derived from the many statutes that gave powers to and laid duties upon them. Many of those statutes were broadly drawn, giving considerable discretion. This apparent strength concealed a weakness in the concept of local government. Local authorities came to be seen as first and foremost agencies for the provision of a series of separate services required by national legislation. The focus was on the services and not upon local government.

While European local authorities have duties laid upon them, which in some cases will be greater or less than in the UK, those duties do not define their role. In most Western European countries, local authorities are given the power of general competence: that is, the right to take any action on behalf of its local community that is not specifically barred to it. The starting point is not a set of defined powers and duties, but a wide-ranging power to which is added national duties. In practice, of course, the bulk of their activities are the provision of national services in accordance with those duties. The importance of the power of general competence lies less in the activities that it makes possible than in the concept of local government to which it gives expression.

It is often argued that to give local authorities in the UK a power of general competence would make little practical difference, and that they had until recently only made limited use of their power to spend the 2p rate (about to be changed to an amount per adult) on 'expenditure which in their opinion is in the interests of their area or any part of it or all or some of its inhabitants' (Local Government Act 1982, s. 137(i)). That is to misunderstand the significance of a power of general competence.

The power of general competence should be seen as an expression of a concept of local government as the community government itself. As Alan Norton has argued:

The commune or municipality in European law is the general body of the inhabitants of an administrative area. The citizens of the commune or of other local territorial authority areas are in law conceived as governing themselves through an elected council as their sole agent. The word 'communal' (and the German equivalent 'Gemeinde') carry meanings of community and common ownership.[2]

As the community governing itself, the local authority is entitled to take actions that are sought by that community. It need not search for specific powers, because the powers derive from the concept of local government itself. Because the local authority is the community governing itself, it is or can be concerned with any needs or problems faced in the community, and not merely the services it provides directly. The identity of the authority does not derive from the services provided, but from the community.

Because it is the community governing itself it recognises the readiness to work with and through others. Joint action with other authorities or working through another organisation is readily undertaken.

Syndicates or consortia of local authorities which appoint their own officers or are served by officers of participating authorities are widely employed in France, Italy, and Germany to carry out tasks which can most effectively be performed on a combined scale and have specific legal forms. Similarly joint authorities are set up in Scandinavia for transport and other purposes.[3]

In the UK it has been assumed that a local authority should not merely provide the service directly but should employ all the staff involved in the provision of the service. It was almost as if the size of an authority should be determined by the specialist skills required. Stated like that, it shows the absurdity of the approach, but that result derived from the concept of local government as an agency for the delivery of services. It has led to local authorities being far larger than in other countries in the world as Table 14.1 shows.[4] The size of local authorities in other countries is smaller because their role is not defined by the services provided, but by the community they serve. The value of the experience of other countries is that it shows that there are many forms of local government and the present form

Table 14.1 Average population size of local authorities

England and Wales	122740
Sweden	29527
Denmark	17963
Australia	14125
USA	12000
Norway	8891
New Zealand	7980
Italy	6717
Canada	5011
West Germany	2694
France	1320

Source: Goldsmith and Newton (see note 4).

taken in the UK is not the only one. Indeed, one can find other traditions of local government in the UK. The strength of urban government in the latter part of the nineteenth century was an expression of the community governing itself. Lacking a power of general competence – although even that was not entirely lacking in municipal government – local authorities used private bill legislation to extend their powers to meet the problems of their areas. Tramways, water supply, gas and eventually electricity undertakings were created by municipal enterprise in response to the needs of urban areas. That tradition was lost as local authorities came to see their main role as the delivery of services specified in national legislation and accepted the stimulus of central government grant and circular as the main spur to action. Past traditions of local government were lost to a much greater extent in the UK than in other countries.

A concept of community government

If one abandons the assumption that the primary role of local authorities is to act as agencies for the administration of a series of separate services, then a new basis for the future of local government can be explored. Because the phrase 'local government' is associated with that assumption – even though too often local authorities behaved as if they were local administration – the phrase 'community government' will be used to mark the new role.

As community government, local authorities' primary role is concern for the problems and issues faced by local communities. They are the means by which communities confront and resolve problems and issues beyond the scope of individuals or of other modes of social action.

The concept of community government is not based on an idealistic picture of local communities. It recognises within communities many differing interests and values. Conflicts exist as well as shared purposes. Community government is achieved through political processes that balance different interests and values. A local authority is a political institution for the authoritative determination of community values, based on public discourse.

Implicit in this concept of the role of local authorities is a requirement for new ways of working. As community government the authority is concerned with the problems and issues faced by local communities. Its aim is to secure that those problems and issues are met in the most effective way. That may or may not require direct provision of a service. In a pluralistic society, there can and should be many modes of social action. As community government, local authorities in the enabling role can sustain those many modes.

The authority seeks to provide services not *to* the public, but *for* the public and *with* the public. The barriers that surround the local authority have to be challenged. The responsive local authority looks outward to the community it serves rather than looking inward to the organisation. It works not merely through traditional departments, but in decentralised offices and with user organisations, community groups and tenants' cooperatives.

The authority recognises that it is responsible to and accountable to the community. That requires the recognition of a governing relationship in which the local authority governs and is governed by the local community. Community government is achieved through citizenship. An electoral process in which only a minority vote is not a sufficient basis of accountability.

Community government challenges past organisational assumptions. The traditional committee system built around services cannot adequately express the wider requirements of community government. Departments built upon the bureaucratic principles of uniformity, hierarchy and functionalism cannot realise the potential of the responsive authority. Existing processes for accountability are too limited to promote citizenship.

The concept of community government suggests roles and ways of working that are very different from those suggested by the Government's programme. Community government is based on the needs and problems faced by local communities. The Government's programmes, while challenging the need for a local authority to provide services directly, still defines their role by their responsibilities for a series of services, and if one of the results of the Government's programme is to reduce those responsibilities then the future of local government inevitably appears uncertain. Whereas the Government's approach is based on the assumed superiority of the competitive relationships of the market, community government recognises value in different modes of social action.

Individual choice in the market provides the model for the Government's programme for extending choice in education and housing. Their approach is, however, limited because they have had to recognise implicitly if not explicitly the limitations of market models and the necessity of collective choice. Thus in education, while apparently extending parental choice, that choice has been limited by the introduction of a national curriculum. The Government recognises in the National Curriculum the need for collective choice – at the national level. For although the Government's programme is based on the assumed superiority of the market, the Government recognises the necessity of collective action.

Problems are created by the market as well as being resolved by it. The growing hazards of the environment are at least in part the product of market forces. Many of the issues faced by society are beyond the capacity of the market to deal with unaided. Thus, the growth in private provision for the elderly has been produced by social security. The reality is that our society is structured by governmental action and the market itself depends upon that structure. The reality is recognised by the Government. Its period of office has been marked more by change in the form of government than by its extent. Even where industries have been privatised, regulation has replaced direct ownership where the result has been to create private monopolies or where wider social interests are recognised. There can be debate about the extent of the

Government's role but the market cannot replace that role, for the market itself depends upon the Government.

The Government accepts the necessity of governmental action, but because it assumes that the market is the means of providing choice in society, it does not recognise that collective choice is itself a means of extending choice and that local collective choice can extend choice further. Community government is based on the assumption that local authorities can be the means for extending choice to local communities. Local authorities have the capacity to give expression to values that cannot be realised in the market whilst allowing diversity in society. Once the need for collective choice is accepted, the case for community government is the case for diversity through local collective choice.

The case for community government

The case for community government has to be grounded in present society – not its past. It is grounded in the needs of government in an uncertain society. Society is changing rapidly and on many dimensions:

- economic restructuring not as a once-for-all change, but as a continuing process
- changing patterns of work and employment
- demographic change altering balances within society
- changing social norms challenging many past assumptions
- growing threats to the environment
- the increasing vulnerability of society
- the recognition of a multi-cultural society
- growing awareness of the discriminations within society

The significance lies less in the particular changes – for everybody can make their own list and give their own emphasis – than in the extent of change and in the many dimensions on which the change is taking place. Uncertainty lies in the interaction between these changes, for in interaction the simplicities of trend analysis disappear.

There is a deeper uncertainty felt at the level of the local community. It is an uncertainty as to the right solution to many of the problems and issues faced. In the long years of growth, services grew in certainty, in response to perceived need and in accordance with the accepted professional solution. There was a 'right solution' to most of the problems perceived in our towns and countryside – pursued by central government and by local authorities alike. Now there is no certainty in the solutions. There are ideas about approaches to be adopted to the inner cities and their problems, but no assurance that they will necessarily resolve them, any more than there is certainty in the response to the changing nature of our countryside or to the scale of environmental problems.

Public uncertainty has grown as the 'certain' solutions of the past have failed to fulfil their promise. While public aspiration remains, public confidence in the capacity of government to deliver has gone. Public doubts have replaced public confidence.

The task is the government of an uncertain society:

- uncertainty as to the issues raised in a rapidly changing society
- uncertainty as to the response to those issues
- uncertainty amongst the public in the capacity for that response

The government of uncertainty has its own requirements. It demands a high capacity for learning both of the nature of the problems faced and from the approaches adopted. But learning is not enough. There is a need for a high capacity for change and adaptation as learning grows. Yet public uncertainty can only be resolved if the public are involved in the learning and in the choices necessary for change and adaptation. The importance of local authorities in the government of uncertainty is their potential for societal learning, for adaptiveness and for involvement.

Societal learning comes from diversity, not from uniformity. In uniformity, the variety of problems and needs can be unseen. From uniformity in approach one may merely learn of failure, while in diversity can be found new possibilities for success. Central government provides for the uniformities of society, while local authorities can be the government of difference both in response to diversity in needs and to diversity in aspiration. Local authorities are built on a scale in which change can come more easily. They can be closer both geographically and organisationally to their citizens, who can be more readily involved in the choices necessary for change.

If the case has been made for the potential of local authorities for learning, adapting and involving, the reality can be very different. The case for community government lies in the need to realise that potential for the government of uncertainty.

Building community government

The changes required to establish community government depend in part upon legislation and in part upon action by local authorities themselves. In effect what is proposed is an alternative reorganisation, but a reorganisation that does not focus on structure, but on role, responsibilities and methods of working.

The role of local authorities as community government

The role of local authorities as community government has already been described. What is required to establish that as the primary role of local authorities? The critical change is to give local authorities the power of general competence – the right to act on behalf of their communities. Such a power could be given by extending the provisions of s.137 of the Local Government Act 1982, set out above. Local authorities are given powers to incur expenditure on behalf of their communities up to a specified limit. That limit could be removed, recognising the general right of a community to incur expenditure on its own behalf.

This would be to achieve the power of general competence within the doctrine of *ultra vires*. Nobody constituted by statute can act beyond the powers given by statute, but general competence can extend the powers. No power of general competence can be unlimited, and in Western Europe limits are set to prevent local authorities infringing individual rights, to prevent them carrying out functions given to other agencies of government or to regulate the terms on which they can engage in commercial activity.

The role of local authorities as community government opens up other possibilities. There is a case for extending the quasi- legislative role of the local authority, giving it much greater powers to lay down regulations or vary the penalties to be imposed for particular offences.[5] Local authorities have two ways of gaining such powers – either as by-laws or by private bill legislation – but the use of such powers is restricted by assumptions about the need for uniformity. It is right that powers which can be used against the individual citizen should be set within a national framework of law, but greater variety could be allowed than has been normal in the UK. The principle should be that the case has to be made for uniformity, rather than as at present where there is a presumption against diversity.

The role as community government gives the local authority a special concern with all the activities of government in their area. The increasingly fragmented system of government described earlier in this book needs to be appraised in its impact on local communities. Community government can be given expression in a right of inquiry by local authorities and in a duty of consultation upon other agencies. But more is required if community government is to be a reality. The issue is whether functions presently carried out by other agencies of government should be carried out by local authorities.

The range of local authorities' responsibilities often appears more as a result of historical accident than of any systematic consideration of their role. The concept of community government suggests two criteria that should be important in determining the functions to be given to local authorities rather than to other agencies of government. The first is local choice and accountability for that choice. Where there is scope for local choice, albeit within a national framework, there is a case for allocation of such functions to local authorities as locally elected institutions, rather than to appointed boards which lack local accountability. The second criterion is the interrelationship of the functions with other governmental functions since community government has a capacity to look beyond particular functions and to consider that interrelationship.

The case for local authorities assuming responsibilities is strong in relation to the health service, the probation service and many of the functions of the Training Agency. To take the health service as an example, the scope for local choice is recognised in the powers given to district health authorities as purchasers of services in relation to need for which there is at present no clear basis in local accountability. The creation of the purchaser role in health strengthens the case for local government assuming responsibility for health, distinguishing as it does the governmental role of local choice from the actual provision of services. Equally important, however, is the close interrelationship between many of the activities of health authorities and those of local authorities. It is not merely the well-understood, if not necessarily always well-developed, relationship on issues such as community care or environmental health. It is that in positive policies directed at promoting health, the whole range of local authority activities have a role to play.

There is a need too to give local authorities a new role in the provision of education, not restoring the previous role, but defining that role by community concerns, taking over the role of the Funding Councils for Schools, while maintaining local management of schools, planning and guiding the provision of education rather than managing individual schools.

The development of community government requires a reappraisal of the complex of agencies that are involved in the government of local communities, raising issues about their accountability to local communities – or indeed whether there is any clear basis of accountability for their actions. The growth of special purpose agencies builds organisational barriers into the working of government at the community level. It reduces the capacity of government to learn, because learning does not flow easily across organisational barriers; it reduces the capacity of government to adapt, because adaptation to emerging problems cannot usually be contained within the boundaries of single-purpose organisations, defined for past problems; it reduces the capacity to involve the public who have little respect for or even understanding of organisational boundaries. Special purpose agencies may be appropriate where problems are known and policies clear, but that presupposes a certainty that does not belong to present society.

Many ways of working

Community government cannot be built through existing patterns of working, since the organisational assumptions built into that system of working reflect traditions of local administration.

The first requirement is to recognise that although the responsibilities of local authorities as community government are much wider than those as local administration, those responsibilities do not need to be exercised directly – there are choices to be made.[6] Once it is accepted that the role is defined by the needs and problems faced by local communities, then it is obvious an authority cannot and should not always act directly. It has to work with others.

Over recent years local authorities have shown a capacity for this role as community government. They have responded to crisis in their local economies and to the growth of unemployment in their areas. At a time of financial pressure, they established a new function of economic development, using their existing powers including s.137 so effectively that as shown in Chapter 10 the Government has given them new powers, so that limits can be set. It is significant, however, that this new function has involved authorities in working in a wide variety of ways to assist other organisations and individuals rather than acting directly. This is community government at work.

The issue local authorities face as community government is what is the most effective way in which community needs can be met. That may involve direct provision, but a local authority can regulate; can provide grants; can use its influence in the local economy as a major employer or major purchaser of goods; can assist others through the knowledge, skills and information it deploys; can bring together organisations, individuals and groups; can build or assist new organisations; can contract with other organisations for the provision of goods and services; can involve users in the running of services; can speak on behalf of its area and those who live within it.[7] A dependence on direct service provision alone limits the role, as does the assumption that the only alternative mode of action is through private contractors.

The role as community government will and should be built in different ways by different local authorities, but national action may be required to increase their capacity by extending their powers. The role needs leverage and leverage implies powers and resources. One such resource is the ability to use contract conditions as a means of meeting community aims. Contract compliance has been restricted by the government and that restriction limits the capacity to act as community government. Community government requires an extension of capacity, not a restriction.

Responsive in action

Community government requires local authorities to look outward, yet past local authorities built organisations that looked inward. Too often in the long years of growth the provision of services became their own justification. A public service orientation is required that recognises that the value of the service lies not in itself but in the value seen both by customers *and* by citizens – whether those services are provided directly or through other agencies.

There has been change in local authorities. Even before the publication of the Citizen's Charter an increasing number of local authorities had come to recognise the need to review their working to ensure responsive services.[8] The Citizen's Charter has stimulated others. However, community government should go further. It involves far more than improving reception arrangements or training staff in dealing with the public, although both are important, or even than setting standards for services. It can involve the whole organisation, because the actions in the field and on the counter are conditioned by the rules and organisation governing them. It can involve the public beyond the organisation not merely as customers but also as citizens on whom the decision to provide services must rest.

To build community government will require that such developments are not merely added on to an existing organisation, but that the organisation is built for responsiveness in action. This cannot be achieved by central government action – it faces the same needs in its own actions. It can, however, release the capacity for initiative by reviewing whether present regulation and legislation meets the test of responsiveness in action. There is a case for a 'free local authority' experiment based on the Scandinavian model.All four Scandinavian governments are committed to reducing controls on local authorities that hinder better service, and have launched the 'free commune' experiments, in which selected authorities are invited to propose controls to be removed by central government – itself an example of learning.[9]

New patterns of organisation

The development of community government requires from local authorities the capacity to work in many different ways. If they are to work with others to build responsive services and to strengthen local accountability, new patterns of organisation must be developed which do not necessarily fit easily into the traditional pattern of committee and departmental control.

Local authorities have already begun to develop new patterns of organisation as they have begun to develop new roles:

- Local authority companies
- Public and private sector joined in new organisations
- Tenants' cooperatives
- User-control of leisure centres
- Decentralisation to neighbourhood offices
- Devolved management

The committee system itself should not be assumed to be sacrosanct or the best means of supporting community government. It focuses attention on the provision of services rather than on other modes of action. Local authorities should be encouraged to experiment. Such experiments have been suggested in the proposals on internal management, discussed in Chapter 5, but as suggested there, those experiments will be limited if restricted to the creation of political executives. That could be seen to be one expression of community government, but much more is required if a local authority is to be the community governing itself. Structures must encompass strategic direction, but also responsiveness in action, scrutiny, effective representation, accountability and community involvement. Yet rather than requiring local authorities to adopt such structures, one should give them legislative space to develop them – if approved or initiated by their citizens.

Rebuilding accountability

Community government requires stronger local authorities, but stronger local authorities are only justified if there is stronger local accountability. It would be hard to regard the present local authorities as an expression of the community governing themselves. There is a weakness in their basis in local accountability. The turn-out in local elections, although increasing slightly year by year, is only about 40 per cent. The local elections, like parliamentary elections, can produce councils on which one party gains a clear majority on a minority of votes cast, or even without the largest number of votes.

The case for proportional representation is, if anything, stronger in local government than in central government. Because local authority areas are relatively homogeneous, the distortions caused by the first-past-the-post system can be greater. There have even been authorities where one party has gained the whole of the seats, leaving two-fifths of the electorate totally unrepresented on the council. There are many authorities where one party is continuously in control for election after election, even though it fails to gain a majority of the votes. Certainty of power can easily lead to an arrogance which does not express accountability in practice. The development of community government can be supported by a system of proportional representation which can ensure the presence on the council of the range of political views in the community.

Electoral reform is a necessary but not a sufficient condition for local accountability. The election is the test of local accountability, but accountability requires the development of an active citizenship with the scope to play a part in local government beyond the periodic election. This will both strengthen accountability in its own right and, by promoting involvement in local government, encourage turn-out. The use of the referendum by local authorities or on the initiative of a specified number of electors is one approach. The development of user involvement in the provision of services or in estate management enables citizens to play an active role in community government. The encouragement of elected neighbourhood councils for the expression of community views and as a source of community initiatives would spread involvement in a country which has fewer councillors in relation to its population than other countries in Western Europe (one councillor per 1800 citizens in the UK compared with a norm of between one per 250 and one per 450 in Western Europe).[10]

Accountability requires from local authority a recognition that more is required than accountability through elections. Accountability is a condition of community government for that is the community governing itself. That must involve a continuing relationship between an authority and its citizens, based on their right to vote, but also their right

- to know
- to be listened to
- to be heard
- to explanation
- to be involved
-

Community government should be built on a charter for citizens as citizens as well as citizens as customers. For responsiveness to customers can never replace accountability to citizens. Public services are provided according to criteria determined by the processes of government. Many public services have to be rationed according to need, rather than supplied according to demand. The interests of different customers have to be balanced. Law and order have to be maintained. While there can and should be responsiveness to the customer within public policy, there remains the need for accountability to the citizens for the policy.[11]

Conclusion

This chapter has set out a concept of community government. It has focused not on issues of structure but on the nature of local government itself. By emphasising role, functions, ways of working and the basis of accountability, it has shown that there are other alternatives to local government apart from that which we have known in the past or that emerging from the Government's programme.

Such changes will not be easily achieved. Central government will have to abandon policies adopted not merely in recent years but in the past. If the development of community government is seen as a means of social learning, then central government can achieve a new role in relation to local authorities in learning with them rather than imposing on them. Change will be required in procedures, controls and in the Civil Service itself to release the capacity for community government.

It may be hard to see any central government ready to devolve power, but wisdom and political sense may lie in a central government that focuses on issues requiring its action, rather than on dispersing energy on issues which can be devolved to local authorities. At present policies are in the reverse direction, for the result of the Government's policies has been a concentration of power in central government, despite a commitment to reducing the power of the state. The continuation of those policies may seem inevitable, but that very concentration can create its own problems in the ineffectiveness of a central government that has overreached and overburdened itself. Trends elsewhere are to strengthen local authorities rather than to weaken them. Other countries have learnt the lesson that may have to be learnt in the UK.

A reversal of past policies demands an alternative scenario for the future. It is not sufficient to expect the restoration of local government to its previous position. The case for community government is a case for local authorities with a new role and a new way of working. Such a case can be argued, but example is more powerful than argument.

It has already been pointed out in this chapter that some local authorities have responded to the challenge faced by building up a role that approaches community government. In response to the problems faced they have established a new role in economic development and in wide-ranging environmental concerns and a new way of working. They are finding support for that role. Many are seeking to develop responsive services, although more are concerned to treat the public as customers than empower them as citizens. The best argument for community government will be made by local authorities which take such measures further and strengthen local accountability by involving their citizens in the choices that have to be made and in the control of their services.

The Government's programme may seem to make such changes more difficult, but that programme makes such developments more necessary. The introduction of compulsory competitive tendering focuses attention on the governmental choice of what is required from a service. A local authority will only maintain control of services by showing its capacity to respond to the public's needs. A positive case for community government can be built on such necessities. Each local authority that seeks to build the case for community government needs to review its organisation and its way of thinking, to ensure not merely that it can meet the requirements of the legislation, but that it:

- has the capacity to speak on and for the community beyond the requirements for the services provided
- uses to the full all the methods available to it to work as an authority on behalf of the community it serves
- builds a responsive authority
- involves the public as customer but also as citizen in the choices to be made, laying the basis for the accountable authority

In present actions of local authorities, the case can be made for the future of local government as community government.

Notes and references

1. Alan Norton, *Local Government in Other Western Democracies* (Institute of Local Government Studies, 1986) p. 24
2. Ibid., p. 20. See also Philip Blair, 'Trends in Local Autonomy and Democracy', in Richard Batley and Gerry Stoker (eds), *Local Government in Europe* (Macmillan, 1991) p. 51.
3. Ibid., p. 42.
4. Michael Goldsmith and Kenneth Newton, 'Local Government Abroad', in *The Conduct of Local Authority Business*, Research Vol. IV, Cmnd 9801 (HMSO, 1986) p. 140.
5. See David King, 'The Next Green Paper on Local Finance', paper given to an Institute of Economic Affairs Conference, 1988, for examples of possible powers.
6. See Michael Clarke and John Stewart, *Choices for Local Government* (Longman, 1991).
7. See Michael Clarke and John Stewart, *General Management of Local Government* (Longman, 1990) for a development of this argument.
8. See Chris Skelcher, *Managing for Service Quality* (Longman, 1992) for examples.
9. See John Stewart and Gerry Stoker, 'The Free Commune Experiment in Scandinavia', in C. Crouch and D. Marquand (eds), *The New Centralism: Britain Out of Step in Europe?* (Basil Blackwell, 1989), for descriptions of these programmes, and John Stewart, *An Experiment in Freedom: The Case for Free Local Authorities in Britain* (Institute for Public Policy Research, 1991).
10. Goldsmith and Newton, 'Local Government Abroad', p. 141.
11. John Stewart, 'Defending Public Accountability', *DEMOS Quarterly* (Winter 1993).

Index